01     $2.00

CHINESE COMMUNISM IN CRISIS

CHINESE COMMUNISM IN CRISIS

Maoism and the Cultural Revolution

JACK GRAY &
PATRICK CAVENDISH

FREDERICK A. PRAEGER, *Publishers*
New York · Washington · London

FREDERICK A. PRAEGER, *Publishers*

111 Fourth Avenue, New York, N.Y. 10003, U.S.A.

5 Cromwell Place, London S.W.7, England

Published in the United States of America in 1968
by Frederick A. Praeger, Inc., Publishers

Library of Congress Catalog Card Number: 68–11318

Printed in Great Britain

CONTENTS

B. Doctrinal and National Policy Texts

Jack Gray is the author of chapters II, III and V, Patrick Cavendish of chapters I and IV.

FOREWORD

THE CRISIS OF the Cultural Revolution is too recent to be fully studied. Its effects are not yet known, and its events have not yet fallen into any meaningful perspective. The sources of our knowledge of it are imperfect. The main sources for the actual events of the movement are reports of Red Guard posters, pamphlets and newspapers sent out by foreign correspondents in Peking. These Red Guard publications are sensational, confused and contradictory; they often represent rivalries and quarrels among groups whose relationship with each other and with the factions in the Chinese leadership we know very little; and what they publish can only be hastily and partially reported by foreign correspondents (mostly Japanese journalists) in Peking.

What we can attempt as historians of modern Chinese politics is to describe the background of the crisis and the issues which are most likely to have been important in its development, and to suggest the uses to which victory on either side may be put.

In dealing with the politics of a Communist country, we have tried to maintain wherever possible in our method of analysis the principle that we should not accept an ideological explanation for events (even when such an explanation is explicitly given by the Chinese) until we have exhausted all possibilities of explanation in terms of practical responses to practical problems. In the same way, we have refused to base our analysis on the naïve assumption that the leaders of the Chinese Communist Party habitually act in order to maintain their power, rather than maintain their power in order to act. We believe that, while the crisis may represent a struggle for power, it marks a struggle based upon concern with real issues of national policy.

We have attempted to bear in mind that every event in China can be seen from three points of view: as an event in the long and unique history of China; as an event in the development of Communist ideas and methods; and as an event in the progress of one among a large number of underdeveloped countries with broadly similar problems. If we have any bias, it is towards the last viewpoint, which is the most neglected of the three. ?

The written text has been kept short and simple, with notes and source-references confined to the indispensable minimum. The Documentary Appendix supplies, as illustration rather than as systematised evidence, some of the most interesting and characteristic of the mass of available source material. Extensive quoting of Chinese documents, however, can be misleading. The reader unfamiliar with things Chinese should be warned that the high moral tone, the philosophical form, the vagueness and the emotionalism of these documents are not expressions of Chinese Communism exclusively. They represent a Chinese form of political rhetoric which antedates the Communists by two thousand years. It is built into the language, and must be discounted, or its form of expression at least allowed for, in interpreting the true import of a given comment. The literary documents which have been included give an impression of the kind of political innuendo alleged by the Maoists. They also provide a little material on the evaluation of history, one of the most important subjects of cultural controversy in recent years.

We hope that specialist colleagues who may read this book will remember that it is a work written for the general reader at a time when the struggles which it describes are still unresolved. We can prove nothing; we can only correct some current misunderstandings, add something to the readers' sense of what is relevant to political and social conflict in China; and, if we have done our work well enough, perhaps increase a little the stock of hypotheses available to deepen research on modern Chinese development.

University of Glasgow   J. G.
December 1967   P. C.

I

THE REVOLUTIONARY BACKGROUND

A BRIEF REVIEW of the main phases and issues of the Chinese revolution over the past eighty years will help to place more recent events in perspective. The imprint of the recent past is particularly heavy in China for, despite the great importance of youth today, it is the experience of the revolutionary veterans, an ageing leadership, which has determined the direction of Chinese policy. They have, moreover, placed very great emphasis on the lessons of the recent past, the correct interpretation of which is regarded as extremely important. It has, in fact, been transformed into a myth in the full meaning of that word, a powerful mixture of truth and fabrication. For this reason, and because we need to see for ourselves what alternatives emerged at different stages and why the revolution took its particular course, it is important to gain as clear a picture as possible.

Modern Chinese history is conventionally dated from 1840, the year of the First Opium War between Britain and China, which brought about the effective opening up of the country to Western economic and political influences. This convention is sound in that external pressures and stimuli have been the cardinal feature of the modern Chinese revolution. This has been so, however, largely because the West, and later Japan, began to impinge upon China at a time when China itself was beginning to suffer from more and more serious internal difficulties. Foreign pressures and stimuli have acted in many different ways. War and diplomacy have led to the impairment of Chinese sovereignty, including the loss of territory, the collapse of institutions and the disturbance of Chinese society. But they have also acted as a stimulant, compelling the Chinese to devise means of saving either their values or their nation from destruction or subjection. 'Saving the country' became the sovereign motive in Chinese politics from the latter part of the nineteenth century, and it remains so today. Foreign sources have also provided most of the ideas and methods which have figured in the various remedies put forward for the plight of China, including the many international features of modern society and politics, Marxism-Leninism among them, which are such important features of China today. In the period between the Opium War and the republican revolution of 1911, a series of humiliating defeats at the hands of the West and of Japan, leading to loss of territory and of full sovereignty, eventually persuaded Chinese leaders that a reform of political, military and educational institutions was necessary if China was to survive. The futility of merely introducing modern technical innovations, such as battleships and the telegraph, was finally demonstrated by the victory of Japan in 1894. The issue of fundamental political change versus technical innovations as the foundation of national defence is still alive today.

In the decade before 1911, the Manchu court began to introduce constitutional, military and educational reforms. Meanwhile a republican revolutionary movement grew up, mainly in the refuge of Japan where many young Chinese were studying. Their social aims were rather vague but they sought to set up a parliamentary regime and to push through nationalist reforms such as had been undertaken in many of the rising nation-states of Europe. Behind all this lay their concern for China's survival. The revolution of 1911, when it occurred, was not an impressive affair. It consisted of a series of mutinies, minor military operations in central China and 'declarations of independence' by provinces. The chief beneficiaries of the revolution were the upper classes of the provinces, who saw their chance to run local affairs without central interference, and the army, which turned out to be the most substantial institution to survive the revolution.

The most outstanding leader of the modernised army was Yuan Shih-k'ai. Called in by the throne to deal with the revolution, he used his power to secure the abdication of the Manchus and his own position in the succeeding regime. He was shortly installed as president of the new republic, but the parliamentary regime did not prosper. The initial period of optimism lasted only until the middle of 1913, by which date Yuan had undermined the republican regime and removed such democratic features as it had acquired. Finally, in 1915, he made the attempt to found a new imperial dynasty. His death in 1916 allowed the revival of parliamentary institutions, but after this date an endless series of attempts to re-establish a constitutional regime on a basis acceptable to all factions produced no lasting result. This was largely because relations between the senior military leaders deteriorated after the death of Yuan, their erstwhile patron and the only leader with paramount authority.

The great militarist cliques spent the years between 1916 and 1928 competing for the control of different regions or provinces or for control of the central government in Peking itself. The political structure of the country, which had not been very closely integrated previously, now disintegrated completely, leaving the Peking government as little more than an address to which foreign powers could send demands or protests. The militarists, usually called warlords by everyone but themselves, were the leaders of local or regional military administrations, some of which were more stable and constructive than others. In many cases, they acquired appropriate civil trappings and worked with the social elite in the provinces; and in some cases, notably in Manchuria, foreign interests played an important part in their operations. They were generally very conservative in outlook, but they did include some men, such as Ch'en Chiung-ming and Feng Yü-hsiang, who were receptive to newer and even to radical ideas and were sometimes prepared to employ progressives in important positions. 'Assuring one's own borders and allowing one's people to live in peace' was a common slogan among them, but few found it possible, even when they wished so, to avoid involvement in the repeated civil wars for any length of time. The disorder of the years after 1916 exacted a colossal price in lives, property and lost opportunities for economic, social and political development.

Meanwhile, during the early years of the Republic, new political forces, the forces of the May Fourth movement, were germinating. It is significant that they were brought out into the open by crises arising out of foreign relations rather than by domestic issues. The first decisive sign came with student demonstrations in Peking over the Shantung clauses of the proposed Versailles settlement on May 4, 1919. The demonstrators sought to dissuade the government from accepting Japanese claims to former German rights in Shantung. When the students were subsequently bullied by the government, business circles and students in other large cities took up the protest movement, directing their anger against the government. The patriotic movement did, indeed, necessarily imply a movement against the bureaucratic-militarist government of the day, and this latter adopted a hostile attitude, not so much because it disagreed with the students' view of the diplomatic situation as because, like most Chinese governments in recent times, it could not tolerate a public political movement.

As a political force, the May Fourth movement's direct effects had been dissipated before the end of 1919. The embryo of the anti-warlord and anti-imperialist movements of the mid-twenties had taken form but had not developed. Nevertheless, this episode had a tremendous influence upon the more radical youths who were now beginning to see the possibility of new political developments. Most important of all, however, was the fact that the anti-Versailles demonstrations had occurred against the background of a cultural revolution—the New Culture or New Thought movement—which can be dated back to 1917. This movement was centred on Peking University and on the radical periodical *Hsin Ch'ing-nien* (translatable as *New Youth*) edited by Ch'en Tu-hsiu, later the first leader of the Chinese Communist Party. Its essence was a violent attack on traditional values and institutions, accompanied by strong advocacy of scientific and democratic ideas. Western literary, philosophical and moral influences were extremely strong, and the movement covered everything from freedom of choice in marriage to the use of the vernacular instead of the esoteric literary language as the medium of literature and education. From this time forward, the cultural revolution was to continue. It was a revolution at a level much deeper than that of politics, but its practical outcome very much depended on the country's political development.

The May Fourth movement had drawn attention to political problems and dramatised the political role of the students, who henceforth were generally at the forefront of Chinese politics. There were, however, many problems standing in the way of further development. Though the students realised from the start the importance of mass propaganda, they and those merchants most involved with them were a small elite largely cut off from the people as a whole, who could not read and understood little of public issues. The student groups were mainly confined to the large coastal cities and they had as yet no permanent and strong political organisation with which to sustain a political movement on either external or domestic issues. Behind this lay a basic confusion over aims. Some of the modern intellectuals believed in avoiding political action and in concentrating on educational, social or technical reform. It was only gradually that an important section turned towards a desire for a decisive political solution to the country's problems, thus turning their backs on existing institutions. Only later, too, did anti-Japanese feeling turn into a more general revulsion against the foreign powers.

The most important influence shaping the political outcome of the May Fourth movement was the new Soviet regime in Russia, which took a close interest in East Asia. After three years of germination, the Chinese Communist Party was formally established in 1921, being at first a tiny group of intellectuals. Two years later, in 1923, Sun Yat-sen—at that moment the rather unsuccessful leader of a local regime in Canton, but with aspirations to the leadership of a reforming national regime—decided to accept Soviet and local Communist help in revitalising his party, the Kuomintang (Chinese Nationalist Party). By the end of 1923, Soviet political and military advisers began to appear in Canton and the first united front of Nationalists and Communists came into being. The two parties co-operated on the basis of securing certain fundamental reforms and, above all, of regaining full Chinese sovereignty. Imperialism was now seen in the terms elaborated by the Comintern. The Kuomintang aimed at setting up a national autocracy which would slowly introduce truly democratic institutions. The Soviet Union was able to impart more sophisticated ideas about political methods, and the Kuomintang became a more effective organisation by drawing on Soviet experience. The two revolutionary parties also gained greater strength from the events of 1925, when a series of incidents between Chinese and foreign interests sparked off an intensified anti-imperialist movement in central and southern

China. Great emphasis was placed upon the political penetration of the masses: a project which was carried out to some extent in the large cities and in the Kwangtung countryside, where the United Front regime had military control.

There were two notable features of the revolutionary regime: the organisation of a new type of army, and the development of 'mass movements'. The Whampoa Academy near Canton, established in 1924 and under strong Soviet influence, attempted to train the nucleus of a modern army under Kuomintang party control, with political training playing a major role. Party representatives, political departments and party branches in military units were copied from the Soviet Union. Though their practical effect on the Kuomintang's expanding armies was not as great as the party had hoped, they expressed an important aspiration. The underlying intention was not only to create an effective fighting force but also to upgrade the status of the soldier, to bridge the gap of fear and hostility between soldiers and civilians and to make the army a positive, constructive force in political reform. At the same time, however, it was a basic tenet of Kuomintang policy that the revolutionary troops should always be under political (party) control. These factors, brought into play in 1924, are still at work today. As regards mass movements, the revolutionary regime from the outset fostered popular organisations of many different types. Trade unions, peasant associations, women's leagues, student unions, and so forth, were established with the dual purpose of furthering the political aims of the revolution and at the same time of providing a solid basis for reforms in each sector of the community. The revolutionary parties and the new public organisations seemed to make possible the development of a revolutionary democracy based on mass participation combined with party leadership. The development of political activities in the countryside was an especially novel and important feature of the movement. It was at this time, too, that Mao Tse-tung, a fairly important figure in the Kuomintang–Communist apparatus, acquired his interest in the peasant movement.

The regime rapidly gained strength during 1925, and by 1926 Chiang Kai-shek, now its military leader, was able to launch the Northern Expedition: a campaign for the reunification of the whole of China, which had been the constant ambition of Sun Yat-sen

6

but unrealised by the time of his death in March 1925. The Kuomintang armies were surprisingly successful; leaving Canton in May 1926, they had reached Shanghai and Nanking by March 1927. Unfortunately, the political divisions within the Nationalist movement had been aggravated during the expansion of the two parties in 1925 and the growth of their regime in Kwangtung. The Northern Expedition at first inhibited and then later accelerated the final break between the more conservative and the more radical forces within the United Front. Basic disagreements over domestic and foreign policy were aggravated by sharp factional conflicts. When the break finally came in April 1927—the most famous episode being Chiang Kai-shek's purge of Communists on April 12 in Shanghai—it was essentially the outcome of a struggle for the control of the Nationalist movement both in terms of party apparatus and in terms of territory, finance and military power. In the course of the struggle within the Kuomintang, the mass organisations were broken up. After many confused conflicts within the anti-Communist section, which eventually turned out to include the great bulk of the Kuomintang and its forces, a Nationalist regime was set up in Nanking early in 1928 under the leadership of Chiang Kai-shek.

The Northern Expedition was completed with the capture of Peking in June 1928, and the old Peking government (by now a mere shadow) finally disappeared. Thus began the Kuomintang's 'tutelary' regime, pledged to the introduction of representative institutions at the local and national levels by 1936. The basic aims of the country's new leaders ostensibly remained what they had been during the revolutionary war: national unity; the development of a strong modern state with effective military, economic and social roles; the fostering of democratic institutions and higher cultural levels; and the development of local initiative and participation. A decisive change in attitude and in the means to be adopted, however, could not but affect the direction of the new state. Partly because of the leadership's experiences during the struggle with the Communists and of the insecurity of the new regime, the democratic development of mass movements and of the party itself was halted, though there were very many Nationalists who wished for a populist regime. The great preoccupations of the leadership were legislation and rearmament. They believed in getting ahead quickly through the use of government machinery and the already existing loci

7

of power—community and business leaders, military officers and so on—and believed that mass participation and initiative under party guidance would be useless as well as dangerous. Thus, the popular anti-imperialist movement was neglected or restricted in favour of ill-publicised diplomatic negotiations; the development of trade unions was halted in favour of the bureaucratic control of industrial relations; and in those villages where peasant associations had existed, control reverted from them to that of local garrisons, police forces and landlords. While increasingly tight restrictions were placed upon public opinion, relations broke down between the Nanking government under Chiang Kai-shek and the new regional military leaders who had risen to power within the regime. Chiang's attempt to integrate and to reduce the size and influence of the country's armies, combined with the repression of opinion inside and outside the party, brought a new round of large-scale civil wars which lasted from 1929 to 1931. In these circumstances, the diplomatic and domestic programmes of the Kuomintang were gravely handicapped.

A new period opened after the Japanese army's invasion of Manchuria in September 1931. By 1932, a new and more stable leadership coalition emerged in Nanking, and the Kuomintang regime entered its brief heyday. Between 1932 and the outbreak of war in 1937, its two great problems were the fending off of the Japanese in northern China and the eradication of the Communist regime in the mountains, first of Kiangsi and then of Shensi. Its achievements during this period have not been fully assessed. Certainly, the country was somewhat more integrated on the eve of the war than it had been five years before (with the exception of parts of northern China, virtually lost to Japan); there were more roads and railways, a more effective army and some improvements in administration, finance and the judicial system. Yet it seems clear that the Kuomintang regime could do little more than scratch the surface of China's problems. It did not have the strength or the methods to implement its reforming legislation, which was laid down without the support of a substantial political movement. It was cut off from the countryside and, because of its cautious policy towards Japan and its repression of political opinion, it did not enjoy much support even in the cities, where its true base lay.

During this period, the Chinese Communist Party, which up to

1927 had been based mainly upon a coalition of young intellectuals and radical trade unionists, became an agrarian organisation based in the mountains of Kiangsi. It virtually abandoned the attempt to maintain a Communist movement in the cities and towns. During the period between 1928 and 1936, when Mao Tse-tung was securing his position at the apex of the Communist movement, the party gained much experience in dealing with the peasants, who form the vast majority of the Chinese population, and in waging guerrilla warfare. Forced by circumstances to base itself upon the village society, it strengthened its position among the peasants by a carefully modulated policy of land reform. From the end of 1931 it also strengthened its claim to be the national movement of the future by adopting a consistently anti-Japanese stance; this, though of no practical significance at the time, was to prove of great political value when a patriotic movement grew up in the cities. Meanwhile, however, it faced encirclement by Kuomintang forces. These were eventually able to destroy the Kiangsi Soviet and to force the party, in 1934, to undertake the Long March, but they were not able to eliminate the movement altogether.

When the Communist leadership, with its troops, arrived in Shensi, where it eventually established its capital at Yenan, the party's fortunes were at a very low ebb. At this juncture, in December 1936, there occurred the Sian Incident in which Chiang Kai-shek was detained by his own anti-Communist forces who could no longer endure the policy of non-resistance towards Japan. He was shortly released with Communist help, for, in 1935 and 1936, the party had responded to the United Front policy of the Comintern and now accepted the Kuomintang once more as the leader of national resistance. The effect of the Sian Incident was to hasten the movement towards a firm and formal anti-Japanese front and to infuse new life into Chinese politics. When the Sino-Japanese war finally came in July and August 1937, it arose out of incidents such as had occurred before; the new element was Chiang's decision that he could give way no further, and he adhered to this decision even after the defeats of 1937 and 1938.

The outbreak of the war was greeted with some relief by many politically minded Chinese, for the years of apparently endless concession were over. The Kuomintang regime retired to Chungking to continue the war, and some of the universities, business firms and intellectuals also retired with it to the interior. Other intellectuals, however, travelled to Yenan where the Communist regime now enjoyed a recognised status as a territorial and military establishment within the United Front. At the same time, the war brought constitutional changes. Chiang Kai-shek's position as sole and supreme leader of party and state was formalised, but minor parties and other political groups were allowed to operate and the domestic political scene opened up.

This relatively hopeful dawn soon darkened. Above all, the relationship between the Kuomintang and the Communist Party turned cold some time before the so-called 'New Fourth Army Incident' of January 1941 finally destroyed whatever trust there had been between them. While the war between the Japanese and the Kuomintang troops had virtually halted, the boundary between the Yenan and Chungking regimes was remilitarised and the political situation in the Kuomintang-controlled areas grew less hopeful. Meanwhile, the Communist regime was successful in waging guerrilla warfare against the Japanese in northern and eastern China, using its long experience of fighting in the countryside, and combining military and political work. While following moderate social policies, it built up a network of guerrilla bases in which army units collaborated with local peasant militia. The Japanese and their Chinese collaborators were largely confined to the main lines of communication and to isolated posts. It seems likely that the very severity of the desperate Japanese measures of repression in northern China strengthened the hand of the Communists who were organising peasant resistance. The war saw the party extend its rule over huge populations in the enemy-occupied areas, while its Kuomintang rival was mainly confined to fixed positions in the west and south-west.

The pieces on the chessboard began to move in 1943 and 1944. The Japanese resumed their advance and occupied Honan, Hunan and Kwangsi, causing consternation in Chungking. Pressure for military and political reform from China's American allies was redoubled. The failure of these efforts to persuade the Kuomintang to institute reforms coincided with closer and, for a time, quite cordial, contact between the Americans and the Yenan-based Communists. By this time, the end of Anti-Japanese War was in sight. The political settlement of post-war China became an urgent problem, and this drew the United States further and further into Chinese politics. When the Japanese surrendered in August 1945, Kuomintang and Communist forces competed for the control of the cities and for possession of the military equipment that was being abandoned by the Japanese. This struggle for the upper hand inevitably weakened the political detente which had been achieved on the eve of victory. While hopes of a democratic coalition regime still persisted, the problem of the disposal of the two armies remained insoluble, and the two sides jockeyed for the most favourable territorial position in the expectation of a renewed conflict. The United States, desiring the emergence of a constitutional regime, placed unrealistic hopes in the minor democratic and liberal parties as constituting a possible 'third force'. The prospect of a peaceful settlement dwindled because of the military problem and because Chiang Kai-shek was confident of success in a trial of strength with the Communists.

The civil war which started in 1946 was to last until 1949; but it was not long before clear signs appeared of the Communists' military superiority. Once again, they were fighting as a rural-based force against the towns, but this time the struggle was one between large and well-equipped armies rather than between guerrilla and conventional forces. Chiang has been frequently criticised for the error of his decision to try to regain and then hold Manchuria, which proved a task too great for his forces. Defeats on the military front were matched by a weakening grip on the political front. Severe inflation, hard conditions and the repression of opinion alienated the public from the Kuomintang regime, which was now suffering from a debilitating loss of morale. A very large number of the better informed began to take the view that there was no alternative to a Communist regime: an attitude which was facilitated by the moderation of Communist policy at this time. By the beginning of 1949, the Communist armies had swept as far south as the Yangtse. While Chiang moved to the refuge he had prepared in Taiwan (Formosa), other groups in the Kuomintang camp unsuccessfully attempted a last-minute compromise. The Communist forces moved on into southern China, and the conquest was virtually complete by the time that the People's Republic was inaugurated in October 1949.

The civil war of 1946–49 gave the Communist Party control

11

of the towns and cities after twenty years in the countryside, thereby presenting it with a new range of problems. The new leadership of China had also developed an intense animosity against the United States on account of the latter's close involvement in Chinese politics after the Anti-Japanese War and its relationship with the Kuomintang regime, then the legal government of China. It was not until the Korean War, however, that this animosity turned into direct hostility and a formal feud. It must also be remembered, moreover, that the Communist regime came to power almost entirely under its own steam. It was not, as some in the West believed in 1949 and for some time after, simply the Chinese wing of a planned international military operation. The Soviet Union had given it no significant help; Stalin, indeed, seems to have had little faith in the future of the Chinese Communist Party after the end of the war, and he maintained correct diplomatic relations with the Kuomintang up to the last possible moment.

From this story we can pick out certain enduring features which are visible in more than one phase of the revolution. First, the nationalist motive has been a constant factor among the political elite, though it was only with the importation of theories of anti-imperialism that the Chinese began to get a systematic view (whether realistic or not) of their country's position. A belief in foreign economic exploitation and undercover political interference became widespread among Kuomintang supporters as well as Communists, and there was throughout the period reviewed a tendency to attribute every conceivable social or political evil to the noxious influence of imperialism. We find both regimes seeking to reassert China's full sovereignty, the Kuomintang through diplomacy and rearmament along conventional Western lines, and the Communists through a citizens' army based on a massive political movement and through the international Communist and anti-imperialist movements. Both faced the problem of making the common people of China aware of the national crisis, but it can be said that only the Communist Party has made any significant impact in this respect.

Despite the enduring nature of the nationalist motive, the modern elite has been very deeply affected by foreign influences and has tended to find much cause for despair and much to despise in their country. Many of its members went abroad and came back knowing much more about other countries than about their own. A widespread tendency is noticeable among unlettered as well as among educated people to feel that Chinese can never match Westerners, and both Kuomintang and Communist propaganda has been concerned with this lack of self-confidence. The response has been to seek to restore self-confidence by reversing the terms of the dilemma. The theme 'we are better than they' is particularly strong today. Both parties, too, have felt a special mission to lead the anti-colonial revolution in Asia, though the Communist Party, with its internationalist outlook, has also been interested in Africa and Latin America: regions previously beyond the range of Chinese policy.

To save and restore China, a strong unitary state has been considered a prime aim by almost all Chinese revolutionaries. To achieve this, a state organisation has had to be constructed rather than captured and remoulded, for the older institutions, much in decay in any case, have provided no basis for further development. The Kuomintang leaders eventually allowed the creation of an administrative and military apparatus to obscure other factors in the political situation, and failed to get very far with development in the local level. They intended the state to support and take the place of China's infant modern capitalism and to break down the crust of 'feudalism'—in other words, to do away with those things which inhibited modernisation as they conceived it. There was a minority among the political elite who believed in piecemeal reforms at regional or lower levels. They ignored the ideologies and slogans of the revolutionary parties and concentrated on immediate practical problems. Even so, and despite the very obvious attractions of such an approach in a time of political decay, the revolutionaries were probably correct in thinking that local or gradual reforms could not provide an alternative to revolution. The results of such efforts were always liable to destruction because of the continuing general instability, and reforms were likely to lack motive power or lasting effect without a general political change and without political organisation. The revolutionaries believed in mending the roof rather than running around with small buckets to catch a few of the drops. Mao's dictum, 'put politics in command', is not, therefore, a new idea.

To achieve a strong state—in one case a tutelary regime leading to a parliamentary democracy, and in the other a people's demo-cracy—elitist and dictatorial methods (in other words 'leadership'), were considered essential. The Kuomintang remodelled itself after 1923 along democratic-centralist lines and tried to become a tightly disciplined organisation. Outside the party, it excercised, in principle, a one-party system and controlled public opinion. Control inside and outside the party has also characterised the Communists, but their effectiveness has been much greater than that of the Kuomintang and, so far as inner-party discipline is concerned, this effectiveness was already proverbial in the 1920s. Political liberalism, in fact, scarcely gained a foothold in modern China. Freedom for different groups to negotiate with each other within a parliamentary framework with established civil liberties, and the protection of individuals through the law, did not characterise the political system. Democracy could not mean such things in an unstable society, weighed down by poverty, war and ignorance, where the consensus which makes Western democratic institutions possible did not exist. Both revolutionary parties, indeed, inveighed against 'liberalism', affirming it to be destructive of the personal and social discipline they considered essential. They were supported in this by the older ways of thinking which failed to draw a distinction between freedom and license. For the Kuomintang, democracy was envisaged essentially on Western lines but as something that could only be built up slowly and only after the country's fundamental problems had been solved. For the Communists, it has meant a party-controlled mass regime based above all on participation. If liberal ideas were influential anywhere, therefore, it was among the literary and academic intellectuals who, despite a strong leftist trend and a considerable involvement in the revolution, were deeply influenced by Western individualism from the beginning of the New Thought movement onwards.

民主主義

Another major and related feature of the revolution has been the great importance of warfare. No political movement without a military arm and a territorial base has made a lasting impact on the course of modern political history. This is not to say, of course, that 'moral' factors have not been important. They certainly have, especially in so far as they have conditioned the attitudes of the educated minority, the active element in political society. The collapse of the Kuomintang between 1946 and 1949 was as much a moral as a military defeat; and even the militarists of the 1920s were sensitive to the attitude of the 'better elements' and did what they could to influence public opinion by 'moral' justification of their aims and actions. Nevertheless, the importance of war in domestic politics certainly coloured the outlook of the revolutionary elite.

It is in this context that we should seek to understand the 'struggle' morality which is characteristic of the present regime in China. It echoes an enduring theme of the past eighty years, for most reformers and all revolutionaries in modern China have stressed repeatedly the need for collective and personal discipline. For this reason, the Kuomintang's political and intellectual leaders in the 1920s and 1930s held up modern military ideals and the military ethos as a model for the whole community. They wished to achieve the standards of public and private discipline—including, for example, obedience to established authority, responsibility, honesty, public spirit and even punctuality—which are largely taken for granted in the modern industrial-democratic West. The Communists have also been concerned with this question, though their ultimate goals are different. The moralistic strand in the revolution has, indeed, been very strong and, as in any genuinely revolutionary movement, has meant the moral renovation, or the attempted renovation, of the individual. The great difference today is that there are now an organisation and methods which can be used to promote the reform of attitudes and behaviour on a significant scale. It is no longer confined to clubs of zealous young patriots.

The chief problem confronting the revolutionary parties has been that of contacting and penetrating the great bulk of the people, who are difficult to reach in both the physical and the mental senses. As we have seen, a significant effort in this direction was made between 1925 and 1927, when propaganda was organised—including oral propaganda, the use of mass meetings and political entertainment. Another significant stage come in northern China during the Anti-Japanese War. It was during these two phases, also, that the radical writers and literary intellectuals acquired the keenest desire to communicate with the masses and to 'throw down the pen and follow the troops'. In the second case—that of the Anti-Japanese War—the intellectuals were prepared for the attempt to participate in politics by a decade of patriotic and left-wing movements centred in Shanghai. The effort to draw the mass of the people into a wider community, and to engender more positive attitudes to pressing problems, has needed the constant prodding of a huge political organisation. The promotion of literacy and education, and the provision of means of communication, such as radio receivers and news discussion groups, have been salient features of the present regime. The problem of reaching the villages and of raising educational standards to even a modest level has certainly not been solved, however, and this fact must always be borne in mind.

The common features of Chinese revolutionaries have been emphasised here, for the Kuomintang and the Communists faced the same fundamental problems and saw these problems in partly similar terms. It was this, after all, that made possible the United Fronts agreed on in 1923 and 1935: the feeling that the great majority of the Chinese people were united under the yoke of imperialism and should therefore work together, and that the major reforms needed ought to be approved by all, or by nearly all. This United Front attitude has remained a feature of the Communist regime until very recent years, despite fluctuations. It would be quite wrong, however, to underestimate the profound differences between the two great parties, for their basic attitudes and political methods were very divergent. The Kuomintang was more genuinely elitist in that it made a less optimistic evaluation of the common man. Again, it emphasised social harmony above all, while the Communist Party has tended to stress the divisions within society. Above all, the Kuomintang believed that the political involvement of the people should be a gradual process and should follow rather than accompany the basic reconstruction of the country. The Communist Party, on the other hand, has seen mass politics and mass social movements—carefully handled, of course—as the key to all development. Whereas the Kuomintang believed in policing society while improvements were made 'from above', the Communists adopted a more dynamic approach. How they tackled the country's enormous problems after 1949 is the subject of the next chapter.

II

PROBLEMS AND POLICIES, 1949–65

THE CHINESE COMMUNIST PARTY entered the final civil war with twenty years of experience of rule in China. It had had a long and arduous apprenticeship in government before gaining control of the central power (an apprenticeship denied to Communist movements elsewhere), and its policies had a degree of caution and realism such as one would expect from a party which had ruled territory ever since six years after its foundation and since the youth of its leaders. In the course of these twenty years, the Chinese Communists had learned to compromise with the political forces they found in the villages of their upland soviets and Border Regions, and to come to terms with the ruling classes in the national struggle against the Japanese. At the same time, it must be noted that the party's experiences had their limitations. It had never ruled a city or had to handle modern industry. Though based on the countryside, it had never (except for insignificant intervals) held power in the agriculturally rich areas, with their commercialised farming and their much more complex rural society. Even in terms of its own peasant policies, while it had gained some experience in the administration of land reform, its attempts at the collective reorganisation of agriculture had been confined to a few experimental mutual-aid teams, mostly created in special local circumstances of economic disaster, natural or man-made, and mostly set up since 1943. Moreover, even in the matter of land reform, the party's experience had been suspended for a decade during the Anti-Japanese War:

a decade during which the Communist ranks had increased enormously. Hence, only a small minority of the survivors of the Long March had had much experience of this basic policy. The supporters recruited after 1936 had been brought into the party primarily on the basis of a patriotic appeal, and their attitudes to the radical social changes they would be called on to support and promote— collectivisation, for example—were not yet formed.

POLITICAL CONSOLIDATION

The circumstances of the Communist victory increased these difficulties of adjustment to unfamiliar problems. The war did not, as had been expected, continue to be one of guerrilla operations and the gradual expansion of Communist base areas, in which political stabilisation would be an essential element. It changed quickly, as the inherent weaknesses of the Kuomintang regime revealed themselves, into a more conventional war of movement in which the People's Liberation Army moved rapidly to seize centres of communication and to divide and destroy the Kuomintang forces in positional battles. The collapse of the rival regime thus came so quickly and unexpectedly—four or five years before it was reckoned on—that the Communist Party was left with the problem of absorbing vast numbers of non-Communist soldiers and administrators, and of consolidating its hold on the country with a very inadequate force of politically trained and reliable personnel.

Some of the gaps between profession and practice which quickly appeared in the policy of the Communists after they came to power may be explained as improvisations which their limited experience and restricted control forced them to adopt. The crudities of the land-reform campaigns in some areas, and the harsh and indiscriminate campaign against counter-revolutionaries—which were inconsistent with Communist conduct since the rise of Mao Tse-tung to the leadership of the party—may not be, as they are often assumed to be, classical exercises of Chinese Communist methods, but makeshifts. For example, the history of land-reform policy between 1946 and 1950 was full of uncertainties and controversies as a result of the changing fortunes and problems of war, and of changing experience as the People's Liberation Army moved south into areas whose social conditions differed from those of the northwest and Manchuria.

With all such allowances made, however, it is true that the Chinese Communist Party came to power with considerable advantages as a result of its long experience. Governing the Border Regions provided it with more than just administrative experience. In the situation in these Communist-held areas, some of the most difficult and characteristic problems of Chinese politics were at a maximum. The necessity for peasant support in guerrilla conditions posed in a sharp and urgent form the question of communication between the educated radical elite and the mass of the population. The scattered nature of the Communist-held territories produced problems of central control which were fundamentally those of the country as a whole, but more severe, more difficult and more urgent. Grouped round these key issues were the ancillary problems of the behaviour of cadres, soldiers and intellectuals, of improvised economic development with inadequate resources in siege conditions, and of the balance of political forces in a revolution at once nationalist and radical. At the same time, the fact that the situation was one of national resistance to a foreign invader meant that there now existed an effective will to overcome these problems. These were the circumstances in which Mao Tse-tung worked out the essentials of his political theory and strategy, much of which is still applicable today on the national scale because the problems are still in many respects the same. To some extent it is true that the problems today may be the same because Mao Tse-tung has willed them to be the same; but, substantially, the basic problems which he faced in the Border Regions are still unsolved in China as a whole. Nor would they have been solved (although their solution might have been simplified) even if Mao had not chosen to thrust China back into siege conditions, comparable with those of Yenan, by his uncompromising policies towards both America and Soviet Russia.

The national political situation in China in 1949 gave the experienced and realistic Chinese Communist Party a milieu of unusual tolerance and goodwill. The Chinese were weary of warfare, which had been almost continuous since 1911, and were willing to pay a high price for peace and strong government. Hopes of reform and of parliamentary government through the Kuomintang party were destroyed by the intransigence of Chiang Kai-shek towards his rivals, Communist and non-Communist alike, by his brutal repression of liberals, and by the futility of twenty years of paper reforms.

Conversely, the Communists had shown in the Border Regions that they could provide the very results which the Kuomintang had failed to provide: democratic local government, fair rents and just taxes. The hyperinflation of the last years of war finally discredited the Kuomintang in the eyes even of its most natural supporters: its own bureaucracy and army.

The new Communist government offered a place for the social-democratic parties in its administration, and passed an Organic Law and Common Programme which, while not concealing its determination to carry through the full programme of Communism, was such as could be enthusiastically accepted by the majority of politically conscious Chinese. Inflation was successfully halted. The Kuomintang remnants, a million strong, were defeated and peace restored. The land was redistributed to peasant tenants, through their own carefully guided efforts, by a campaign which was turned into a process of political education and recruitment, and in which representatives of non-Communist parties and social groups were involved on a large scale. Taxation was unified and made reasonably just. Economic relations between city and country were restored and, with the double stimulus of growing urban markets and the restoration of the incentives of peasant proprietorship, the economy boomed. A new and representative form of local government was set up as a preparation for the formal establishment of an electoral system. By the end of 1952, it was believed that production levels had been restored to those of the best pre-war year (1936), and the stage had been reached when an attempt at planned economic growth could begin.

FIRST FIVE YEAR PLAN AND COLLECTIVISATION
1953–57

The First Five-Year Plan was launched in 1953: an ambitious project and one which would require the full utilisation of China's resources. It was China's first and, so far, its only attempt at centralised planning of the Soviet type; and this lasted, in effect, not for five years but for three (1955–57). In common with other Communist economic programmes, it assumed that no effective planning was possible without the degree of control which a fully developed socialist system would provide; and, therefore, the plan coincided with a new policy, described as the 'General Line for the

Period of Transition to Socialism'. A system of compulsory purchase of staple crops was immediately introduced, and the tentative and experimental steps taken since the end of 1951 to introduce co-operative farming were speeded up.

Any system of planned, rapid economic growth in an under-developed economy—or, for that matter, in a well-developed economy in wartime—has certain consequences which have political implications. It is obvious that the rate of savings must normally increase sharply and consumption must be controlled. It is also obvious that the creation of credit cannot be a major means of providing capital because of the inflationary consequences, so that taxation and price-controls must play a major role. In a peasant country, rapid industrialisation usually means rapid urbanisation, together with a sharply increasing demand for marketed agricultural products from an agricultural sector which cannot hope, even at the best, to increase total production as rapidly as industry can be developed, and which cannot much increase its marketed surplus by cutting down on the farmer's own family consumption. The price of food will tend to rise, and might well, if left free, rise to such an extent as virtually to wipe out the capital available for economic growth. Food prices must, therefore, be controlled, as the most essential step in the prevention of such an inflationary situation.

It is likely that the effort to industrialise—especially in a country which is not only poor but which feels threatened and must, therefore, make the maximum effort to strengthen itself in defence—will be greater than could be called forth by any level of economic incentives that the state can afford. This will be especially true of the crucial food-supplying sector, where the first increases of production probably involve the investment of considerable amounts of additional labour by a population used to much leisure, where (especially in a precarious monsoon climate) security of subsistence tends to have a higher priority than increased incomes through crop specialisation; and where many farmers are so poor that any increase in income through increased production or higher prices may well be devoted largely to the further consumption of food, with the result that the marketed surplus may actually fall as production rises. Also, the growth of urban markets for products from the countryside other than staple agricultural crops, such as cereals and cotton, may provide an incentive to concentration upon peasant sidelines and handicrafts higher than it is possible to provide, within any likely plan, for the production of staple crops. Inevitably, therefore, economic incentives have to be eked out by patriotic and ideological appeals, and to a greater or lesser extent by forms of social and political control of consumption and marketing; and there is necessarily constant experiment to find the lowest level of economic incentives which will serve. Once the decision to rely upon planned rapid growth is taken, the rest follows, and provides the co-ordinates of planning policy thereafter. It is also true that in a system of economic policy which asks citizens to forego some short-term economic advantages—which demands, in fact, sacrifices for the good of the community—there will be more or less pressure to ensure that sacrifices will be equally shared as far as possible. This is one of the most important political consequences; egalitarian demands are bound to become significant.

The point is sometimes made (though it is forgotten again with remarkable regularity) that Communist economies are analogous to wartime economies, and that to judge them by the yardstick of times of peace is to falsify them.[1] In China's case—where, for 250 years, economic growth has lagged appallingly behind the growth of population; where malnutrition has been endemic and widespread famine regular; where even in bumper years there is hunger in some part of the country; and where population increase is now such that the economy must run almost as far as it can in order to stay in the same place—it is idle to expect anything but an all-out 'total war' on poverty and in developing national resources to the point where food supplies are both adequate and secure. Similarly, in a country where, as is the case of China today, the national territory along several thousand miles of almost defenceless frontier and coastline is encircled by the bases of hostile, if still mutually antagonistic, powers, and when one enemy is the first industrial power in the world and the other the second, it would be equally idle to suppose that any national government would feel able to ease the situation at home by sacrificing to consumption what might be spent on industrial development necessary for defence. We shall misunderstand the significance of the Chinese system, and falsify the nature of political controversies in China, if we suppose, without further thought, that any responsible Chinese government would behave differently from the Communist government in any essential respect, as far as economic priorities, the speed of planned economic advance, and the imposition of the consequent political controls, are concerned. The room for manœuvre is not great.

During the years of the First Five-Year Plan, the model for economic growth and organisation in China was naturally the Soviet Union. Industrial organisation was built up on the Soviet pattern, largely with the advice of Soviet experts. Collectivisation sought to create agricultural institutions which were on paper little different from the kolkhoz. The new Chinese Constitution put into operation in 1954 was explicitly a copy of the Stalin Constitution of 1936 (with some modifications necessary because China, with its relatively small non-Chinese racial minorities, did not adopt the federal plan of the USSR). In law and the law courts, in art and literature and in education, Russian advice was taken. The Chinese army, equipped by the Russians, changed its own former revolutionary character and structure to a professional and hierarchical organisation.

In the key process of the organisation of agriculture, China followed in general terms the precedents of the People's Democracies of Eastern Europe, all of which, in order to avoid the disasters which the forcible and ill-prepared collectivisation of agriculture had brought upon the Soviet Union, had adopted a gradualist policy and made, in varying degrees, concessions to the voluntary principle. Chronologically, China was the last of the then Communist countries to attempt collectivisation, which had already broken down in Yugoslavia and was on the point of dissolution in Poland.

Collectivisation in China went on nevertheless, and resulted in virtually universal organisation of agriculture: a result which no other post-war Communist revolution has achieved. Elsewhere in the Communist world, the collectivisation of agriculture was supposed to follow after the mechanisation of farming; and in fact, although this was not so, the process of collectivisation was at least accompanied by policies which sought to provide an adequate technological basis for the new scale of farming. In China, while the party began with the same orthodox assumption, it was quickly rejected. At the existing stage of economic development in China, rapid mechanisation was neither feasible nor of much economic value. Chinese farm labour was underemployed for much of the year; there was no pressing need to economise on agricultural labour in order to find labour for industrialisation. The problem was one of increased yields rather than of increased output per manhour. The most obvious and pressing reforms in agricultural technology—the repair and extension of defences against flood and drought, the increase of the irrigated area, the diversification of crops, the increase of the humus content of the soil—could all be met most economically by the use of existing underemployed labour. What was required was the mobilisation of local labour through a system of co-operative farming; and Mao Tse-tung stressed that the basis of agricultural advance during the First Five-Year Plan would be *social* change, not *technological* change.

On the whole, the more general arguments for co-operativised agriculture in underdeveloped countries apply in China with particular force, if they apply anywhere. The dissemination of improved farming methods in a country of 100 million farms, each with too small a margin over subsistence to permit ready experiment, is a task which in itself suggests the need for grouping the peasants in larger units. The very great difficulties always experienced in providing agricultural credit at tolerable rates of interest to very small farmers, most of whom are bad risks, dictates a need (long felt by the farmers themselves) for the setting up of groups within which the risks would be spread. More fundamentally, the waste of capital and its uneven distribution represented by a system of tiny farms— each separately, and inadequately, equipped—is intolerable at Chinese levels of income and saving.

There were existing forms of co-operation in China which met these needs, but they were confined almost entirely to the top 10 per cent of farmers, and left the other 90 per cent helplessly isolated and unable to increase their efficiency. The most obvious step for the improvement of Chinese farming was to set up a co-operative system which would bring into association the underemployed rural poor and the equipment and savings of the more prosperous. This did not perhaps demand full collectivisation; but it certainly pointed strongly to a degree of co-operation which would make possible the unified working of larger areas of land and the effective mobilisation of local labour and capital.

The alternative policy, that of encouraging the development of the 'rich-peasants' (4 per cent of the rural community) into large-scale employers, and the transformation of the rest into agricultural labourers and urban workers—this is a solution in which few Chinese have much confidence. The underemployed masses in the countryside have to be kept alive, and urban industry cannot expand at a rate which will provide employment for all of them; they must either be put to work on the spot or kept on charity. Moreover, although they may have little or no employment for much of the year (at the present level of farming technology), the labour is urgently required at the busy seasons of agriculture, so that, even if they could be employed in the cities, they cannot be wholly severed from the countryside. Only in future conditions of highly developed industry and labour-saving farming technology would it be possible in China to pursue, without unthinkable human misery, the direction of capitalist agriculture; and such an attempt at present would, one can be almost certain, merely call forth afresh the radical discontents and the collectivist demands on the part of the poor majority in rural areas, demands through which the Chinese Communists were able to grow to overwhelming strength. The poor rural masses are the majority of China's citizens; the more democratic the system of government, the more directly and effectively their demands would dominate the system. It is a question whether the Chinese Communists have acted as a spur or a curb upon the utopian aspirations of the poor; certainly, they have as often had to fight to contain egalitarian and collectivist extremes, such as arise naturally in the villages, as they have had to push to the left against conservatives and pragmatists. Struggles in the villages and in the party hierarchy have been carried on in the context of a general agreement that the problem is to balance social justice, as envisaged by the poor majority, with economic rationality.

This may not continue to be the fundamental question in the countryside. Increasing prosperity and widening opportunities may already have eroded away the opposing positions of poor peasants and prosperous peasants, and may already be tending to produce a sort of village solidarity against extremes of collectivism represented both by a high level of collectivism within the village and a high level of national collectivism represented by grain-procurement policy. It may well be true that, in contrast to what has happened elsewhere in the Communist world, Chinese Communist agrarian policy is threatened less by its failures than by its substantial success in raising the incomes of the majority of the villagers, as the security

c

provided by collective grain-growing releases the surplus energy and resources of an ever-growing sector of the peasants for the private pursuit of profit through side-occupations and commerce in local free markets. The poor are still at a disadvantage in these respects; but for how much longer? The fate of the Cultural Revolution may depend in the last analysis on this question.

The socialisation of trade and industry was an easier task politically. The state already dominated industry through its inheritance of the industrial base built up in Manchuria during the Japanese occupation, the establishment of new state industries with Soviet help, its control of supplies of staple raw materials, its domination of the market, and its monopoly of labour organisation in the cities. The 'Three-Anti' and 'Five-Anti' campaigns of 1952, although aimed primarily at forestalling the development of corrupt relations between private business and state servants, provided an opportunity to destroy the Chinese business class as an organised political force. Mass campaigns of great mental cruelty were used in an attack upon the owners of industrial and commercial enterprises between 1951 and 1953. This campaign was perhaps inspired partly by fears of a Kuomintang revanche as a consequence of the Korean War—fears similar to those which had inspired the equally severe campaign against counter-revolutionaries in 1951.

In 1955, parallel with the speed-up of the co-operative campaigns in agriculture, a movement was launched to induce the owners of business to give the state a half-share in their enterprises. This campaign, menacing and irresistible though it was, was carried on in the carefully face-saving form of a patriotic-socialist appeal for the voluntary action of business men, enabling them to make a virtue of necessity and take some pride, if they chose, in having sacrificed their independence for the common good. With this step complete, the owners were then gradually and quietly bought out, at 5 per cent interest for twenty years. Many of them remained in their firms in a managerial capacity. The higher standard of life which they have continued to enjoy (some of them still live like merchant princes) is one of the anomalies against which the Red Guards have demonstrated.[2]

The economic basis of the dramatic local successes in increased production upon which the successful collectivisation of agriculture was founded was simple, and was consonant with Chinese conditions, with Communist wartime experience and with Chinese traditional methods in land reclamation and water conservancy. In essence, it was the labour-intensive construction scheme undertaken in the off-season of agriculture, and designed to pay off in increased production at the next harvest. In conditions where, both in construction and in normal production, considerable increases could be expected from the greater use of labour-intensive methods, there were opportunities almost everywhere for such schemes, and there was usually the possibility of continued development by these means from year to year. In this way, it was possible to develop agriculture without very much investment of capital as opposed to labour, and the labour did not need to be paid while employed in construction; it would be rewarded by increased incomes following increased production in the next harvest, and the increase in incomes would accrue each year permanently thereafter. This method of development presupposed, of course, a co-operative organisation and the sharing out of a single collective income. It also presupposed, in practice, that such small amounts of capital as were required could be provided mainly by the collective itself, and this meant largely by the more prosperous members of the collective.

These schemes were not equally attractive to all members of the collective. Work in construction increased the total number of labour-days for which the collective owed remuneration; and so, other things remaining equal, depressed the value of the labour day. The increase in production following the construction scheme had to pay off well enough to keep the remuneration of a labour-day sufficiently high to offset this. If the scheme were unsuccessful, the only result would be a redistribution of existing income in favour of those who had actually participated in construction work, at the expense of those who had not. On the whole, the more prosperous might well prefer to put their enforced leisure between the busy seasons into private enterprise in side-occupations rather than to participate in collective construction, and it would be the poorer members who would welcome the employment opportunities which construction work afforded—and might welcome them as a means of redistribution of income, whether the construction increased total collective income or not. This risk could be overcome, as it apparently was in the case of the best examples in China, by full and free 'mass-line' discussion at every stage.

The results of the First Five-Year Plan in industry were dramatic. China put up a rate of growth which was unprecedented in any comparable country, and can be said to have achieved a break-through in the development of heavy industry, which, by 1957, was very nearly in a position to sustain its own further growth.

Agricultural progress was more problematic. Farming statistics in a country as vast and varied as China can hardly inspire much confidence, supplied as they were during the First Five-Year Plan by local Communist cadres who were usually themselves natives of the village, and whose interests as villagers conflicted with their loyalties as party members; statistics, moreover, which were compiled in a most primitive manner without field samples or other physical checks. Farming statistics are notoriously unreliable even in advanced countries; China's figures, although there is no doubt that they were compiled conscientiously and did not represent mere propaganda, are probably only very approximate. It is even possible that the increase of about 4 per cent per annum in agricultural production which they show represented to a very great extent the improvement, not of agriculture, but of the ability to collect statistics. On the other hand, the technological possibilities of rapid improvement in Chinese agriculture are so tremendous that it is difficult to believe that Communist efforts, on the whole well-directed, could have produced little or no result. Observation suggests a sharp rise in the well-being of the rural population at this time; and figures for incomes, savings and purchasing power, which are not open to the objections directed against agricultural statistics, suggest that observation was not misleading. However, much of the increase in incomes may have resulted, not from increased productivity of agriculture, but from side-occupations which the evidence suggests were very profitable at this time. Whatever the precise figure for agricultural production, the very rapid development of industry put a strain on the ability of agriculture to feed the cities. This was one of the two main problems which emerged from the first plan. The second was the problem of population.

During the period of the First Five-Year Plan, China was absorbing the lessons of the 1953 census, which had shown that the previous estimates, suggesting a total population of about 450 million, were wildly wrong, and that the population was nearly 600 million. As this enormous population was heavily weighted towards the young,

28

the population increase could be expected to accelerate rapidly during the next generation. The first response was to launch a birth-control campaign; and this in various forms and in varying degrees of intensity has gone on ever since. It is unnatural, however, for Marxists to accept the necessity for birth-control; the labour theory of value and the emotional opposition to Malthusian ideas make such a position uncomfortable for them. Moreover, the Chinese party, with its Border Region experience of labour-intensive economic development, and its subsequent experience of similar policies on the collective farms, was disposed to put a high value on the possibilities of continued development of food production by means of the exploitation of underemployed labour. Mao's statements began more and more to emphasise 'our six hundred million people, who are our greatest resource': statements which implied that, if this resource could be fully employed, the problem of population would disappear. He put very great emphasis on his conviction that, if collective economic activities were adequately organised, the problem would be one, not of a labour surplus, but of a labour shortage.

Indeed the problem of population was clearly regarded less as a problem of food supplies than as one of employment. The Chinese government believes that China's land, properly exploited, can maintain by the end of this century 1,000 million people at a good level of diet. The immediate problem is how to provide productive employment. In this respect, the Russian model of growth, with its emphasis upon urban, capital-intensive, labour-saving forms of growth, was not appropriate to Chinese conditions. Conversely, the Border Region tradition, developed in the collectivisation campaigns, provided a Chinese alternative.

THE RECTIFICATION CAMPAIGN AND GREAT LEAP FORWARD, 1957–61

During the latter stages of the First Five-Year Plan, in 1956 and 1957, political circumstances also forced new choices upon the Chinese government and party. The year 1956 was one of malaise throughout the Communist world, as a consequence of the repudiation of Stalin in Russia. There was widespread demoralisation and the beginnings of revolt in the Communist countries of Eastern Europe, while their collective system in agriculture was threatened with collapse. In China, there were fainter but not insignificant echoes of these events elsewhere, with strikes, withdrawals from the new collectives and unrest among students. There was also a dangerous degree of demoralisation among intellectuals and technicians. In May 1956, three months after the condemnation of Stalin at the Twentieth Congress of the Soviet Communist Party, Mao Tse-tung initiated an attempt to give the intellectuals greater freedom: his 'Hundred Flowers' pronouncement.[3] In early 1957, after the Hungarian rebellion (to which, at first, he seems to have reacted with a certain amount of sympathy), he invited and urged the Chinese people to voice their discontents and criticisms. This invitation, made in a speech at the Supreme State Conference, was the basis of Mao's essay *On the Correct Handling of Contradictions Among the People*, published in June 1957.[4]

After some natural hesitation, the more articulate classes of the population responded to this invitation. The party presumably expected that they would do so by criticising particular policies or their application, and particular persons or institutions; but the intellectual critics attacked head-on the Communist Party's monopoly of political power, and demanded in effect a parliamentary system with competing parties, an independent judiciary and real freedom of expression. Even students educated wholly under the Communist regime joined in these demands and used the language of Western democratic politics in expressing them. The strength and boldness of the criticism alarmed the regime. The 'Rectification campaign' was switched into a campaign against 'rightists', and the most prominent critics were denounced. Many were sent to the rural areas 'to participate in the revolution' (a cure which Mao is reported in early 1967 to have suggested again for opponents of the Cultural Revolution). The speech *On Handling Contradictions* was now published, with how much alteration in the light of these events since it was made it is impossible to tell; but probably the strict limits to discussion which are spelled out in the published version were additions.

The Rectification movement appeared to Mao to have shown that the causes of discontent in China were connected with the bureaucracy which he and the party had built up since they came to power, and especially since the period of the First Five-Year Plan. The contradictions among the people, the leadership concluded, were largely the consequence of bureaucracy and of a bureaucratic manner of administration; they sprang from the difficulties put by bureaucracy in the way of an appreciation by the masses of the identity of their own long-term interests with the interests of the community and the state. The events which followed, the Great Leap Forward and the creation of the Communes, may be seen in their political aspects as an attempt to short-circuit bureaucracy and to demonstrate that the proper alternative to a Stalinist bureaucracy was, not liberalisation, but the full development of Maoism as demonstrated in the Border Regions, the land-reform and the collectivisation campaigns.

The first step taken was a major measure of economic decentralisation. At the end of the First Five-Year Plan, the figures before the party were that the productivity of the agricultural sector as a whole had risen since 1952 by 24 per cent, and peasant incomes by 13 per cent. Procurement and agricultural taxation—the biggest issue in 'contradictions among the people', and the key point in the 'worker–peasant alliance'—had remained the same throughout the first plan, the intention having been to defer until the Second Five-Year Plan the revision of norms upward in proportion to the growth of production in agriculture. A debate now apparently took place among the party leaders as to what should be done. The assumption was that the taxation and procurement norms would be increased, and the increased revenue and food supplies used to develop state industry. Mao now argued, according to the official history of the agricultural taxes (written at the end of this year, 1957) that the new surplus should be left in the hands of the collective farms, and that the peasants should be induced to invest it for themselves in the development of local resources.[5]

This major and unprecedented concession was the financial basis of the Great Leap Forward. A tremendous campaign was mounted to induce the villages to exploit fully all available resources of nature, labour and capital, in an effort to transform the local economies in the course of three years. There were good economic arguments for the idea, although not for the hectic pace which was set. The state could not provide sufficient capital to provide adequate employment in the countryside. To try to provide employment opportunities in the towns would have involved heavy investment in the creation of the social overheads and the amenities necessary to sustain a vastly increased urban population. Without mechanisation of agriculture, rural production would have been injured by the permanent withdrawal of the underemployed from the villages where their labour was indispensible for sowing and harvest. The transfer of additional food supplies would not automatically occur when rural workers were transferred to the towns, and the process of transporting and processing grain for the urban population was, and is, enormously wasteful; it is better to employ and to continue to feed the rural population where it is.

It is possible that, by the end of 1957, there was another argument for the decentralised economic system represented by the Great Leap Forward. There were already signs that the Soviet Union was exploring the possibility of achieving better relations with the United States; this might, from China's point of view, have the consequence of reducing Soviet support for Chinese efforts to improve the country's security in the Far East. While the Chinese, from obvious motives of national interest, had been the most strenuous defenders of the unity of the Communist bloc, they were now faced with the possibility that their main international prop would weaken, and that they would perhaps have to rely on themselves. They might have to face a situation in which they would face an American or American-supported invasion without the modern equipment and aircraft which the Soviet Union had hitherto supplied. In such a case they would have to fall back upon a guerrilla defence of the kind used against the Japanese: sacrifice the cities to the invaders (or to their atomic weapons), and fight on in the countryside. The importance of military considerations in the Great Leap Forward is suggested by the prominence given not only to the creation of self-sufficient local economies, but to local ability to manufacture steel and to the attempt to arm the whole people as a vast militia. It is not without significance that the one leader dismissed in the controversies over the future of the Communes and the Great Leap Forward strategy was not an economic planner, but a soldier: the Minister of Defence, Marshal P'eng Teh-huai.

The Communes were created as the institutional framework of the Great Leap Forward. One need not be altogether sceptical about the official explanation that the Communes arose from spontaneous examples of the amalgamation into new and bigger units of groups of collectives in Honan and elsewhere which were taken up in three months by the whole of China after Mao Tse-tung had approved them.[6] There had been for some time before a steady movement in the direction of enlarging the collectives; indeed, increasing scale was one aspect of their development throughout the collectivisation movement, and the diversification of the economic activities of the collectives had plenty of precedents.

The Commune—essentially an amalgamation of all the collectives within the *hsiang* (or parish, the lowest unit of administration in Chinese local government)—provided a unit within which it was possible to mobilise capital and labour on a larger scale, and extend over a much wider (and usually therefore more diversified) area the principle of using the surplus of the more prosperous to put the underemployed poor to work. Resources of groups of villages, and not simply of a single village or a part of a village, could now be pooled, and some of the very great disparities between adjacent villages in incomes and in potential investment could be ironed out. The Commune was a unit large enough to provide a high degree of self-sufficiency. It would make possible a greater degree of crop specialisation and help to break down the stubborn survival of the old subsistence pattern of cropping. It would provide for the planning of water conservancy on a less inadequate scale. In these respects, the Commune might provide the foundation of a local economy sufficiently diversified and prosperous to give full employment to its inhabitants, without the wastes of urbanisation.[7]

By the end of 1958, the year of their origin, the Communes had already been the subject of controversy within the party leadership, and plans made for them had been seriously modified. In the three years of natural disasters which followed, the Communes—and even the collectives which were their foundation—were threatened with complete breakdown. The Communes that were to emerge in 1962 were something very different from the original, although still preserving most of the potentialities of the original.

One of the disabilities from which the Commune suffered was the free-supply system associated with it, by which each member of the Commune was guaranteed his subsistence (on the assumption that he worked), and only part of his remuneration was paid in respect of piecework or contract work. There has been much speculation about this, but we know so little of how it worked (if, indeed, it was ever widely applied) that it is difficult to explain its purpose and

33

significance. Was it simply a social security measure to ensure a minimum standard to all rural citizens? Was it actually, under all the ideological extravagance which accompanied its advocacy, simply a means of rationing? Was it intended primarily to even out disparities of income, not so much among individual members within each collective, as among all the constituent collectives in the commune? Was it inspired by ideological considerations, representing an attempt to push ahead of the Soviet Union on the road to Communism? Is it possible that the creators had such confidence in the Great Leap Forward that they believed the age of abundance was at hand and that the necessities of life could be provided free to all? Probably all these factors were involved.

The problem of those families which, while not classifiable as in need of welfare payments, were in chronic distress because they had little labour-power and many dependants, was and is a serious one. The free-supply system would bring up to a tolerable minimum their standards in the necessities of life. Free supply would also perhaps provide a check, if not a means of full control, over the peasants' own consumption of grain, by making the level of consumption a communal matter subject to discussion and therefore to party influence. There can be no doubt of the anxiety of the creators of the Communes to produce as far as possible, by this means and others, an equalisation out of standards among different villages; much trouble had been taken during the development of the collectives to secure this result among the brigades which constituted the collective. The claim that the free-supply Commune was a long step towards Communism—made at a time when, in the eyes of the Soviet Union and the rest of the Communist world, China was merely on the road to socialism—is unlikely to have been made without an appreciation of its implications for Soviet leadership of the world Communist movement, and is therefore most unlikely to have been made simply as internal propaganda. And in the euphoric hopes of the year of the Great Leap Forward, as manifest in the extravagant overestimates made of the subsequent harvest, it is not impossible that some members of the party believed that the Communes would ensure an immediate break-through into a new world of prosperity.

The free-supply system, after a struggle in the Central Committee, was virtually abolished by the end of 1958 on the grounds that it would prejudice incentives to labour. It remains an episode difficult to explain. Mao was personally closely associated with the creation of the Communes, and the indifference to material incentives, which the free-supply system seems to express, was completely inconsistent with his past attitude.

The 'break-up' of the Communes, however, was not complete. The three-level system of ownership which emerged provided great flexibility, and it could solve some of the difficult problems of scale and control involved in community-development projects and in local government in developing countries, in China and elsewhere. Every form of local government represents a compromise; the best scale for road-building, for example, does not yield the best results in education. In a country where, as in China since 1958, so much of the responsibility for economic development rests upon these local governments, the compromise is a more painful one, and the results of failures and inefficiences consequent upon such compromise are liable to be very much more serious. The original unitary Commune proved to be on too large a scale to conduct day-to-day farming, which reverted to the original small collective; this was too small for effective agricultural planning, and such planning was left in the hands of the brigade. Local water conservancy, communications, education, medical services and industry, were operated on the more adequate Commune scale. The main advantage of the system was its very great flexibility, and it is this very fact which makes the Communes so difficult to study. They vary widely from place to place, according to crops, terrain, resources, and political and economic possibilities. On the whole, however, as the ample evidence derived from almost daily press descriptions of the operations of individual local communes shows, it is obvious that, while in special circumstances (such as in highly intensive and highly profitable suburban horticulture) the Commune might be the real economic unit—the enterprise, many-sided but unitary—in normal circumstances the Commune played its restricted part only in the background. The news is always of such-and-such a brigade of such-and-such a team, and the Commune is named simply as a geographical expression. Comparisons made between adjacent teams (members, therefore, of the same Commune and often stated to be so) show such disparities of methods and results as to suggest that the Commune administration had little control or influence.[8]

By 1962, the Chinese economy seemed, by a process of adjustment which threatened collectivised agriculture, to have recovered from the difficulties of the preceding three years. A large private sector had been created; rural trade fairs flourished. The Communes had been articulated into a three-tiered system in which the Commune itself had become primarily the political government of the area—the *hsiang* government once more—but charged still with the responsibility for the development of the overheads of the local economy, with funds supplied from the lower levels of organisation. The Communes were split into production brigades; these were for a time the units of farming, but they had ceased to be so on the whole by 1961, and thereafter retained merely the function of planning the work of their constituent teams which now became the unit of accounting and of contracting, on behalf of the teams, with the state. By 1961, the cadres of the production brigade had lost the power to impose plans and contracts upon the teams, because they were deprived of the power to determine the distribution of the income of the teams. Brigade cadres protested about this, but had to accept it.

READJUSTMENT AND PREPARATION FOR REVOLUTIONARY RENEWAL, 1961–65

With the worst of the natural disasters over in 1961, in that year a process of stock-taking began, under the 'Eight-Character Guideline on Adjustment', with the slogan 'adjustment, consolidation, reinforcement and improvement'. This involved the readjustment of priorities as among heavy industry, agriculture and light industry—mainly in favour of agriculture, which was now given first place. It also involved, as a consequence, an attempt to make the fullest use of existing industrial capacity to cut down on the need for new construction. From the point of view of political reactions, perhaps the less comforting aspect of this policy was the adjustment of relations between economic and cultural growth. Expansion of educational facilities was to be slowed down, 'so as to facilitate the diversion of a part of manpower and financial resources towards strengthening the economic construction front', together with the reduction of urban population so as to increase the labour force (especially the educated labour force) in agriculture.

It must therefore be noticed that this period of 'relaxation' was not by any means all relaxation in effect. The personal interests and ambitions of millions of people, mostly young people, were prejudiced by the massive diversion of population to the countryside from the schools and factories. School students lost their anticipated opportunity of a higher education; those workers in industry who were diverted to agriculture lost their higher urban standard of living; and both these groups, and the professional people who were sent to help build up rural amenities, lost their enjoyment of the amenities of the towns. These discontents were a major factor in the crisis of the Cultural Revolution in 1966, although the response to them varied in its effects according to the background of the individuals concerned.

It should also be noticed that, even when Mao Tse-tung's Commune idea was heavily at a discount, the problems which it had been designed to solve still remained, and had to be tackled in ways not entirely dissimilar, involving as the Communes did a major shift in the relations between town and country. It will not do to put too strong an emphasis on the difference between the Maoist and the opposing line; on these basic questions of the allocation of resources between town and country, the party did not have great freedom of manœuvre. Even as far as the Commune system itself is concerned, the policy of 1961 may have been merely one of adjustment and not of retreat. Our interpretation of what happened to the Communes after 1958 depends entirely upon what we choose to believe to have been their most essential characteristics. If these were the free-supply system and Commune-scale unification of farm management, then there had undoubtedly been a drastic retreat. If, on the other hand, one believes that the essential characteristics of the Commune system represented an attempt to redefine the relations between town and country, both economic and political, then the changes after 1958 were not fundamental. As we still know very little about the details of the working of the Communes, the question cannot be answered with any confidence. Existing answers express no more than personal prejudices.

Economic rationalisation was accompanied by an attempt at ideological adjustment, in which a balance was sought between the mass-line techniques of 1958 and the need for responsible management and technical advice. The key to this was the reinterpretation of the slogan 'red and expert'. There was a spate of writing about the place of the technician:

More and more facts have shown that industrial development and technical progress depend on people who have scientific and technical knowledge and technical experience . . . assignment of improper jobs would mean a very great waste of technical resources. . . . We must not confuse technical views with political views. . . .[9]

This was justified ideologically by quoting Marx to the effect that technicians are not a separate class, but merely 'a superior class of workmen'. A balance was also sought between the mass campaign in industry and the system of defined individual responsibility:

Some people think that if the responsibility system is strictly enforced . . . we will return to the old path of depending on administrative orders and on a small number of people. . . . The mass line is the fundamental line of the party in all kinds of work . . . the mass campaigns in the factories, mines and enterprises are able to develop a tremendous force because they are not antagonistic to the demand for centralised leadership. . . . It is a proven fact that a rigid system of responsibility must be established . . . to enable everyone to understand clearly the specific aim of the struggle. . . . But if we push the responsibility system by administrative orders, it may be unacceptable to the masses. Consequently . . . the mass line must be followed. . . . The responsibility system must be formulated in this way before it can be made realistic, be easily understood by the broad masses, and be carried into practice smoothly.[10]

Much attention in these discussions of 1960 was paid to the implications and the practice of democratic centralism, and most of the discussion was carried on in the pages of the party's youth journal, *China Youth (Chung-kuo ch'ing-nien)*. This material therefore spells out for the 'revolutionary successors' in a simple form the norms of political behaviour in China. The theoretical basis of the discussion is that democracy and centralism are not mutually exclusive, but mutually reinforcing. One is a condition of the other; democracy needs centralism to realise itself, but real centralised unity is possible only on the basis of the summation of divergent views and of the strict preservation of equality between men. Bureaucratism is the opponent of the achievement of this kind of democracy, and bureaucratism is 'mainly due . . . to the inadequate cultural standard of the labouring masses'.[11] This is why intellectuals must be particularly careful in their relations with the masses. Great stress is put upon the preservation of the *appearance* of democracy in these circumstances, and on the personal behaviour and manners of leaders. But the main content of the argument is concerned with the necessity of full and free discussion. 'The mind of a leadership is nothing more than a processing factory which has to obtain its raw materials and semi-finished products from the masses.' It is also stressed that not only should divergent opinions arising from partial knowledge and limited experience be listened to, but also dissident opinions based upon divergent interests. The methods of persuasion are, as they always have been, spelled out in sufficient detail to make it certain that they were meant to be applied.

Throughout the readjustment phase, the necessity of the mass line is, in fact, stressed as much as ever. It is accepted as the inescapable condition of successful social improvement in China; and, although extremes of practice may be condemned in some quarters, there is general agreement on it. Where the discussions of 1961 and early 1962 differ from those of 1958 is in the lack of any reference to the class struggle in the later discussions. This is the more significant in that one would expect reference to it to occur precisely in the context of discussions which stress that the expression of views arising from divergent interests is legitimate. However, in September 1962, the Tenth Plenum of the Central Committee once more reasserted the need for class struggle. (See Documentary Appendix, page 172, for abridged text.) According to Mao's later statements, it was he who took the initiative in this. The new slogan was 'production struggle, scientific experiment, and class struggle' and the question of class struggle must be looked at as a part of this whole new line.

What the Tenth Plenum was mainly concerned with was economic policy—in particular, how to prevent a recurrence of the disasters of the preceding three years. Agriculture was to be given priority in economic planning, with the specific aim of building up areas of stable high yields through water-conservancy construction, mechanisation and the development of the production of chemical fertilisers. The place, and the limits, of class struggle in this context

39

are fairly obvious. In the renewed drive for agricultural improvement which would require the fullest possible mobilisation of the
resources of the countryside, the now flourishing private sector in
agriculture would have to be brought under control. The decision
of the Central Committee was defended soon after in an article in
Red Flag (Hung-ch'i) on November 16, 1962, in the form of an
analysis of Lenin's statements concerning the continuation of class
struggle in the period of transition between capitalism and communism.[12] The article is significant in several ways. First, it lays
stress upon the peasantry as the majority of the petty-bourgeois
representatives of capitalism, and as the most important problem
during the transition. Secondly, it implicates the bourgeois intellectuals in resistance to the further advance of socialism. Thirdly, it
is clearly designed to give the authority of Lenin to Mao Tse-tung's
own exposition of the problem of continuing class-struggle in China.
As a further illustration, an analysis of the fate of agriculture in
'revisionist' Yugoslavia was also published.[13]

China Youth promptly came out (on December 1, 1962) with a
further article on democratic centralism, "On the Correct Interpretation of Democracy and Freedom", laying a heavy stress on the
necessary limits of freedom:

> There is always a governing condition for the democracy and
> freedom we propose. . . . It is that democracy and freedom are not
> contrary to the interests of socialism, or in other words, to the
> six political standards set by Chairman Mao. . . . Democracy and
> freedom can only be the means. They cannot be the ends. . . .[14]

As far as the fundamental problem of the peasants' capitalist
tendencies are concerned, *China Youth* applied the new class-struggle
line to them, condemned the speculative activities of the former
well-to-do farmers, and ended: 'It is essential . . . to establish the
political predominance of the poor peasants and lower-middle
peasants under the leadership of the proletariat . . . and to wage a
resolute struggle against the remnant force of the exploiting class and
the spontaneous forces of capitalism.' The rural cadres were involved
in this: 'The majority of basic cadres in the rural areas are of
peasant origin . . . the dual character of the peasants is still found
among many of them.'[15]

It is not immediately obvious why, in a collectivised system, there should still be poor peasants in China. Two answers were given. First, that while incomes had been evened up by the improvement of standards, memory still played a part in social and political attitudes. The former poor were grateful to the collective, believed in it, and would work harder for it. Secondly, it was argued that in some ways the former poor peasants were still at a disadvantage:

> We still see that part of the poor and lower-middle peasants who were worse off at the time of land reform are still not well off at present, and a handful of them are even experiencing difficulties. These are caused by historical factors as well as new ones. Some of them, owing to poor living conditions in the past, got married late, and their children are still young. They have a big family but little labour power. Others, due to difficult family conditions at the start, have no savings so far, and when they encounter natural calamities [and] weddings or funerals, they find it hard to cope. . . . After co-operativisation . . . the poor . . . took the lead . . . warmly participating in social and public undertakings, putting the public first and themselves last. . . .[16]

This article described, as an example of how the poor peasants might be helped, the case of a production team that had supplied the poor peasants of a certain area with piglets, building styes for the animals with communal funds to be paid back at cost after the harvest. In general, it said, the method of assisting those in such difficulties was to enable them to participate in auxiliary occupations, more or less under communal auspices, thus incidentally strengthening the collective sector.

In January 1963, *New Construction* (*Hsin Chien-she*) published a long article on the question of the private sector of agriculture. It challenged the argument that, because this private sector operated in the shade of successful collectivisation, it was therefore in nature socialist, and it emphasised the dangers of permitting the private sector to develop freely. Certainly, it granted, the private sector should be allowed to exist because it satisfied certain needs of consumers which the collective economy could not yet cope with, and because it brought out 'positive factors' which otherwise would not operate. Nevertheless, it must be controlled in case it should lead to domination over the collective and the large-scale diversion of resources to the pursuit of speculative profit, as distinct from limited private production and trading on a small scale. This was not a fierce attack on the private sector; the author took pains to emphasise that it was a problem which fell within the scope of 'contradictions among the people'. He advocated no specific measures, and implied what is no more than a vague degree of control.

In February 1964, *Red Flag* published an unusually long and fully argued article on the Commune system by T'ao Chu, the vigorous and successful ruler of south China (abridged text reproduced in the Documentary Appendix, page 179). Its tone is such that it could almost have been written for a foreign audience, which immediately suggests that the readers of *Red Flag* themselves were not thought to be fully familiar with the theory and practice of the Commune system. The publication of the article at this time has an obvious significance, and it has an additional interest in that it may give some clues as to why T'ao Chu was prepared to support the Cultural Revolution in the summer of 1966, but apparently only up to that date. (He was to come under fierce attack, in company with Liu Shao-ch'i and Teng Hsiao-p'ing, by the end of the year.) T'ao Chu says nothing about class struggle, but his insistence on the fundamental question of the Commune's ability to use the surplus of the more prosperous production teams to raise the productivity of the less well-endowed teams is almost in itself a justification for the renewal of 'Socialist Education' in the countryside.

The Socialist Education movement was now (by early 1963) well launched. It is still formally taking place, and can be regarded as the Cultural Revolution of the rural areas. It does not seem to have led to any very serious policy changes. With the passage of time, it has become more concerned with the immediate problems of apathy and corruption among rural cadres than with the state of mind of the population. Nevertheless, it is plain that the whole movement of these years—including the Cultural Revolution—was very much concerned with overcoming social and psychological obstacles to the further development of the Commune system. The pace, however, was slow, and the tone of most of what was published was moderate. Little was said about the Communes as a means of eliminating the 'Three Great Differences' between town and country, industry and agriculture, and mental and manual labour. These issues continued to be treated in a practical way: in the greater diversification of Commune enterprise, the shift of trained man-power to the countryside, and the renewed insistence on the par-ticipation of cadres in productive labour.

At the same time, however, several institutions were being much publicised as examples of the elimination of the 'Three Great Differences'. Of these the most important was the Tach'ing oilfield (see Documentary Appendix, page 222). Here, in this large new industrial complex in the north-west, no city was built, the workers being housed in spaced-out village settlements where their depen-dants cultivated the farms and provided services. In the refineries, the People's Liberation Army's system of 'democracy in the three main fields' was applied, and all decisions were taken by committees which included managers and technicians, party representatives and workers from the shop floor. Every member of the staff participated in manual labour, and the schools ran a system of part-work, part-study. It is clear that Tach'ing was built up as a model of practical Maoism, the more convincing in that, with the withdrawal of Soviet technical assistance, the Chinese had been forced to rely on their own efforts to create the oilfield and the refineries. The publicising of Tach'ing (in early 1966 Peking radio had a daily 'Tach'ing half-hour') was a clear pointer to the future.

Although the advocacy of changes in policy and institutions was muted and cautious between 1962 and 1965, perhaps because of strong opposition within the party, there were other developments in the field of ideology which were eventually to flow together to form the flood of the Cultural Revolution.

Of these developments, the most significant was in the People's Liberation Army. The assertion of party control over the army was a salutary victory over the militarism which had destroyed civil government in twentieth-century China; but it could not, in the circumstances in which the People's Liberation Army was created, produce a professional army of the normal kind. During the years of struggle against the Kuomintang and then the Japanese, it was an indoctrinated army engaged in revolutionary and guerrilla opera-tions, an army in which military and political duties were insepar-able. Its relationship both with the population and with the state (represented by the party) was peculiarly close. It operated as the political and military backbone of an armed population. Its forces were dispersed and not in close touch with the 'central' Communist government at Yenan. In both these relationships, upwards to the party centre and downwards to the population, success depended upon the political awareness of its cadres; while, as far as the rank and file were concerned, recruitment depended upon indoctrination in that radical 'mass nationalism', with its revolutionary implications, which the Communists advocated and invoked in their struggle against the Japanese. The ambiguity of the relationship between the Kuomintang and the Communist forces was a further reason for political indoctrination by the army.

In the years of the final civil war (1946–49) and of the consolidation of Communist power in China, the People's Liberation Army was again deeply committed to political action, mainly through the land-reform campaigns. Thereafter, when internal peace was restored and the turbulent process of the destruction of the power of the landlords was over, there was an inevitable tendency for the army to become a professional army of a normal kind, a tendency accelerated by two factors: the Korean War, in which the Chinese forces for the first time fought an orthodox campaign against a well-equipped professional army; and the Soviet ascendancy of the early fifties during which, in military as in civil matters, Russian organisation and methods were accepted. The organisational change, and the increase in modern equipment which promoted the development of technical units, were developments which were not easy to reverse, especially as the vested interests which they created were connected with a degree of hierarchical privilege, on the absence of which the Yenan armies had prided themselves.

In 1958, as part of the Commune line, with its revival of the idea of guerrilla defence based on an armed population, an attempt was made to revert to the former organisation and system of the People's Liberation Army, with systematic party control at all levels and intensive political training. The idea seems to have had sufficient support (even among those leaders who were highly dubious about the Communes themselves and the economic policies associated with them) to secure the dismissal of P'eng Teh-huai, the Minister of Defence. The Commune line withered away in the army as it did in civil life; but the conditions in the lean years that followed, which produced the relaxation of political control in economic and cultural matters, produced in contrast a renewed emphasis on 'politics in command' in the armed forces. The bad harvests of 1959 to 1961 produced a serious threat to public order, if not to the stability of the regime; and this was further complicated by fear that the Kuomintang might seize the opportunity to invade from Taiwan.[17] Distress in many parts of China also affected the morale of recruits.

In 1961, Piao, successor (in 1959) to P'eng Teh-huai as Minister of Defence, intensified political training in the army. He also put it firmly on the basis of a cult of the thought of Mao Tse-tung: a curious fact, considering that Chairman Mao's influence in every other side of Chinese life was then at a low ebb. It is difficult to explain except on the assumption that, for whatever reason, Lin Piao was willing to accept the fact that, in using the authority of Mao in the indoctrination and reform of the army, he would eventually contribute to the possibility of Mao's reassuming the active leadership of events. His motives are not known; his record does not suggest that he had any burning interest in ideology; he was, and is, believed to be in poor health, and to have been brought out of retirement to take over from P'eng Te-huai. In spite of Lin Piao's comparative youth, it is not easy to suppose that he saw himself as a potential successor to supreme leadership of the party. Without evidence to the contrary, it seems reasonable to think of him on his record as primarily a soldier, and to look first for an explanation in his professional interests and activities. Of these, if there was previously any doubt, his speech in September 1965—"Long Live the Victory of People's War"—removed all uncertainty. (See Documentary Appendix, page 191, for abridged text.) The speech was an unequivocal endorsement of the idea of an armed people, of a guerrilla defence, and of the political concomitants of such a defence. This support for Mao's military ideas must have come with particular force from a man who had fought the key campaign against the Kuomintang from Manchuria to the Yangtse and from the Yangtse to the south, and who is the only senior commander in China to have had the responsibility, in the Korean War, for fighting the kind of 'war of hardware' against America—a war on America's terms—the advisability of which he now so roundly repudiated.

Guerrilla defence involves not only military but civilian morale. It was therefore natural that, by 1964, the People's Liberation Army,

45

having undergone three years of intensified indoctrination on the basis of the study of Mao's thought, should be held up as an example to the civilian population, and a campaign to 'learn from the People's Liberation Army' launched. This campaign was directed most intensely at two groups; the militia, and educated youth (the cadres of tomorrow). The text of the movement was the booklet *Quotations from Chairman Mao Tse-tung*, which had been compiled by Lin Piao for the use of the army.[18] By the end of 1965, in fact, the People's Liberation Army was playing the dominant role in the developing Cultural Revolution. Lin Piao's 'People's War' speech marked the new phase, and the army newspaper took the lead in the mounting criticism of the writers associated with the Peking party branch, the attack on which led, in May 1966, to the forcible removal from office of the Peking party secretary, P'eng Chen, and precipitated the crisis which followed.

Before examining the background and course of this crisis, it is necessary to make an appreciation, albeit briefly, of the principal elements in the 'Thought of Mao' which are the governing inspiration of his vision of Chinese society, and hence of the objectives of the Cultural Revolution.

III

THE THOUGHT OF MAO TSE-TUNG

THE POLITICAL THEORY of Mao Tse-tung is represented for the purpose of the Cultural Revolution mainly by the little red book carried by the Red Guards, the *Quotations from Chairman Mao Tse-tung*, produced by Marshal Lin Piao for the indoctrination of the People's Liberation Army. There are dangers in accepting this compilation as representative of Mao's thought. The 400 brief extracts which make it up cannot represent every side of Mao's large output of writing, and it is also possible that the selection is slanted to make a particular case, representative perhaps more of Lin Piao than of Mao. As far as can be seen, however, the selection is broadly true to the spirit of Mao's writings. The only obvious distortion is that the more controversial issues of the last few years receive much less space than one might have expected. The issues of the polemic with Soviet Russia are not stressed, nor is the demand to put politics in command applied in detail to civilian concerns. It is not that revisionism and the place of politics are ignored; they are there, but they are not in any way expressed as a challenge to a putative opposition.

It was clearly the aim of the book to avoid contentious matters as far as possible, in the interests of unity. The original function of the collection as the basis for the indoctrination of army cadres and, through them, of recruits probably accounts for this stress upon unity; but, as the book was accepted for general use as a sort of testament of Maoism, presumably the aim of unity was preserved

47

when the campaign to learn from the People's Liberation Army merged into the Cultural Revolution. The book is a brief and simple restatement of what its compilers took to be the consensus, the view of politics acceptable to the vast majority of those in Chinese public life.

The *Quotations from Chairman Mao* represent a distillation of general statements from an output of writing which was almost all manifestly connected with particular events and situations, and which therefore usually aimed at quite specific and practical results; and even if the *Quotations* are read as theory, their practical bias is very obvious. Even in his theory of knowledge, even in the elaboration of the idea of contradiction which is the most abstruse part of his writing, Mao's concern is not with the theory for its own sake, but with the severely practical question of how to learn about, understand and manipulate the endless variety of social circumstances, economic conditions and political patterns of China. Moreover, his emphasis on the empirical study of actual conditions is not wholly concerned with social investigation, but is closely related to his prescriptions for political behaviour, summed up in the idea of the mass line.

Mao constantly condemns empiricism, but he is the most empirical of Marxists, and in spite of his insistence that practice, and the knowledge that flows from participation in practice, depend upon a theoretical framework (Marxism), the emphasis of his whole philosophy is on the investigation of facts.[1] What he condemns as empiricism is a particular kind of pragmatic behaviour which fails to relate the parts to the whole, or which loses sight of ends through absorption with the means. The faults which he attacks, the problems he has in mind, are Chinese problems, and although like all philosophers he writes as if he wrote for eternity, all his writings are a response to the practical problems which arise from the proclivities of a particular group of men forming the political leadership of a radical movement in a society with its own particular problems. This is not to say that Mao Tse-tung's theories are of interest only to Chinese. The problems of China are unique only in their emphasis and their pattern; the elements of which these problems are composed are common to all human societies beyond the most primitive level, and many of the problems of politics to which Mao seeks answers are universal and fundamental, even if they have taken special forms in China.

His prescriptions for political behaviour, however, are a response to Chinese circumstances, and this is why they are so generally misunderstood in the West. The mass line is discounted as a figleaf of party absolutism, a piece of hypocrisy, or at best as a form of democracy so primitive and uncertain as to be unworthy of serious attention. Similarly, his writings on public morality, which form so large a part of the propaganda of the Cultural Revolution, strike the Western reader as pious platitudes which, occurring in a totalitarian system, are interesting only because they are fraudulent; or they are discussed as a curious survival of moralistic Confucianism in a Marxist system which is by definition one based on amoral analysis and the repudiation of appeals to altruism. Before the force of his insistence on practice and on the mass line is appreciated, however, one must appreciate the strength and persistence of China's elitist, bookish and bureaucratic habits of thought. Before the relevance of his moral appeals can be appreciated, one must see that in a society in which social conscience and public spirit were in many important ways undeveloped, and in which the collapse of traditional values through revolution, civil war and foreign invasion had all but destroyed such public spirit as had existed, any revolution had to be a moral revival, whatever else it was.

THE MASS LINE

The *Quotations* anthology gives the gist of Mao's statements concerning the mass line, and there is a wealth of information about its practical application. The mass line means, first, that political action should conform to the wishes of the majority of the members of those classes which the Communist regime claims to represent. This is not, however, as in developed parliamentary countries, simply a question of acting upon the political opinions of the electorate; nor does it, in a one-party system, permit competition between different groups of aspirants to power in order to influence the opinions of the electors. Its purpose is not merely to influence mass opinion, far less merely to record it; the application of the mass line is a process of mutual education of leaders and led rationalised in Mao's theory of practice, and institutionalised in the procedures of the administration. To paraphrase Mao's own prescription in terms which will relate the concept more closely to the real problems of a backward society with a bureaucratic–elitist tradition, it is the

49

process by which the politically conscious leadership puts itself in direct contact with the inarticulate, largely illiterate and politically undeveloped mass of the local community, learns from the members of that community what are their aspirations, their sense of possibilities, their doubts and problems; sums up these ideas in terms of the wider experience and responsibilities and of the theory of the leadership; returns them to the masses in an articulate form, and poses new questions; then, with the agreement of the majority, puts the consequent decisions into practice, and studies the results in the same terms. The advantages of this political method are that it prevents rule by *fiat* and elitist pretensions, it involves the whole population in active discussion and explicit commitment to policies, and it forms a process of education by which the mass of the people gradually overcome their inarticulateness, their suspicion of change, their ignorance of modern technical and organisational possibilities, their narrow family and clan outlook, the extreme shortness of their economic perspectives, their ignorance of comparable situations elsewhere, and their ingrained fear of governments. It has had substantial success both in minimising elitist tendencies and in increasing the articulateness of the population.[2]

It is less important to condemn this political concept out of hand as unsuitable for importation into Britain or America than it is to recognise it as a possible solution to problems which are common to a number of underdeveloped countries and are particularly acute in Chinese society. In China, it has solved—partially at least, and certainly much better than in any other comparable country—the problems of bringing the peasants into a real and continuing dialogue with the national leadership, of achieving labour discipline in factories largely staffed by rural recruits, and of creating a sense of national unity. The claim of the Chinese leaders that adherence to the mass line has been the main reason for their successes is probably justified. Perhaps the most fundamental problem of all which the mass line has to solve is that, in pre-modern countries, obedience to new legislation is not automatic, and obedience to authority even in familiar matters is incomplete. New laws and new policies proclaimed at the centre will be effective only if they are based on the summation of local experience and followed by campaigns in the local communities in which, as a result of discussion, each local community affirms its acceptance and commits itself to obedience.

Perhaps the simplest problem it solves is in minimising corruption by subjecting local officials to perpetual scrutiny of their actions and regular accounting for expenditures which the local community has itself sanctioned, because the method involves the continuous discussion, modification and development of local projects and the participation in execution as well as in discussion of a large number of the local community.

THE CLASS STRUGGLE, THE PARTY AND UNITY

In applying the mass line, it is assumed that class conflicts are involved. But Mao's concept of continuing class struggle in a socialist society cannot simply be equated with the crudity of Stalin's rationalisation of his oppressive policies. In practice, the idea of class struggle in China is partly concerned with specific conflicts of interest with which Mao attempted to deal in his pamphlet *On the Correct Handling of Contradictions Among the People*, published in 1957. At the other extreme, it is a catch-all phrase condemning undesirable social attitudes; but its main content in the 1960s, in Mao's own thinking, has concerned his belief in the growth of a 'new class' of the kind described by Djilas. Mao, of course, does not use this phrase; instead, he talks of the bourgeois political superstructure outlasting bourgeois economic power, of bourgeois ideology outliving even bourgeois political forces, and of the transmission of these bourgeois attitudes to the new generation of revolutionaries. What he means, however, is that the revolution is producing in China, as he believes it has in Russia, its own establishment which has adopted some of the behaviour of the upper classes which it replaced.

Mao insists that the resolution of 'contradictions among the people' is a form of class struggle, and one of the charges frequently made against those purged in the Cultural Revolution has been that they denied that these non-antagonistic contradictions constituted class struggle. One can sympathise with the victims, because the classical idea of class struggle is not readily applicable to all the present social problems of China. The problems are real enough, and they concern essentially, as suggested, the creation of a new class with interests in conflict with those of the ordinary citizen; but it is not a class as Marx defined classes. It does not own the means of production. It is the class which Marx forgot: the bureaucracy, which may own nothing and enjoy everything.

The groups particularly under attack in the Cultural Revolution include the 'bourgeois royalists' and 'bourgeois authorities' in education and culture. These were partly bourgeois in origin, in a Marxist sense; but those 'taking the capitalist road' were not bourgeois in origin, or, if a few were individually, this was immaterial. They were members of the bureaucracy created by the Communist regime, members of the party, who, in Mao's view, now stood for a form of government and for related economic policies which he identified with Soviet revisionism. Using the language of Marxism, he is attacking an urban elite of educators and administrators who stand over against the uneducated masses, and form an obstacle to further change in the interests of the masses. In this respect, as in connection with the mass line, we can say (without committing ourselves on the question of the truth of Mao's analysis or accepting his values) that he is dealing with a problem which is at once a general one in underdeveloped countries, and one with particular relevance in a country with a tradition in which education leading to public office was the basis of social position. The greatest obstacle to the development of democracy in any real sense in China and in comparable countries is the opposition of an elite or a group of inter-related elites who, by virtue of education or political authority, or both, are in a position to defend their own sectional interests very well; and, on the other hand, a simple population, scattered, ignorant and inarticulate, which cannot bring its influence to bear.

As far as rural China is concerned, however, class struggle also indicates something more orthodox. It refers to the familiar idea of the 'spontaneous capitalist tendencies' of the peasants, particularly the more prosperous peasants, and the obstacle which this puts in the way of the further development of collectivism. This is the other great issue which, along with bureaucratism, is probably foremost in Mao's mind, and it is difficult to tell which is primary. The attempt to strengthen the collective side of agriculture, and the first moves to attack the 'bourgeois royalists' in cultural life, originated at the same Central Committee meeting in 1962, and the two movements have developed side by side. They are linked by the supposition that both problems could be solved by the full employment of the mass line in mobilising the poor peasants and workers against the private sector of agriculture, and their student sons and daughters in the cities against the establishment.

Throughout Mao Tse-tung's career, there has been a source of tension in his thinking between the divisive implications of class struggle and the integrating influences of nationalism. It is a perplexity inherent in the twentieth-century Chinese situation, and Mao's constant attempts to redefine the area of agreement have been more than exercises in tactics. The May Fourth heritage and the Marxist heritage clash and have constantly to be resolved. On the whole, Mao throughout his career has usually been on the side of breadth in the course of controversies which have involved the question with which his *Selected Works* begin: 'Who are our friends? Who are our enemies?' In the early days, during the alliance of 1923–27 with the Kuomintang, he was under suspicion in the Chinese Communist Party of collaborating too closely with his Nationalist colleagues.[3] In Chingkangshan, he attempted to base his soviet on as wide a social foundation as the party's theory then allowed, and defied the Central Committee in doing so. In the Juichin soviet, he deplored the party's refusal to support the left-wing but non-Communist rising in Fukien. His administration in the Border Regions subordinated Communist objectives to the creation of a mass nationalist resistance to Japanese invasion. During the Third Civil War, he opposed egalitarian extremes in land reform and insisted that the reform must not be carried out by poor-peasant leagues, but through representative village governments from which only the landlords and those rich peasants who were also landlords were to be excluded. The elaboration, in 1957, of the idea of non-antagonistic contradictions, and the insistence that 'in the objective conditions of China' even the antagonistic contradictions between the remaining private employers and their workers were capable of peaceful resolution, were partly an attempt to find a new level of unity. And, as has been suggested, the *Quotations* anthology itself was designed to restate the consensus. Throughout his long leadership, of the party and then of the country, Mao has constantly laid it down as the aim of successive campaigns that 95 per cent of those involved are capable of being brought to support them. This was repeated even at the height of the Red Guard movement. His confidence in this high proportion of 'winnable' adherents has sometimes been misplaced, but it is not so much a prediction as an instruction. It is at once an expression of confidence in massive support and an injunction to secure this degree of support, if necessary by compromise.

The tension between unity and class division expresses the fact that the Communist Party in China has a dual role, and this should never be forgotten. It is a Communist Party, but it is also the nationalist movement of China, analogous to the nationalist movements in the former colonies. The fact that China was never, formally, anyone's colony does not alter this. The party, therefore, not only inherits the emotions of the nationalist movement, but also its responsibilities, among which is to create and to maintain national solidarity on the basis of a consensus. The hostility of most of China's capitalists to privileged foreign enterprises, and the experience of the war against Japan, strengthened the idea of the possibility of the unity of 95 per cent of the nation, but more important perhaps was twenty years of practical experience during which the Chinese Communist Party, working in the rural areas, learned that it was possible to unite the majority of the village behind a revolutionary programme, and learned what degree of compromise and what type of organisation were necessary to secure this.

Our knowledge both of Russian and of Chinese rural society on the eve of revolution is very imperfect, but present knowledge suggests that their characteristics were very different, and that the difference may go far to account for the contrasts between Soviet and Chinese policies towards the peasants.

In general, the Russian village consisted of a mass of poor peasants (up to 80 per cent of the village population), broadly equal in economic status and sharing the egalitarianism of the *mir* and of their common status as former serfs. This mass faced a minority (perhaps 10 per cent) of *kulaks*, whose superior prosperity was very recent, and who were as a class largely the deliberate creation of Stolypin. They were bitterly resented; very often they were even physically cut off from the village in their own individual steadings. The middle-peasant group in Russia was generally insignificant. In China, there was much less polarisation, and a much stronger middle-peasant group. Moreover, on such issues as tenancy and indebtedness, many Chinese middle peasants shared the grievances of their poorer neighbours. The middle-peasant group was, in fact, too large to be bullied, but varied enough to be split by carefully designed policies on particular issues. In Russia, the *kulak* minority produced the bulk of the marketed surplus of agriculture. In China,

[handwritten marginal note: DIFF. BET. RUSSIAN & CHINESE PEASANTRY.]

54

poor, middle and rich peasants, each as a group, made an equal contribution to the surplus. It was therefore impossible in China to control the surplus by attacking and expropriating a small minority of the village.

In the course of twenty years of experience, the Chinese Communist Party came to terms with this situation, and very seriously modified its originally doctrinaire policies. Its class analysis of the village had to be, and eventually became, much subtler than the Russian model, its methods inevitably more dependent on persuasion, and its attention to economic incentives much more close and realistic.[4] Such was the basic lesson drawn by the party during its twenty years in the wilderness.

The nationalistic, as opposed to the class, responsibilities of the Chinese party made this lesson easier to absorb. But perhaps the most significant influence of the nationalist heritage of the party has been on Mao himself. He has shown in a dramatic way, as the national leader of China and the inheritor of the nationalist democracy of the May Fourth period, that he is willing to destroy the party he has created by an appeal to non-party citizens, because he believes that the party has become bureaucratic and an obstacle to national and democratic aims. The analogy with other partisan leaders—Tito and Fidel Castro, for example—hardly needs elaboration.

'Unity' in relation to class divisions and to ideology is a word which needs definition. Whatever the practice of Communist cadres may be, in Mao's thinking it is not equivalent to uniformity. He stresses throughout all his writing that differences are to be expected, that they are the driving force of history, and will continue to exist for ever. His pamphlet of 1957 on 'contradictions' was an attempt to define the pattern of social differences in China. In the course of it, he put forward the phrase which is officially translated as 'unity, struggle, unity', as the formula for dealing with these differences. This translation has made it easier for some commentators to write as if uniformity were the aim. But the phrase in the original Chinese does not say 'unity, struggle, unity'; it says 'solidarity, criticism, solidarity', and immediately after using it Mao Tse-tung goes on to make it quite plain that he is concerned, not with uniformity of opinions, but with the idea that all controversies inside the party, and between the party and the population, should start from *a will*

55

to solidarity. Far from being a formula for the mass production of 'blue ants', this is a universally accepted rule for successful government by discussion, as anyone who has ever been on a committee knows. Without a consensus on fundamentals, without agreement on aims, basic priorities and general method, discussion is pointless. In his 1957 pamphlet, Mao demanded that criticisim should be based on six criteria. It should help (i) to unite the various nationalities of China, help (ii) socialist construction, (iii) the people's democratic dictatorship, (iv) democratic centralism, (v) the leadership of the Communist Party, and (vi) international socialist unity. The issuing of these rules after, and not before, the party had been so roughly criticised was not, as is so often said, a ruse to catch the 'rightists', but simply a restatement of the consensus already enshrined in the Organic Law and the Common Programme. Mao's fault was in assuming that potential critics still interpreted them as he did.

POLITICS IN COMMAND

For most of the period during which Mao has been in power in China, there has been, in spite of 'brain-washing' (a much exaggerated phenomenon), more freedom of expression permitted than in any other Communist country before the East-European thaw of the last three or four years. The only periods of Chinese Communist rule when there have been stringent and general attacks upon writers, for example, are the anti-rightist campaign which succeeded the Rectification of 1957, and the present Cultural Revolution. The idea that intellectuals, including scientists and technologists, managers and planners, have been under constant restriction is very largely the result of failure to appreciate what is meant by the apparently sinister slogan 'let politics take command'. Although, like everything else in China, this has its extravagant applications, on the whole it is simple enough. The *Quotations* anthology begins by insisting that administrators must not forget policy, that they must remember the broad direction in which their specialised and local efforts are supposed to be aimed. This is the germ of putting 'politics in command'. At the broadest, it means that one must work within the consensus; but it is more than this, and has many ramifications.

China is a country of enormous size and endless variety, with a population far greater than has ever before been brought together under a single unitary government. Physical communications are still scarcely adequate. Social communication is still very far from perfect; indeed, it is surprising how ill-served the rural majority still are by the mass media, in a country popularly supposed to be in the grip of an almost universally effective thought-control dictatorship. (This point is amplified in chapter 4, page 81.) It is impossible to legislate at the centre for the whole of China, and utopian to expect the localities to carry out the centre's orders without constant pressure upon them. In this respect, China is still as it was in imperial times; in spite of the impressive volume of instructions coming down and reports going up, its unity is still largely an ideological, not an administrative, unity. To put politics in command means, among many other things, to carry on provincial and local affairs in response to policies which can be usefully stated by the central administration only in the broadest terms: terms often so broad that, in practice, they can have little more than the force of recommendations—hence the supporting barrage of ideological reiteration (which China-watchers read), and in addition the barrage of innumerable reports of local examples of good or bad application in varying local circumstances (which China-watchers too often ignore).

In science, technology, planning and administration, it has a related significance, and a simple one. We are accustomed in the West to the theory that technical advisers and civil service administrators should not make policy, but should merely advise the elected policy-makers. We are equally habituated to the idea that these technicians and civil servants frequently enjoy in practice more influence on policy than the theory suggests. This is a problem in China, as it is anywhere else, and a greater problem because intellectuals are few, and the layman (including the party functionary) often does not have the education to enable him to deal with the specialist. Hence, the special slogan within the context of 'politics in command': 'be both Red and Expert'. The specialist must know and accept policy, and the party-member policy-maker must know enough about the special fields which impinge upon his work to be able to communicate with the specialist without being at a disadvantage.

There is another and vitally important field for the application of politics in command. In local economic development, in the application of science, in medicine, in education—in almost every

E

branch of social endeavour—successful reform must involve a clash with the social or personal habits, and the apathy, ignorance and suspicion, of the poor masses. In medicine, for example, the basic need is for the prevention of disease by the improvement of hygiene, and a doctor who goes to a village to deal with these problems is going to be involved from the start in criticising the habits of the population. He will need politics: the art of persuasion. He will most probably be a member of a mobile medical team, which must leave behind in the village a rudimentary part-time organisation for providing first-aid and instruction about hygiene: an organisation chosen from the villagers. He must influence the villagers' choice, which once more means politics. He may be a bright young specialist who, with prospects of a lucrative practice among senior cadres in Shanghai, has been pressurised into volunteering for rural service. Contemptuous of the peasants, sick of the food, nauseated by the stench, bored with the monotony and terrified of infection, he yet must remind himself of his duty. This, in the Chinese Communist sense, means politics. What we would call social conscience (if we did not take it for granted in doctors without giving it a name) is, in Maoist parlance, a matter of political attitude. This is the simplest and widest application of the slogan.

There is more, however, to 'politics in command' than this. It implies a positive and progressive attitude on the part of people in authority or in positions of influence: an attitude which is the antithesis of what we in the West think of as bureaucratic. Routine is not enough. The party is the engine of social change; it cannot just idle, it must pull. Since 1959, stalled by the failures of 1959–61, it has not functioned as a revolutionary party. The essential meaning of the Cultural Revolution since it began at the meeting of the Central Committee in September 1962, lies in the attempt to get it going again. It represents a reaffirmation of the insistence on 'policy' with which the *Quotations* anthology begins; and, in fact, if one substituted 'policy' for 'politics' throughout, the slogan 'let politics take command' and its derived slogans would be immediately comprehensible.

The complement of this insistence that administrative and all other work must be informed by knowledge and understanding of the broad questions of policy, is that the administrator must be able to relate policy to ever-varying local conditions. Hence the restora-

tion of emphasis since 1962 on Mao's empirical theory of knowledge, the criticism of academic philosophers, and the attempt to
induce the ordinary citizen to study and even to write 'philosophy',
in the sense of recording his own application of Mao's theory of
knowledge to whatever work he is engaged in. This has led to an
enormous amount of naïveté and extravagance, and one could very
easily, by overstressing this side of the movement, string together
from the records of the lunatic fringe a characterisation of the
movement which would make it appear quite ludicrous. But to do
so would be to miss the point.

CONTRADICTIONS

In this renewed attempt at philosophical education, Mao's theories
concerning 'contradictions' play a very large part, and this makes it
easy to dismiss much of what is written as some sort of mystical
theology. One has, as usual, to examine Mao's own applications of
the idea to appreciate its practical significance. In spite of the
philosophical form of the essay *On Contradictions* (officially dated
1937), it is quite perfunctory as a systematic development of the
Hegelian-Marxist idea of contradiction. It does little more than
use the authority of Marxist language to provide a mnemonic
formula for a simple and practical analysis of situations, useful to a
political leadership composed of a mass of village cadres and former
guerrillas who are politically unsophisticated and mostly subliterate. It may lead to a crude form of analysis with built-in
distortions; but at least it *compels to a habit of analysis*, and this is its
main function in practice.

The term 'contradiction' is used, in the first place, for the opposed
interests of social classes in the orthodox manner; but it is employed
for such a variety of relationships that it has ceased to have any
meaning which, in a Western sense, or even a Marxist sense, could
be called philosophical. It is used in almost any situation in which
Western writers would use such words as conflict, contrast, dicho-
tomy, antithesis. It is applied, not only to situations in which there
are conflicts of interests, but also to situations where the problem is
one of priorities or of marginal utilities, and to situations in which
differences of opinion occur as a consequence of the partial knowledge, one-sided experience or imperfect sympathies of the individuals involved. It is a useful metaphor, and one which can provide

a common language between the educated and the ignorant.

Even the more abstruse expressions of the idea have their practical point. The 'principal contradiction' and the 'principal aspect of the contradiction' seem to take us into realms of intellectual juggling. But what is the point they seek to make? *On Contradictions* states:

> At any one time there can only be one central task. . . . Consequently the person with over-all responsibility . . . should not act upon each instruction as it comes from the higher organisation without any planning of his own. . . . It is part of the art of leadership to take the whole situation into account and act accordingly. . . .

The humblest subliterate Chinese village leader promoted to responsibility from the population of his own village is faced daily with all the problems of government in microcosm: conflicts of interest among individuals and groups; conflicts of interest between personal, or local, aspirations and duties to the collective and the state; conflicts of opinion; cost-accounting of plans, problems of disparities between different kinds of resources, short-term versus long-term gains, the difficulties of setting piecework norms in agricultural work—a complex of inter-related problems. The simple mnemonic of 'contradictions' compels analysis, provides a common language, and gives the village leader confidence in his own judgement. In the innumerable examples quoted for the application of the formula, there is little sign of distortion as a result of its use; it can be applied well or badly according to the quality of the empirical investigation which lies behind the conclusions expressed in terms of it. We should not despise it or misunderstand it because we are too literate to need such mnemonics, any more than we need the reiteration of number-slogans, like the Four Goods, the Five Firsts, the Three-Antis and the Five-Antis, the Three-Eight working style, the so-many do's and the so-many don'ts. The Chinese may not need them much longer, and then perhaps the contradictions formula may become just an old, bad joke to the mass of the population; but that time has not yet come.

DEMOCRATIC CENTRALISM

There is, however, one aspect of Mao's use of the idea of contradiction which has very real vitality, and that is his interpretation of

60

the 'unity of opposites'.[5] In those conflicts in which one desideratum conflicts with another, he refuses to accept the easy solution of compromise. The most important application of this is his attitude to democratic centralism, and this is the problem which includes all others. Effective central control militates against effective democracy. The freest of governments represents a gross and crude restriction on the freedom of citizens. It is a universal problem, but it is also one of particular severity in China because of the enormous size and variety of the country, and also because of the almost universally accepted need for a strong government whose writ runs everywhere. It is also a problem which Mao himself feels particularly keenly because of the enormous stress which he puts upon the possibilities of local and popular initiative, which are bound to be reduced by the existence of a strong government, especially a one-party government. Most statesmen in most countries accept what they find in this respect, or in the course of the process of government continue to strengthen centralisation in the interests of smooth administration without usually being more than half-conscious of what they are doing. It is one of Mao's distinctions that he has never let this problem rest.

Torn between the desire to assert the fullest possible party influence and the belief in the fullest possible freedom for local initiative as well as the fullest possible popular control over cadres, he has sought, not a simple compromise, but the creation of new institutions which will produce both a higher degree of centralisation and a more effective degree of democracy. These new institutions were represented by the Communes. This is why the Communes have been interpreted in the West in such contrasting ways. They represented a drastic decentralisation, on the one hand; but, on the other, they also represented more direct party control of the local community. The local collective and the local state organs were merged, but the unit remained small enough for effective direct democracy, while the hierarchical apparatus of the state was largely put out of commission. China was to become a country composed of an agglomeration of 23,000 self-sufficient, self-governing communities, responsible for their own economic plans, determining their own levels of consumption, contracting freely with the state, capable even of defending themselves independently (for the first three months the Commune administration had whole and sole command of its own militia) and of determining their own levels of welfare expenditure and investment, and governed by an administration elected by direct universal suffrage. At the same time, an ideologically united party—whose awareness of policy depended less upon its hierarchical structure than on its direct exposure to mass-media instructions and propaganda from the centre—would provide a more effective form of unification than the bureaucracy. The historical relationship with the guerrilla administration of the Border Regions is obvious; and, indeed, Mao's critics at the time dismissed the Communes as 'guerrilla stuff'. But Mao also believes that the Communes represent the society of the future, not only in China, but throughout the world. Democrats throughout the world who are worried by the steady growth of the power of the state, even in the most democratic of countries, cannot but sympathise with Mao's bold and imaginative attempt to solve this fundamental problem of politics, even if they do not accept it.

INCENTIVES AND ECONOMIC ORGANISATION

Political issues in China, as in any planned society, are usually based upon economic issues, as Mao stressed when, in writing *On The Correct Handling of Contradictions Among the People*, he gave the principal place to conflicts of economic interest among the individual, the collective and the state. The fundamental problem is one of distribution of the economic product between, on the one hand, personal incomes, collective welfare and investment funds, and state revenue and supply on the other. Mao's theories concerning the economic aspects of social organisation are as important as his theories concerning political leadership, but they have been almost totally ignored in the West. Even a commentator as well-informed and judicious as Richard Harris can write that Mao 'has no interest in problems of economic development'.[7] Mao's own description of the Border Region economy between 1940 and 1943 is seldom referred to, and has never been analysed or translated, except for its preface. The official Chinese Communist history of agricultural taxation, which was written in terms of Mao's essay *On the Correct Handling of Contradictions* and to defend his policies in this respect, has never been analysed. The comments written by Mao himself on the development of individual co-operative farms, and interspersed through the *High Tide* anthology (1956) are worth a volume of analysis in themselves,[7] but they have not been systematically studied and are hardly regarded in the West as a significant part of Mao's writings, although they express all the ideas which underlie his policies since 1955.

The first maxim of Maoist economics is that production must precede taxation and procurement. The cadre's task is to increase production, and only then and secondarily to collect for the state. This is emphasised in the preface to his account of policy in the Border Region and has been consistently emphasised in advice and instructions to cadres throughout the regime. This is in complete contrast to the policy associated with Stalin, in which (as we now know more clearly than ever as a result of the work of Soviet scholars since Stalin's death) the villages were pillaged to support industrialisation by levels of procurement which took little account of costs or consumption norms.

Again in contrast with Stalin, Mao Tse-tung has consistently attached importance to material incentives. His attacks on dependence upon material incentives since 1962 have been directed, not against their existence, but against their operation in an uncontrolled private sector. Since he first held the responsibility of ruling a territory in the Chingkangshan soviet, he has been more ready than many of the other party leaders in China to compromise on ideology to protect the incentives to production. In 1957, he pointed with pride to the fact that taxation and procurement in China were moderate and stable, and such research as has been done on this in the West tends to support him.[8] His policy has always been to keep these norms down so as to permit the retention in the hands of the local collective of most of any increases of production, and to ensure that collective income was divided in such a way as to maintain a rise in personal incomes for most of the population from year to year, while permitting the accumulation of collective funds for investment on a modest scale (not more than 5 per cent of gross income). His stress on short-term construction schemes that envisage paying for themselves, if possible, within the year is in itself a recognition of the necessity for very strong incentives in capital construction in agriculture.

Mao's recent attacks on material incentives are not a reversal of these policies. They are concerned with three things: (i) high differentials in industry resulting from incentive bonus schemes in a situation in which the higher standards of living of city workers are a cause of serious discontent to the rural population; (ii) uncontrolled profits in the private sector of agriculture which lead to competition for land, labour, and fertilisers with grain production because (as always in China) vegetable farming is enormously more profitable than grain farming; and (iii) with Libermanist ideas on the organisation and planning of industry.* They are in no sense an attempt to replace price policy with moral exhortation in economic life. Price policies may not always have been effective in China, any more than they are always successful anywhere else, but they are the most important form of control.

His writings, and the policies which they express, have always assumed that the chief value of collectivist organisation lies, not in the collective as a tax-gatherer, but in the collective as a means of mobilising local capital and labour for the development of production. He emphasised throughout the collectivisation movement his belief that social reorganisation in China must precede technical reform and is the first condition of successful technical reform. This, indeed, might be said to be his obsession. In every major campaign of social change, it has been explicitly stated and stressed that the increase of production was the purpose of the change; in land reform, by the removal of the harsh rents and the insecurity of the old system and the full restoration of the incentives of ownership: in collectivisation and in the community construction schemes which collective organisation made possible; in the Communes; and in the Cultural Revolution, the main end of which is to 'liberate the productive forces'.

Mao Tse-tung combines his belief in the value of collectivist economic organisation with a belief in the importance of entrepreneurship. This is a combination that Western commentators find it difficult to understand, because, for historical reasons we associate entrepreneurship with economic individualism. The problem of how to create an atmosphere that will maximise the spirit of enterprise is one on which a great deal has been written in the past few years; but no one has attempted to analyse what it means and how it works in socialist systems. In China, it is difficult to see how

---

* See Documentary Appendix, page 238, for the abridged text of one of the attacks made during the crisis on Sun Yeh-fang, one of China's senior economists who was made a whipping-boy for the 'economists' in the party.

economists can ignore the question. Its records are everywhere. In the innumerable accounts published of economic success and failure in agriculture and industry, enterprise is the factor most stressed. The profits of such enterprise may be collective, the motives ascribed to the individual or group which produces or backs a new idea may, as a matter of course, be represented as altruistic; but the starting point is almost always the individual's or the group's ingenuity, far-sightedness and willingness to take a risk in the interests of increased production or increased efficiency. Enterprise may not always bring great material rewards, but in a society where status is dependent upon reputation, and where successful contributions to production are a major factor in the gaining of reputation, there is no reason to assume that the incentives to entrepreneurship are inadequate. In the most successful Communes, life has been transformed for their members by successful innovation; the Chinese believe that this has occurred on about one-tenth of the Communes. Mass-line techniques of stimulating enterprise in the communal use of local resources— especially for projects with a gestation period short enough to obviate the need for sacrifice of consumption or for the extention of credit— probably represent China's most valuable contribution to the solution of the problems of economic development in poor countries; and there is little doubt that Mao Tse-tung must be given the main responsibility for originating the idea and maintaining its application.

It is often said that Mao is a romantic, who exaggerates the power of the human will, and discounts natural and economic obstacles to change; and that perhaps he discounts the obstacles which human nature itself presents to the sort of changes he seeks. But Mao has nothing to say about 'will'. What he talks about is 'consciousness', which is rather different. He believes (and his belief in the possibilities of initiative and enterprise among the mass of ordinary people is a reflection of this) that when human beings become conscious of 'the direction of history', their energies are liberated, and that these energies are enormously powerful. This probably springs from two sources. On the political side, there is his experience of the explosive force of popular discontent in China when, through radical agitation, it was given a rationale. On the economic side, there is his concern over the fatalism in the face of nature which is the general attitude of a population that has always lived more or less precariously at the mercy of the monsoon, with flood and drought alternating, and never a year when some part of the country did not experience disaster and starvation. To remove this ancient conservatism of fear and ignorance, and to persuade the Chinese people that from a scientific point of view their problems are already solved, that man can control nature if he chooses to organise to do it—this to Mao is the fundamental problem; once this bondage of fear and hopelessness is broken by education, the Chinese people will respond *en masse* to the challenge of taming their environment. In the event, perhaps they will, and perhaps they will not; but there is nothing fanatical in expecting that they will.

It is also said that Mao is a romantic, a utopian, in expecting the Chinese people to follow him to extravagant heights of collectivism. We must ask, before we can accept or reject this, just what heights of collectivism he expects in reality. It has been suggested already that the moral exhortations in Mao's writing are not platitudes in the context of Chinese society, but are directed against the real evils of a country in which social conscience had decayed and public honesty had been corrupted; and we can ask whether Mao expects from the Chinese any more than human nature gives without too much complaint in other societies. When we examine what is held up for praise and what is subject to censure, it is very hard to sustain the idea that what is demanded is extravagant. The expression of morality in the Chinese language is always overstrained, and it is always overtranslated; this is as true of traditional or Nationalist pronouncements as of Communist statements. Mao himself, however, studiously avoids the conventional extremes of language, and even in his moralising essays—*Serve the People* (1944) and *In Praise of Norman Bethune* (1939)—the language is moderate.[9] The heroes of the Maoist cult, although they may be surprisingly given to reading the works of Mao, are not wildly heroic. They were, if they did what they are said to have done, brave and conscientious men; but the only possible reason for making such a fuss about them is that their sense of responsibility is not too widely shared in Chinese society; and anyone who has lived in Chinese society does not have to be told this. There is nothing in the substance, as opposed to the frills, of these stories exemplifying social conscience and public spirit that asks for more than the degree of co-operativeness, respect for public interests, and common honesty which we would normally regard as

66

the self-discipline necessary to sustain a modern society. The attempt to impose this discipline in relation to unfamiliar institutions which demand wider loyalties than the narrow family loyalties of traditional society puts a strain upon the conscientiousness of the majority of the population; while the demand for humility and democratic attitudes from leaders who, in spite of their lip-service to the new values, instinctively adopt the traditional attitudes of the mandarin, complicates the problem; but it is not a problem created by absurdly unrealistic ideas of what human nature is capable of.

We can now sum up what Mao Tse-tung has sought consistently throughout his career in politics. His objectives have been: an empirical style of work which applies national policy in terms of local conditions throughly studied; a mass-line technique of work which secures the mutual education of leaders and led, and which maintains the maximum participation of the majority of the population in decision-making at the local level; active, positive leadership by the party's cadres in every aspect of social progress, carried out in such a way as to make the process of change at the same time a process of education which aims to free the mass of citizens eventually from the tutelage under which they now inevitably work; the creation of a system of national government which both maximises local initiative and enterprise, and also maximises direct exposure to the ideology that provides the framework of effort; a decentralised economic system which makes a reality of the identity of self-love and social by bringing the benefits of modern technology into the village in the form of industries created and run by the village itself; preparation for the defence of China, in the absence of adequate modern military equipment, by a nation in arms.

To all these developments, bureaucracy is the threat. In reacting against the bureaucratic tendencies of his own party, Mao is not doing so on the basis of some private utopian vision. He is reacting to the bureaucratic decay of the Nationalist movement of which he was once an enthusiastic, although critical, member: a decay which is one of the great tragedies of modern politics and one of the great political experiences of Mao's own life. He shares at least one conviction with Western liberals: that, while the difference between paternalistic socialism and fascism is a real one, the line between

them is easily crossed. The Kuomintang crossed it; Mao believes
that the Soviet Union has crossed it; and he fears that his own
party is only a few short steps from it. He believes that his own
administration, if the continuation of mass-line revolution is halted,
could turn into a Kuomintang-type bureaucratic elite, governing
the country by fiat from the towns, building up their urban amenities out of the hard-won surplus of the peasants, content to maintain
the peace and collect taxes, forming a new class with privileges
almost as unshakeable as those of the old ruling elite, and in the end
perhaps, like the Kuomintang, becoming corrupt, parasitic and
incapable even of defending China from invasion.

"NEW CLASS."

To both Mao and his liberal opponents in China, the enemy is the
same: bureaucracy; but they diverge entirely on the means by which
it should be combated. The liberals believe, essentially, in gradually
improving the elite. Mao believes in destroying the foundations of
the elite. He faces one of the fundamental problems of politics: the
tendency for a levelling revolution to produce its own new privileged
establishment. But he does not hope to defeat this possibility, as is
widely believed in the West, simply by perpetually recurrent,
disruptive mass protest. The Cultural Revolution is meant to be the
prelude to the full application of a specific solution to the problem,
on the lines of a refined and extended Commune system which will
cut down bureaucracy and minimise the 'Three Great Differences'—
the differences between town and country, between industry and
agriculture, and between mental and manual labour—which he
rightly sees as the most inhibiting discontinuities in Chinese society.

DIFF. BET.
"THIRD ROAD"
n MAO:

IV

THE REVOLUTION IN CULTURE

THE TERM 'CULTURAL REVOLUTION' is familiar today as the short form of 'the Great Proletarian Cultural Revolution': the ambitious and far-reaching political campaign which began in the summer of 1966. This campaign has, of course, deep roots and a long background. In tracing here the specifically cultural aspects of developments since about 1962, an outline is required, if we are to gain an intelligible view of the Chinese Communists' present cultural policy and its place in the party's strategy of revolution, of the general cultural development that has been taking place under Communist auspices over the past thirty years. Only against this background will the debates and disputes between 1963 and 1966—the main subject of this chapter—make any sense at all.

'Cultural revolution' is a term that has been current in China ever since the May Fourth movement of 1919. It stands for an accelerated and comprehensive change in all fields, from science, public health, education and academic research to personal morals and relationships, social *mores*, entertainment and the arts. It means, for example, the introduction and application of modern agricultural and medical science, the provision of universal education, the establishment of a 'popular' literature and the substitution of late and free for early and arranged marriages. In Marxist terms, all these aspects of life are part of the 'superstructure' of society: secondary social institutions which ultimately rest on the 'economic base', the prime factor determining social development. Not all of these many facets

69

can be discussed here; the main emphasis will be upon literature, an aspect which has been very prominent since 1964, with a necessarily more cursory survey of education and academic research in the humanities.

No aspect of life in China today is independent of politics, at least in principle, and this is held to be particularly relevant to those facets of cultural life where apolitical, specialist or private attitudes tend to persist. It is therefore necessary for the party to remind people that stories and films (to take two examples) should not be regarded as mere pastimes. Specialists are also warned that the neutral pursuit of a special interest or the neutral practice of a skill tends to lead to political error. The reasons for this attitude will appear below; at this point it is only necessary to stress the fact that the division of life into largely self-contained compartments, to which we are accustomed in the West today, is not accepted in principle by the Communist regime in China. The most important fact about contemporary Chinese culture is, indeed, the political control and direction which integrate cultural with other activities. It can easily be understood that political trends and changes are bound to affect cultural activities at all times, and that an understanding of the political scene is a primary requirement before considering, for example, literature or education. This is, in some sense, true of every society, but rarely to the degree found in China.

The substantive issues raised by cultural problems in China are to a greater or lesser extent universal. For this reason we are quite entitled to judge Chinese views, policies and achievements on the basis of our own criteria. If such judgements are to have much value, however, they must proceed as far as possible from an examination of the actual product and its social context as well as of the statements and commentaries put out by the Chinese; we must endeavour to pick out effects and functions as well as intentions. Secondly, judgements which fail to take into account the past experience and present problems of Chinese society and government—which lack, in other words, an awareness of the possibilities and alternatives open in China—will be unsoundly based. It is important, in particular, to remember that China is an underdeveloped country. Twenty years of single-party regimes and military coups in newly independent states have persuaded a good many of us that Western political institutions will not necessarily work in poor and badly integrated societies; yet, because of our tendency to regard politics as something 'on its own', this lesson is less readily applied to the educational, literary and technical life of such countries.

At a deeper level, we must surely be aware that the values of our own society on many of the fundamental issues are somewhat confused, the relationship between the individual and society, in particular, being the source of many unresolved dilemmas. In the cultural field, there is the continuing and tacitly accepted gulf between the 'high-brow' and the 'popular'. Hence, if we are to have a balanced view of Chinese culture, we must avoid narrow views of our own culture. This is very important, for most Western comment on Chinese culture is based on an implicit comparison between Chinese culture as a whole and only the 'best' of our own. Thus, Chinese literature is measured against the product of our established literary world rather than against popular literature—for example, the material printed in the popular press. There is, of course, no reason why any Chinese work of literature should not be judged by our highest standards but, once again, such a judgement may have a limited interest. In sum, an examination or criticism of contemporary China should be made from a position of self-awareness; if possible, from a consciously held and well-founded point of view, but at the least from an awareness of the problems inherent in the material being considered.

Our main concern here will be with the 'intellectuals', that relatively small but immensely important sector of Chinese society which played such a vital role in the revolution. The term has a rather vague and restricted use in Britain and America, and is often essentially subjective in character. ('He's an *intellectual*.') It is not an apt translation of the Chinese equivalent (*chih-shih fen-tzu*), which literally means 'knowledgeable element', essentially those with any education. It covers all those with a secondary or higher education. The same term has been used recently to include graduates of higher primary schools, but the more restricted definition will be used here. The intellectuals have an extremely important place in Chinese society; they may have sufficient education to form opinions and to influence others, and they are also essential for national development. The accelerated development of education, and of technical, professional and administrative services since 1950, has served to increase their importance still more. They are therefore too important for the regime to leave to their own devices. Hence, it is they who are the real target of the unending stream of explanations, exhortations and polemics, and it is they who, as educated cadres or activists, must pass the material on to the mass of the people. For these reasons, and also because they are a relatively small and easily identified group, they are subject to more pressure and are less 'free' than other members of society.

There are also historical reasons for the great attention given to the remoulding and correct orientation of intellectuals. Before 1949, education was restricted to a small minority; the great majority of those with any education in that year, therefore, were of bourgeois origin, and probably only a fraction of these had any real sympathy with the new regime and, above all, with its methods. The 'consensus' of 1949 was a negative rather than a positive one. Great pains were therefore devoted to the remoulding of the intellectuals after 1950. It was not so much a question of rooting out opposition as of eliminating 'non-political' attitudes and of mobilising intellectuals for service in the revolution. In the party's estimation, however, many have continued to have a 'petty-bourgeois tail concealed beneath their clothes'.[1] Since 1949, moreover, the socialist system itself has produced a new generation of young educated people; and here again there are manifest problems. Since 1960, and especially after 1963–64, much has been written in China on the spontaneous generation of a 'bourgeois' elite through the very success of socialism: a bourgeois elite being understood, not as a propertied class, but as a privileged group that puts private, professional or group interests over those of the party and society as a whole. It is believed that such an elite will acquire reservations about the political system itself; that it will come to resemble the older post-liberation intellectuals, but be even more dangerous because of its links with and roots in the new system. The apprehensions of China's leaders on this score are easier to understand in the light of the widely held assumption in the West that such a development will, in time, sap from within a collectivist and autocratic system which is successful in raising standards and expectations.

The intellectuals, therefore, both old and new, are regarded as a problem. The final solution, the creation of a 'proletarian intelligentsia' (a subject much discussed in 1958 and since about 1964), means that the existing intellectuals will be replaced by a generation of educated workers and peasants fully integrated with the masses and not forming a special stratum. Such an ideal is part of the vision of Communism and is therefore rather remote. For the time being, the integration and control of the intellectuals is the main task in hand.

CULTURE, LITERATURE AND THE COMMUNIST REGIME

What is the role or the importance of the cultural 'superstructure' within the Communist frame of reference? Culture will be taken here to refer mainly to literature, education and moral values. Communist writers generally see the role of culture, first and last, as educative or formative. They emphasise its power in the formation of opinion, attitudes and convictions, and distinguish this role of culture from that of coercion. There are, they say, many aspects of the 'superstructure' which lie beyond the scope of law or force. In the realm of morals, social opinion and criticism hold sway. Art, again, is a potent force for reform and education, reaching far beyond the scope of any administrative or legal action, for it has to do with 'likes and dislikes'—or, in other words, with emotions. A good cultural trend will consolidate 'the base'; it will reinforce the revolution in the economic and political spheres by strengthening the people's support for the revolution with new moral values and new emotional attitudes. This view takes on added weight in China, where Mao Tse-tung has put great emphasis on 'consciousness' and 'spontaneity'. He has stressed persuasion rather than violence in dealing with all but 'enemies of the people'. The distinction cannot, of course, be watertight, particularly if we admit the concept of psychological violence. Thought reform, a process applied to the intellectuals 'inherited' from the old society, has indeed been called 'coercive persuasion'. Nevertheless, 'administrative methods' have generally been regarded as inappropriate for the solution of ideo-logical and cultural problems, and discussion and criticism, within strict limits and within an atmosphere of control, have been impor-tant features of Chinese cultural life since the Communists came to power. The atmosphere in this respect has depended very closely on the political situation.

Culture, therefore, has to do with motivation, and correct motivation is the essence of 'redness'. 'Redness' means doing the right thing for the right reasons because you think and feel the right way. 'Redness' is primarily acquired through 'study'. This means the tempering of the individual, and it is achieved through work and social experience as well as through theoretical study. 'Redness' is commonly balanced by the term 'expertise', particularly in discussions of education or job. Ideally, the two should be complementary, but with 'redness' coming first. It means willingness to accept correct authority, rejection of egoistic motives, possession of positive motives, and adherence to the relevant professional code. The first element provides an opening for the cynical view that it means no more than political expediency; yet, there is no doubt that Mao values spontaneous and correctly motivated acceptance of authority ('leadership').[2] In many practical situations, 'redness' appears to be the equivalent of 'good character': a quality which, in many fields in the West also, is in some cases rated higher than proficiency.

The important formative role of education in the narrow institutional sense needs little explanation. The future of the revolution is clearly bound up with achievement in this field. It is a means of breaking down the barriers to communication within Chinese society, especially the barriers reared by illiteracy, superstition and the dearth of elementary general knowledge. It is a means of making the population aware of social and national needs and priorities, and of making technical advance possible over an extended front and over a sustained period. And, of course, beyond this there is the paramount role in China of education, in the formal sense used here, as a medium of political instruction.

The formative importance of the arts can be illustrated on two levels. So far as the individual is concerned, the arts are credited with an inspirational or therapeutic role. Drama, in particular, has been used to stimulate unworthy or 'backward' persons to reform themselves, to air everyday problems or conflicts, and to create model characters for emulation. The writer is, indeed, seen as an 'engineer of human souls', in the famous phrase attributed to Stalin and also used in China. On a larger scale, the arts can serve as 'the drummer of the age'. Revolutionary literature and art must 'help the people to make new history'.[3] Such is the grand role of the arts in relation to their era: the role, not only of a barometer showing incipient changes and those already in progress, but also of a lever helping to produce change. For exactly the same reasons, on the

74

other hand, art and literature of a wrong tendency can, it is maintained, do untold damage to the revolution; they can herald and facilitate a 'bourgeois restoration': a theme repeatedly descanted on in China since the beginning of 1966. And the better a harmful work is, in terms of artistic, persuasive or psychological power, the more dangerous it will be.[4] The functions ascribed to culture, including the arts, are, in short, too portentous to allow it to operate without political guidance and interference.

Another important general conception is the subordination of the individual to the collective; this principle is made to apply throughout society, and it is a leading component of 'redness'. The social and national responsibilities of the writer, the student, the doctor and so forth, are emphasised over any private or individual motives or aspirations. Once again, this principle has many applications which are far from being unfamiliar to Western experience; but its main implication for most Chinese intellectuals is probably both as a concept of service and also as a justification for direction in choice of career and in appointments to jobs. Thus, a medical worker (doctor) should welcome being sent away from a modern hospital to humdrum medical work in a backward rural area. The writer must not cultivate his talent in a study or an attic, but must enlist in the revolution and write and live 'for the people'. One of the most problematical applications of this principle is the direction of middle-school or college graduates to job-assigments. They are at a time of life when personal choices seem to come to the fore; and, in the case of the middle-school graduates, there are enormous numbers who must be refused college places and sent to work in the countryside. Though individualism has been regarded as a problem among the peasantry, who had been schooled for centuries in the tough struggle for their own families' survival, it is also regarded as the great and characteristic burden of the intellectuals: a burden which, in the case of the older intellectuals, the thought-reform campaign was designed to remove. And of all the intellectuals, the creative writer or artist was the most individualistic, the natural effect of his life and work being reinforced by foreign influences from the time of the May Fourth movement: influences which increased his alienation from Chinese society.

The party's prejudice against the 'expert'—in the sense of the person who will appeal to the inner logic or requirements of a profession or job to question the application to it of political leadership —is a related feature of the cultural scene. 'Experts' in China, no doubt, have had to be reminded frequently of the broader context of their activities, of the difficult problem of the application of these to the needs of society, and of the narrowness of the economic margins within which they must operate. The misguided application of overadvanced practice in an undeveloped environment has become a familiar problem in many countries. Tradition also forms a peculiar background, for education, literature and knowledge in general were previously very restricted in China. Education tended to be 'bookish' by modern Western standards, and literature was esoteric. These characteristics were, in some ways, aggravated by Western influence. The proposition that the common man can acquire education and training, increase his knowledge of complex matters and apply his knowledge in a practical fashion, was a novel point to make in the Chinese context. It should not be overlooked of course, that the anti-expert bias in the Chinese Communist Party produces its own dogmatism and bigotry. This is the more conspicuous precisely because a limited autonomy cannot in fact be denied to experts under any effective system. As the party itself points out, culture can lag behind or anticipate political developments: a fact which allows all kinds of complications. In the arts, artistic criteria are admitted to exist even though they must be subordinate to the political, and this sets up a most important tension. Culture must be autonomous at least to some extent, and this means that the expert, in the sense in which the word has been used here, cannot be entirely eliminated.

The fundamental text on literature, and by extension, on culture in general, is Mao's *Talks at the Yenan Forum on Literature and Art*, delivered in May 1942. The function of the *Talks* was to lend Mao's authority to certain views elaborated in Communist circles in the Soviet Union and in Shanghai over the preceding decade. The basic aim was to produce a literature which would serve the revolution and which would be able to get through to the unlettered peasants of northern China. This had been the unrealised aspiration of progressive writers for twenty years. So far as the *Talks* advocated a political and social role for literature, the weight of Chinese tradition was also behind them; the novelty they advocated was an extension of the audience to be addressed.[5]

76

+ fact that concern w/ politics in general is greater in china than in west

Several consequences flowed from these two premises: the need to stress political and social ends, and the need for effective communication. Content was put before form, which tended to be regarded as the preoccupation of the bourgeois literary elite; and the effect of a work in social and political terms was rated above the intentions of its author. The writer, artist or educator had to get out among the people and study their language and habits, so that he could gain a knowledge of the community he lived in but had not previously been a part of. An attempt was made in the Yenan period to get the intellectuals to spend some time in the countryside with the peasantry or the army. Since all were of bourgeois origin, it was hoped that they would achieve a 'change of heart' such as Mao has described in his own case: a transformation of bourgeois feelings (likes and dislikes) into proletarian feelings. The emphasis on popularisation was very marked during the anti-Japanese struggle and the Civil War, and was to come to the fore again in 1958 and again after 1962. In literature, it has meant a stress on quantity, speed and small-scale work. During these three periods, journalism, songs, one-act plays, story-telling and so forth, have been put first. The danger that such methods may result in shoddy and ineffective work is recognised, but the benefits of wider participation and dissemination are held to outweight this. In education, popularisation takes the form of an emphasis on spare-time, part-time and rural education, with a tendency towards decentralisation—all of which features were established in 1958.[6]

The opposite pole to popularisation is 'elevation', the raising of cultural standards. Elevation must proceed upon the basis of popularisation: a sensible enough view. Tension arises between the two concepts mainly because of the limitation of resources. Thus, the widest provision of educational facilities is certainly regarded as being to some extent an alternative to the raising of educational standards on the existing scale to still greater heights. In literature, the skilled personnel must be directed towards the provision of a mass of popular material and away from the further refinement of the literature addressed to the better educated. As in any field of endeavour, however, too little spread too far may be effort wasted. In the three periods mentioned, the emphasis was on popularisation; the opposite trend was noticeable in 1956 and in 1957, and between 1959 and 1962.

The most important consequence of popularisation was the decision made between 1938 and 1942 to make use of 'national forms'. To reach the people of the interior, it was necessary to use those media, such as opera, which were familiar to them. The foreign genres and styles introduced since the May Fourth movement, and which had preoccupied the left-wing writers of the 1920s and 1930s, would be of little value in the village or the army unit. On the other hand, 'national forms' were also, by definition, 'feudal' forms, expressing the values of the past; for that reason they needed considerable adaptation. As will be apparent later, the nativist motive has been strong once more in the last three or four years, and this time Soviet influence also has been rejected.[7]

After 1950, a great deal of attention was paid to the 'critical inheritance' of traditional culture, both of the popular and of the 'orthodox' gentry tradition. The reform of opera, especially important in view of the popularity of this art-form, consisted mainly in the eradication of its more obviously anti-modern elements (for example, in the treatment of women). In 1958 and again from 1963, however, there was an attempt to promote new operas on modern, revolutionary themes and so make positive use of this traditional form. The 'disinfection of tradition' was also carried out in the 1950s in the reappraisal of the great poets and writers of the past. The line taken was generally indulgent; if there were any elements in such figures which could be regarded as progressive, these were given full weight. This tendency reached its apogee by the early 1960s, when even some of the great rulers of the feudal past were being re-evaluated in a positive light.

During the same period, in 1956, the policy was introduced which is summed up in the slogan: 'Let a hundred flowers bloom and a hundred schools of thought contend.' It was intended to allow freedom of expression within definite limits. The fate of the short-lived episode of 1956–7 is well known; but by 1960 a kind of relaxation was reappearing. It is important to realise, nevertheless, that this slogan is also used to refer to the encouragement of mass creativity and participation, not merely to relaxation for the intellectuals.

A second concept, 'revolutionary romanticism', was publicised, appropriately enough, in 1958. It had been established as a literary norm in the USSR between 1932 and 1934. It is regarded as having no connection with 'bourgeois romanticism', condemned as an anti-social phenomenon. The writer pursuing 'revolutionary romanticism' seeks to perceive and write about those newly forming phenomena which will change the present and usher in the new society. He will use his skill to describe the 'new things and the new men', and so evoke feelings of optimism and resolve. The typical product of this approach is the heroic literature, 'hero' in this context meaning one who is ahead of the stream and is therefore to be admired and imitated. The products of revolutionary romanticism most often cited are the new revolutionary folk songs and Mao's poems. The problem in the more complex literary field of prose work is that of succumbing to stereotyping and formalism, which produce dull and unconvincing work. It was the tendency to write in 'black and white' which gave rise, about 1962, to the idea of writing more about 'middle characters': non-heroic figures who were neither good nor bad, and therefore expressed all the conflicts involved in the socialist revolution. It implications will be discussed later. Here we come up against the problem, at present insoluble, of popular taste. Given the objective of a didactic literature aimed at the maximum effective dissemination of socially acceptable views rather than at the deeper examination of the individual psyche, what is the best way of getting the messages through? Should the approach be direct or indirect? It is at least a plausible point in its favour that the simpler 'black and white' approach has a deeper appeal to the mass audience: a fact of literary communication which is true to a large extent of our own much more educated and complex society.[8]

The usual formulation which calls for 'the combination of revolutionary romanticism and revolutionary realism', indicates that literature must also be realistic. This depends, therefore, on the faith that the future so much desired is in fact developing in the present. The main implication of 'revolutionary realism' is the rejection of bourgeois 'critical realism'. It means that the writer, while a realist, must affirm the revolutionary regime and society; he must not perpetuate the literature of exposure, attack and dissent which bourgeois realists developed in the old society. The attitude of assent is to be as important now as that of dissent had been before. It was the questions of realism and of historical evaluation which were behind the great literary Rectifications of

79

1951–57.* These campaigns were part of the remoulding of the intellectuals and were conducted mainly through the press. The Rectification of 1964 (discussed below) is regarded as their successor.[9]

Another feature of the last decade has been the increased hostility to all forms of 'humanism': a term that had acquired an exclusively negative value by 1960. It is used to describe any interest in fundamental, general or enduring human factors to the detriment of class analysis and political criteria. It may be used, for example, to describe works on revolution or war which indicate the tragedy for the 'positive' characters, or the people, arising out of the events themselves or out of the action of the 'correct' side as well as that of the enemy. 'Humanism' may cover works which show members of different classes, or 'positive' and 'negative' characters, as sharing certain psychological traits; or works which imply the existence of an apolitical altruism or conscience as a general human trait. As the last feature of our brief survey of basic literary concepts, we should note that the rejection of humanism also constitutes the most fundamental chasm between the Chinese Communist approach and all varieties of liberalism.[10]

In the field of education, the most characteristic policy, (apart from the inclusion of political study in the syllabus) has been that of 'work-study' and the emphasis on spare-time education. These ideas were finally put into effect from 1958 onwards, when the educational system was decentralised. Work-study has worked in many different ways, but typically it entails a certain proportion of the students' time being devoted to physical labour. Every year, students are supposed to spend one month or six weeks in a factory or mine or, most often, in a village, where they practice the 'Three Togethers': eating, living, and working with the masses. 'As our skin is tanned, our hearts turn red.' It is also applied to staff as well as students and to all white-collar workers. Work-study, it is maintained, has an educational and sometimes a specific technical value for the student, through the improvement of character and the marriage of theory with practice. It is also seen as a first step towards breaking down the

---

* The campaigns of the 1950s were the following: the criticism of the film *Life of Wu Hsun* (1951), criticism of Yü P'ing-po's, *Studies in the Dream of the Red Chamber* (1954), the attack on Hu Feng (1955) and the anti-rightist movement (1957).

barriers between mental and manual labour which have been particularly marked in China. For this reason it contains the 'germs' of true Communism.[11]

There are several points to be noted about the provision of education in China. In the first place, the problem of resources places definite limits upon the level of education that can be supported. This is particularly so because the local communities must take on most of the responsibility for primary and secondary education in their areas. Because of the problem of resources, it is possible for a Commune to be held up as an example of 'overeducation', as was the case in one area where one person in four was at school. Another feature is the educational backlog, the enormous effort that has to be made in adult education, working upwards from the attainment of literacy itself. Higher education has its own special problems stemming primarily from its restricted scale, with only about a million places. Nine out of ten middle-school students must therefore be turned away and sent to work. Because of the general restriction of education in the past, the children of the former bourgeoisie have tended to be over-represented in higher education. The party has therefore shown some concern about the failure to alter this state of affairs. In 1962, for example, only half of the graduates of that year were of worker and peasant origin. They had been estimated as a third of the total student body in 1958.[12]

The key to policy in the entire cultural field is the question of communication. The problem is to find means of raising levels over the broadest possible front: an urgent problem in a poor and ignorant society attempting to make a rapid and sustained advance. Even a modest achievement and a relatively slow rate of progress depend upon a continuous effort at popularisation. Given the gap between the educated elite and the mass of the people, it is not likely that such an effort can achieve much except in connection with a political movement.

CULTURE AND POLITICS, 1962–66

The immediate background to the recent and more revolutionary phase, the Cultural Revolution initiated in 1966, is to be found in the period between 1959 and 1962. For three years from 1959, China suffered severe economic setbacks and accompanying political tensions attributed at the time to climatic difficulties and to opposition. An unfavourable international situation was the other leading feature of this period, marked by the withdrawal of Soviet personnel in 1960 and the ending of genuine Sino-Soviet exchange in mid-1963. It was in these circumstances that fear of 'modern revisionism' began to exercise an important influence on public statements from 1960 onwards. 'Modern revisionism' is defined in China as 'the result of the attempt to cater to disintegrating imperialism'.[13] It means that long-term Communist aims are abandoned in favour of dealing with short-term problems, and it implies a relaxation of effort and vigilance. During this period, therefore, a 'great anti-China chorus' (to use a term still employed by spokesmen of the regime) arose outside China, in the Communist as well as the anti-Communist camp. The leadership declared at the time that, in such circumstances, China could be infected by revisionism. Chou Yang made this point in an important speech in 1960, in which he pointed to the danger of a 'bourgeois restoration' should a qualitative change in the 'climate' within China take place. Concern was also expressed at that time about the younger generation, who might be open to bad influences.[14] The difference between the view then put by persons in authority, but now in disgrace, and the retrospective view now held by the Maoists is that the latter hold that such an infection did, in fact, take place on a large scale. By the end of 1962, on the other hand, there had been talk of China's 'turning the corner', and in 1963 no great concern had been displayed. The Maoists also naturally present this whole episode in more vivid and dramatic colours in order to reinforce their point.

The social and cultural life of China, the Maoists now maintain, was deeply affected by these adverse currents. In the wake of economic difficulties, collective work and collective motives were weakened in favour of individualist preoccupations, in the villages, in industry and among the intellectuals; everywhere cash incentives, greater differentials in rewards and old-fashioned values reappeared. A new elite, reared by the socialist system itself, took advantage of the domestic and international situation to fasten its hold upon the leadership levels in every sphere of life and work, including the party itself. A cult of the 'expert', the Maoist case now runs, was built up in opposition to the orthodox emphasis on correct political motivation and leadership. There was, most serious of all, a danger of losing the loyalty of the younger post-war generation. Meanwhile, in the cultural field, 'unhealthy' trends were expressed in a flood of dangerous films, plays, stories and academic writing; while in the countryside, the old feudal culture enjoyed a revival. The class standpoint was replaced by the 'humanistic approach'. In short, the 'correct emphases' in all the concepts outlined in the previous section of this chapter were reversed. In terms of the theories explained earlier, such a cultural trend could be regarded as presaging a political change, though such an accusation was not made until four years had elapsed from the time of the height of the 'bourgeois infection'.

How far can this dramatic view of the years between 1959 and 1962 be substantiated independently? What evidence is there of opposition, criticism or revisionism, or of the fattening of a new elite and the decay of collectivism? A comprehensive answer to this question has still to be made, but there is much evidence giving support to the Maoist view. Several Western writers have picked out particular aspects of industrial, agrarian, academic and educational life which point in the same direction, that is, towards a more cautious, more elitist, and relatively more liberal approach.[15] The rehabilitation between 1959 and 1961 of leading rightists censured in 1957, and the entry during these years of many older figures in the cultural field into the party, are also symptoms of relaxation.[16] We can also find in Chinese sources statements which emphasise elevation over popularisation, and give an otherwise unconventional weight to 'expertise' in relation to 'redness'.[17] Such views tend to substantiate the idea that the internal difficulties of the 1959–61 period provided an opportunity for a return to elitist, and a flight from mass, methods. In the academic field, there was something of a 'renaissance' in which a non-political ethos was allowed to develop. In historical studies, a nationalistic trend was discernible; and in literature, there was an interest in more subtle methods. A certain nostalgia, indeed, could be discerned in the cultural field. These observations are made on a rather insubstantial basis, but a definite picture does emerge from a sampling of the most varied evidence. This 'relaxation' was, of course, a relaxation recognisable as such only within the Chinese context.

The beginnings of the present movement in the cultural field are now officially traced back to the Tenth Plenum of the Central

Committee, held in September 1962. This noted a slight improvement in the economy and called for the renewal of 'class struggle', and also emphasised the importance of effective work in the countryside. The Tenth Plenum is now presented by the Maoists as Mao's counter-attack on the massed bad influences then prevailing, and is considered to mark the inauguration of the 'Great Socialist Cultural Revolution' which got under way in 1963. The centre of this 'revolution' was the Socialist Education movement: a mass campaign for political education, or indoctrination, and renovation of political work. Concentrated primarily on the countryside, it promoted the cult of Mao, the inculcation of collectivist values and the revealing to the 130 million young people of China of the evils of the past: evils which they had never themselves experienced. In 1964 and 1965, this Socialist Education movement developed into a campaign to improve the local cadres. By the end of 1965, the reform of the *hsien* (district) party committees had become the focus of attention. Party cadres were criticised for being timid, self-indulgent and neglectful of their work, even in places which had experienced the Socialist Education movement.[18]

Meanwhile, the People's Liberation Army—reformed by Marshal Lin Piao in a Maoist direction from 1961 onwards—entered the political field through the 'Learn from the Army' campaign which began in February 1964. The army was already regarded as a major formative influence upon the youth, though only a small proportion of those eligible for military service have been taken into its ranks. Having been a test-bed for methods of mass political work, its 'working style' was now recommended for imitation on a national scale. From this time forward, too, the army's cultural establishment began to play a more prominent role, and its influence has grown steadily since 1964. By the spring of 1966, the army's daily journal, *Liberation Army Daily* (*Chieh-fang-chün Pao*), was acting as the pacesetter in the press attacks on the Peking party organisation.[19]

All these developments took place against the background of an improvement in the economic situation. By the end of 1964, at the Third National People's Congress, a mood of confidence was discernible; there was talk of a new 'great leap forward' and of the projected Third Five-Year Plan. Since then, many claims for great leaps in different fields have been made. The Third Five-Year Plan was actually inaugurated at the beginning of 1966, though no details of it are available at the time of writing. Some possible analogy with the Great Leap Forward of 1958 seems to have been in the air, but it was also declared that a great leap would be more difficult now than before, and that more ideological preparation was necessary.

Against the background of the mass ideological movement, a new Cultural Rectification movement was launched in the summer of 1964. Although many of the subjects dealt with during this new phase had been discussed over the preceding four or five years, this was a 'movement' because of its breadth, duration and publicity. In a movement of this kind it becomes difficult, though not necessarily impossible, for more than one point of view to be heard. The object is to sort out a cultural problem in one particular direction and to disseminate the points and the material needed to establish it with the reading public. The press plays a vital role, not only on account of its direct readership, but because it provides the material needed by discussion leaders and propagandists. Thus, it was reckoned in Kwangtung in 1963, for example, that between fifty and seventy peasants could be reached through a village news-reading. Keynote articles, published in several national organs, are followed by a mass of local articles on the subject in hand. Discussions are convened at places of work, and selections of mass opinions are disseminated in the press.[20]

The present official account of the Cultural Rectification movement highlights the personal role of Mao Tse-tung and of Chiang Ch'ing and other figures in the leadership of the Cultural Revolution. Chiang Ch'ing's speech at the revolutionary drama festival of 1964, for example, was widely publicised in May 1967, but it had not been considered important enough to be published prominently at the time of its delivery.[21] The Rectification, however, was conducted until mid-1966 by the established propaganda apparatus under Lu Ting-yi and Chou Yang, who were subsequently denounced for 'waving a red flag to oppose the red flag'—in other words, for insincerity and treachery. Some aspects of the campaign have therefore been denounced as camouflage, but its content still stands. Brief views on the cultural scene, now said to have been put forward by Mao in addresses delivered in December 1963 and June 1964, are now termed "Instructions, Numbers 1 and 2." In the first, he criticises the cultural circles for their lack of achievement and for

85

the survival of bourgeois values. In the second "Instruction", he criticises the cultural work of the previous fifteen years for its neglect of the mass line and for the prevalence of bureaucratic, elitist attitudes. The publicity belatedly given to these statements makes it easier to present those subsequently criticised as direct opponents of Mao.[22]

The Rectification of 1964 marked the end of an era of relative indulgence in the cultural field, particularly in the assessment of the past. The older left-wing generation of the May Fourth movement had continued to occupy important positions and enjoy influence, while older scholars of non-leftist background had been relatively influential in academic circles. Now the cultural organisations were reformed, the cultural journals were remoulded and dismissals made—notably of Mao Tun, the Minister of Culture and a veteran novelist and critic, and of Hsia Yen, a vice-minister and a veteran playwright and doyen of the film world. The main criticisms of the cultural establishment were that it had fostered elitist trends, undermined the mass line and allowed the growth of revisionism.

The Cultural Rectification of 1964 continued in 1965, but it entered a more intensive stage in November of that year with Yao Wen-yüan's censure of Wu Han's opera *The Dismissal of Hai Jui*. From that moment, serious political accusations (though always implicit in earlier criticisms) were levelled explicitly against a growing number of writers and historians. Finally, in May, June and July 1966, these disputes in the cultural field were submerged in a full-scale political upheaval. The substantive moral and historical issues involved in the material criticised, the main object of discussion in 1964, have remained the same since then and are still under discussion, but the overtly political question has come to the fore since the spring of 1966.

This point reached, our endeavour now will be to discuss the most important objects of criticism in mainly chronological order. This will reflect the course of events and will mean working from the substantive issues, always easier to understand, to the evaluation of the political accusations, which is a much more difficult matter.

The essential content of the 1964 Rectification was formulated in the criticism of three theoretical writers: Yang Hsien-chen, Feng Ting

86

and Chou Ku-ch'eng. Of the three, much the most important was Yang Hsien-chen, who had been principal of the party's highest institute of political theory. He was criticised for his presentation of dialectics; it was alleged that he had overemphasised the unity of opposites within contradictions, and had minimised, or even denied, the essential conflict involved in the concept of contradictions. Yang's formulation 'combine two into one' was to be replaced by the slogan, 'divide one into two'. The campaign against him, which began in May 1964, was taken to great lengths in the press, and discussion of the issues was organised among the masses. 'Divide one into two' became a familiar slogan; its practical significance lay in the new emphasis on 'struggle' and in the increased aversion expressed for all forms of compromise. It meant, first of all, that the 'class struggle' was to be stressed, thereby countering the 'class harmony' theory which, it was alleged, was the political implication of Yang's philosophical views. As conveyed to the mass audience, the secondary implications of the slogan were the need for constant analysis of all problems, including those of everyday life, and for the avoidance of complacency about the *status quo* or present achievements.[23] (See, in this context, pages 59–60 above on 'contradictions-analysis'.)

Feng Ting, like Yang, is a Marxist with a long career in the partys' propaganda and academic service. As the author of several works popularising Marxist theory, he was criticised for having ignored class analysis in his treatment of human history and of the relation between man and his environment. Feng, it was alleged, had discussed man and his needs and characteristics in the most general terms, without introducing the class factor into the argument. Chou Ku-ch'eng, a well-known non-Communist historian, attracted a little more attention because of his views on aesthetics, which had been the subject of discussion since 1962. He was alleged to hold the view that art transcended the realm of conflict and that it reflected the spirit of its age: a spirit which was the product of an amalgam of all the social life of a particular era, not that of a particular class. He was criticised for having a subjective approach to art and its relation to society. It is not easy to follow Chou's critics if reference is made to his original essay of 1962, which appears quite orthodox.[24] The criticism of his views, however, provided some theoretical material for the literary and artistic Rectification of 1964.[25] It is clear that all three of these theoretical writers merit much fuller discussion, yet the issues of 1964 will emerge more clearly from an examination of the chief works of literature criticised, the main themes being the firm drawing of class lines and the attack on humanism.

Writings on history provided a great deal of subject-matter for the Rectification, the theory of history having been the theme of intensive debate for the previous decade. Though the evaluation of peasant wars was probably the most publicised historical debate, the most essential question of pre-modern history was the problem of the 'honest' or 'good' official: those paragons of Confucian virtue who were scattered throughout the length of Chinese history and who were revered in the popular memory as well as in the tradition of the Confucian establishment. In 1959, the eminent historian Wu Han (also vice-mayor of Peking) had expressed the view, implicit in much of the work on the cultural heritage carried out in the 1950s, that certain features of the morality of the 'good officials' in history were worthy of consideration in the present age. This was particularly true of their frugality, courage and altruism and, in some cases, their patriotism. His work, *The Dismissal of Hai Jui*, a new Peking opera written in 1959, illustrated this theme. Wu Han subsequently put his views in a more systematic form in articles written in 1962. He was criticised in August 1963, and by 1964 a wide circle of comment had emerged. The debate came to the fore once again early in 1966 after the opera had become the subject of a criticism campaign of unparalleled intensity.[26]

The basic question raised in the 'good official' controversy is whether there could be any such thing as a 'good official' in view of the fact, which serves as common ground in China, that feudal society was divided into the two classes of rulers and ruled. For, as Wu Han himself pointed out from the beginning, the virtues of good officials had been exercised in the service of the feudal ruling class and had served to strengthen the system of exploitation. In the view of Wu's critics, such good officials were a self-regulating device of the system. In their treatment of the people, the good officials merely 'reared chickens and produced eggs' while the bad officials 'killed the chickens and took the eggs'; it was a difference in means not in ends.[27] The 'good official' theory is also held to imply a denial of the role of the people as the motive force of history. This is certainly its general effect; in Wu Han's work the people appear only as suppliants or as a force off-stage. Somewhat similar points to these have also been made about the 'knights errant' (*yu-hsia*) of the ancient period, whose well-loved role as 'Robin Hoods' acting on behalf of the people and against tyrants and exploiters has been denied.[28]

Within the framework of contemporary controversy, Wu Han's position has certainly been equivocal, though it is no less true that his critics have often been crude. (The general tenor of their censure is often little more than the assertion that it is quite impossible to find anything positive at all in the values of a class exploiter.) The most substantial point made by Wu Han, one which he tried to base on Marx's authority, is that the values and the cultures of the two classes in feudal society were not independent of each other, and that both classes influenced one another. A more circumspect formulation of his is that, while the values of the ruling class poisoned the people, popular values were able to enrich individuals of the ruling class. Some of his critics, on the other hand, have asserted that the concept of the 'good official' had no basis whatever in fact; it was a fantasy built up from popular values and was essentially a reflection of the class struggle. This debate cannot be pursued any further here, nor can we do more than refer to the closely related question of peasant wars, which has been the theme of an interesting study.[29] To sum it up briefly, the essence of the 'good official' controversy is the conflict between the strictly class view and the more humanistic view that the class-struggle concept cannot, without many adjustments, be applied to pre-modern society. The strict view had prevailed by the end of 1964, although the historical establishment in China was not reformed until 1966. The practical relevance of the controversy is the official Maoist view that the people should have a popular version of their long history: a version which presents the people, not the ruling class, as the 'motive force of history'. The deep-seated traditional reliance on benevolent rulers should be replaced by confidence in the abilities of the people and in the necessity of popular action: a confidence which, it is hoped, will be bolstered by a more positive presentation of peasant wars and other historical symptoms of the people's energy and creativity.

The evaluation of modern history was the problem involved in most of the films, novels and stories criticised after 1964. The importance placed upon the interpretation of modern history, and particularly of the period since 1919, has been stressed by Mao himself. The approved version is an idealised story of political and moral value related in some respects to various deeper truths of modern China. The purpose of criticism and the trend of Maoist thinking since 1964 has been to extrude from this myth any complications, equivocations and nuances in order to enhance its power. It is interesting to note that arguments over modern history, unlike those over earlier history, have been confined to the world of fiction. Academic writing on the period after 1919 has been relatively sparse and controversy has been avoided. Films predominate in the material discussed here, with opera-plays in the second place, while prose literature is absent. This balance reflects that of the Chinese materials, and emphasises the importance of the cinema as a medium today.

The cinema seems to be very popular among the urban population, and great efforts have been made in recent years to make more films available in the countryside. In 1965, the peasant film audience was estimated at 2,000 million per annum, a figure which reveals the considerable success of popularisation.[30] The cinema is probably particularly influential with the large younger generation. The leading authority in the film world until 1964 was Hsia Yen, a famous playwright and cultural figure of the May Fourth generation. He was an expert in the ideologically difficult art of adapting works of the post-May Fourth period to the film medium in the socialist age. Two films—*Early Spring in February*, an adaptation of a novel of that period (1929), and *A Chiangnan in the North*, a new work about the socialist countryside—were subjected to fairly intense criticism in 1964. Hsia Yen himself became a leading target of criticism in 1965 and remained so in 1966.

The first great campaign, beginning in July 1964, was aimed against *Early Spring in February*. This film was made in 1962 from a script by Hsieh T'ieh-li based on the novel *February*, written in 1929 by the young revolutionary, Jou Shih.* Jou became a Communist shortly afterwards, and was caught and shot by the Kuomintang in January 1931. The story concerns Hsiao Chien-ch'iu, an escapist, melancholy and ineffectual young teacher who nourishes vague artistic, romantic, progressive and altruistic sentiments. In 1926, he takes a post in a school run by an old friend in a country town, hoping for peace and quiet. There he is torn between the attractions

* All remarks here relate to the filmscript text, not to the novel itself.

of T'ao Lan, the headmaster's glamorous younger sister, and those of an impoverished young widow named Wen. (Her husband has recently been killed in the south fighting for the revolutionary Kuomintang.) Both women—the brazenly self-indulgent T'ao Lan, and Wen, a figure of tragic beauty, purity and strength—are attracted by Hsiao. With obviously complex motives, he befriends and supports the widow and her two children. When her ailing infant son dies, Hsiao decides, after a struggle with himself, to rescue Wen and her little daughter by marrying the widow, thus abandoning T'ao. Wen, however, realises the conflict that has ensnared her benefactor, and commits suicide. Under the pressure of these events, and upset by local gossip, Hsiao leaves town and disappears.[31]

The negative character of Jou Shih's novel has been pointed out by Lu Hsun (the great master of the progressive literary scene in the 1920s and 1930s, who died in 1936), and it is not surprising that Hsia Yen felt that its adaptation presented problems. A shrewd critic has aptly described young Hsiao as 'a shirker who unwittingly becomes a scoundrel. . . . Mr Hsiao was probably meant as a type of Chinese intellectual whose capacity for action was inhibited and whose futile goodwill could be tragic in its consequences.'[32] The moral content of the film seems ambiguous by any standards, let alone those of its Communist critics, who see it as 'humanistic', immoral and 'Western-style'. The figure of T'ao Lan, in particular— with her egoistic and romantic outlook on life and her obsessive ambition to travel abroad—has attracted hostile comment. The love scenes in the film, the tempestuous piano music (Western of course) and the Wertherian posturising of Hsiao have made *Early Spring in February* an easy target for criticism. Of course, it is precisely the sentimentality of the film, one can safely assume, which has appealed to Chinese audiences and particularly, one suspects, to the intellectual youth. The adapter did his best with this unpromising material. Hsiao's character was improved in the film version and T'ao's egoism was toned down. She and Hsiao are made to display some interest in the current revolutionary journals. Most important, the film gives the story a positive twist by presenting Hsiao's departure as the product of a new resolve on his part to start a new life and to join in the revolution.

It is unreasonable on contemporary Chinese grounds to criticise the adapter for 'touching up' bourgeois characters. Such changes will almost always be necessary today if works of the 'democratic revolution' (1919–49) are to be presented at all. It is a valid point to make, however, that the adapter has destroyed the consistency of the original and created a confusing hybrid. Characters whose actions, in contemporary orthodox terms, are historically pointless and morally indefensible are treated with sympathy, and their progressive and retrograde aspects are not convincingly related to each other. It would surely have been wiser either to stay closer to the original and perhaps make the characters uglier, or, better still, to leave Jou's work alone and create a new, more inspiring and less ambiguous story about the groping of young bourgeois intellectuals towards revolution in the mid-twenties. The foreign reader may well think that Hsiao's story contains some of the truth about young intellectuals in the 1920s, but he will approach the film with a totally different point of view from that of the contemporary Chinese critic, who is interested in the truth about the 1920s as it relates to present tasks and current policy, not about that truth 'in itself'.

Somewhat different problems were raised by *The Shop of the Lin Family*, which came under criticism in May 1965. This film was adapted in 1958 by Hsia Yen himself from the story of the same title written by Mao Tun in 1932. It was apparently re-exhibited early in 1965.[33] Lin, a shopkeeper in a small town near Shanghai, suffers from the activities of the anti-Japanese boycott, the effects of the Depression on his peasant customers and Shanghai creditors, and the oppression of the local Kuomintang boss. His one sure support is his assistant Shou Sheng. He eventually marries his daughter to this reliable lad when the local tyrant attempts to get hold of her through exploiting his difficulties. Lin, a sympathetic character in the story, finally flees the town to avoid total ruin. His predicament is portrayed with the intention of showing that all but the largest capitalists with foreign backing shared the masses' suffering under exploitative imperialism. Hsia Yen felt that this 'united front' tale would show the past in its true and gloomy colours to those of national- or petty-bourgeois origin and thereby fulfil an 'educational' function. Even so, changes had to be made, for Lin in the story is so sympathetic a character that his role as a capitalist exploiter is not apparent. 'To show his profit-motivated class nature and to prevent the audience from having excessive sympathy for him, I added the aspect of his ill-treating those below him', explained Hsia Yen.[34]

Critics, however, pointed out, first, that Lin was presented as being forced to extract payment from his debtors only by adversity, not by his very class nature; and secondly that his debtors were themselves small-time capitalists. The essential conflict between capitalist and masses was therefore obscured. As in the case of *Early Spring in February*, adaptation could only be carried out to a certain point within the existing framework of the plot and characterisation; above all, nothing could be done about the important relationship between Lin and his employee Shou Sheng, which according to the class analysis should have been one between exploiter and victim. This relationship, severely handled by the critics, appears convincing to the outsider, for such relationships were characteristic of small family firms, but it is easy to see that it obscures the myth of the revolution.

The question remains: Why adapt these works at all, given the contemporary context? The answer is twofold. First, by 1964, an important change was taking place in the general political trend, namely, the replacement of the old, broader outlook, in which the United Front was still a valid concept, by a narrower view which emphasised once more the divisions in society. Because the old bourgeoisie was no longer in the important position it had occupied in the 1950s, and because the rise of a new elite was feared by the adherents of Mao in the party leadership, the history of the revolution had to be reinterpreted. Secondly, these two films of Hsia Yen's were adapted from works of the May Fourth era, which was undoubtedly a period of absorbing interest to the creative writers in the film world of the early 1960s. There was much preoccupation at that time with diversifying and refining film art and with drawing on the 'revolutionary tradition' of the 1930s.[35]

Before passing on to films which deal with socialist society, two films dealing with the Civil War of 1946–49 are worth noting, for, though not criticised until 1966, they display problems similar to those we have encountered in the two just mentioned. *Laying Siege to the City* (adapted about 1962 from a stage play written in 1959 by Pai Jen and others),[36] describes the defection of a Kuomintang military unit in Manchuria. The second, *Red Sun*, adapted (probably in 1961) by Ch'ü Pai-yin from Wu Ch'iang's novel of the same name, describes the tribulations and the final victory of a unit of the People's Liberation Army in Shantung.[37]

Like *The Shop of the Lin Family*, these works seem relatively convincing to the uncommitted historian. *Laying Siege to the City* shows, however faintly, that the dividing line between friend and foe was not sharply drawn in the Civil War, and that the inner conflicts of the enemy and certain human, and even political, factors held in common by besiegers and beseiged alike were important elements in the national situation between 1946 and 1949. In depicting the human and private motives of the leading defectors from the Kuomintang, the film has been criticised for blurring the class line and reducing the significance of 'armed struggle'—this latter being another doctrinal concept on which the Maoists place great weight. *Red Sun* not only shows the People's Liberation Army displaying some minor flaws in adversity, but also, to heighten the drama, brings out the overconfidence and old-fashioned heroism of the doomed Kuomintang commander. Relations between army and people are treated in such a way as not to exclude altogether the bitterness of war. Such an equivocal treatment, from the Maoist viewpoint, of the historical role of the People's Liberation Army is in marked contrast to that recently favoured by the official policy of the regime.

We now turn to works which are held to have distorted socialist society. At the centre of this question is the problem of the 'middle character' mentioned earlier in connection with heroic literature. In the retrospective accounts of the critics, the idea of writing about middle characters was first systematically promoted by Shao Ch'üanlin at a literary conference held in August 1962. The publication of a number of articles on this theme in the weeks following seems to confirm the fact that it was a matter of considerable concern in literary circles at that time. After a period of quiescence, the subject was revived in the autumn of 1964 during the literary Rectification campaign (when it was linked with specific works) and again in 1966.[38]

Advocates of the idea criticised the monotony and weakness of the literature and film plots based on heroic characters, and called for the deployment of a wider range of human material. Such a broadening of scope would correspond to the realities of a society in which most people were neither 'advanced' nor 'backward'. Middle characters were also the chief location of the contradictions in society. The middle-character approach would also, they maintained, have a greater educational influence than the rival 'heroic' method, for the reader would see himself in the characters portrayed and would thereby be more powerfully moved to reform himself along the lines suggested by the writer. Another feature of this approach is the open-ended conclusion in which the future development of the character is not spelled out but is left unstated. But defenders of the heroic method held that readers and audiences, particularly young people, wanted and needed models to emulate; that literature and films should concern themselves with the 'newly sprouting elements' as well as with the predominant phenomena; and that the educational impact of middle characters could not match that of heroic figures. The concept of middle characters was itself attacked on the grounds that people are, in fact, either advanced or not advanced, and that there can be no such intermediate categories as 'neither good nor bad, or both good and bad' in a true analysis. More recently, the view has been expressed that the majority of people are, in fact, advanced and are not 'middle' at all. Defenders and critics have agreed that heroes and middle characters are both essential in literary and film stories. The critics, however, have taken the line that the prevailing heroic method must not impoverish creative writing; while the defenders have accused their rivals of being hostile to the heroic idea itself, arguing that middle or minor characters may and must figure in fiction, but not to such an extent that a new style of literature emerges. At the same time, the opposite extreme—the view that one class at any given period has only one ideal type—has been rejected. The middle character view was strongly criticised in 1964, and the works admired by the Maoists since then have adhered strictly to the heroic approach.[39]

The other important feature to be mentioned here is the emphasis on rural themes, dating from the end of 1962. This policy reflected the general policy of the party. It also coincided with a renewed interest in more subtle methods and subject-matter. From one point of view, this was quite appropriate in that the Chinese village was indeed the scene of many conflicts and ambiguities, and hence provided good material for didactic literature and films. On the other hand, there were obvious risks in concentrating on the equivocal aspects of this material and in dealing with it in a less than straightforward manner. If the fruits of culture were now to be disseminated on a really large scale, then the tastes and attitudes of peasant readers and audiences would have to be taken into account. Which was the more effective with the mass audience: the simple and direct, or the complex and the devious?

The most extensively criticised work in the 'rural theme' genre is the film *A Chiangnan in the North*, based on a screen play by Yang Han-sheng.[40] Issued in 1963, criticism of it began on July 30, 1964. Chiangnan, the Lower Yangtze region, is as well-known for its fertility as the northern region of China (in this case the Kalgan area) is noted for its unpredictable climate, its great droughts and cold winters. The film deals with the transformation into a flourishing community of a village often subject to unpredictable droughts, under the leadership of the local Communist leader. Its purpose quite clearly is to depict the success of the collective efforts of poor villagers.

The story of *A Chiangnan in the North* revolves around the family of Wu Ta-ch'eng, head of a higher-level co-operative near Kalgan, and also secretary of the local branch of the party. The action takes place sometime between 1956 and 1958. Wu's main concern is to see to the digging of wells during the slack season in mid-winter. This is a very arduous task for the villagers and their morale deteriorates, especially when a saboteur secretly shifts the marking stones and most of the wells dug fail to draw water. The problem is aggravated by the unfriendly attitude of the villagers to Wu, whom they regard as crude and unsympathetic in his methods of dealing with them. The other key character is Yin Hua, his wife, who is also a party member. She is portrayed as an extremely sympathetic figure, not least because of her courage in the face of failing eyesight. A teenage orphan, Little Wang, is brought up in the Wu household; he is open, however, to the influence of his uncle, formerly a prosperous small tradesman who now harbours resentment against the collective. The uncle is still trying to ply a little undercover trade with the reluctant help of his friend, the carter; and this, combined with his resentment at criticism and his belief that the collective will prove a failure, leads to his seeking to withdraw his share from the collective and to get permission to join his daughter in the city. He is keen to persuade Little Wang to leave his foster family and go with him. Little Wang, already a somewhat indolent youth, is eventually infected with his uncle's hatred of 'this damned place' and falls in with the plan. How is he to tell his benefactors?

He is very fond of Yin Hua, Wu is a strong character, and his girl friend is unwilling to leave the village. She thinks his behaviour is reprehensible on public and family grounds and tells the Wus. Little Wang prepares to leave in a strained atmosphere, but his plans are forestalled by the dénouement of the class-struggle in the village. His uncle's private trading has made him vulnerable to blackmail by Ch'ien San-t'ai, a counter-revolutionary living in the village and the man who shifted the well-markers. Wang's uncle is almost persuaded by Ch'ien to poison the draught animals, but he 'wakes up' at the last moment and reports the whole situation to Wu. The affair comes to a head just as Little Wang is ready to leave.

Secretary Wu is criticised in the film for his inflexible character and lack of concern for the everyday private problems of the villagers. He also fails to detect the 'class struggle' that is going on under his nose. It is Yin Hua and the *hsien* (district) secretary who finally convince him of the need to mend his ways and alter his obstinate refusal to admit mistakes. Wu comes to realise that he has been lacking in vigilance in spite of the *hsien* secretary's warning to him that the class struggle is still going on. He is fairly effective in keeping the well project going, but only at the cost of much unpopularity and a row with Mrs Cheng, the wife of his deputy who is also the other important Communist in the village. He publicly embarrasses Mrs Cheng when she wishes to leave the work at the wells and attend to domestic affairs. Yin Hua subsequently has an argument with Mrs Cheng about her refusal to continue with the work, as a result of which Yin Hua's eyes get still worse. This unfortunate outcome then causes a *volte face* in the attitude of Mrs Cheng and some of the other difficult women in the village towards the Wus and their project. It is shortly after this that Yin Hua criticises Wu and receives hard words in return, for he does not know of the change in her condition. His eventual discovery of this has a lot to do with his decision to improve himself.

The film is interesting to the foreign reader for its relatively subtle treatment of the conflicts and motives of villagers confronted by a large and unpleasant collective task. The morale of the villagers, the differences between young and old, the occurrence of ridicule and the fear of criticism, the concern with 'face' and the importance of personal bonds, all combine to enhance the interest of the story. Humour also occurs in the treatment of Old Cheng, Wu's party deputy, a tenacious but bombastic old man who is rather afraid of his wife until towards the end of the story. Even Ch'ien San-t'ai, the counter-revolutionary, is allowed some amusing sarcasm at Wu's expense, though he is severely rebuked in consequence. For these reasons, it is not difficult to see why the film was censured as being 'negative teaching material' in 1964. The most serious criticism is of the humanism embedded within it. Vigilance and 'struggle', the thorough criticism of oneself and others, if necessary in public, are undermined by personal considerations throughout. Wu rejects the idea of a 'struggle' against the uncle after the first discovery of the latter's private trading. Even though he is privately upbraided by a foster-daughter for his tendency to compromise, all that Wu does is to tell Little Wang to 'help' his uncle—which is no solution of the problem since Wang is already under his uncle's influence. Similarly, Wu and Yin Hua will not allow any real pressure to be brought to bear upon Little Wang; they hold that he will understand it all one day and come back to the village. And the changes in attitude made by Wu, Mrs Cheng and Little Wang are all made mainly through the personal moral authority of Yin Hua. To the chagrin of the critics, the change in the 'capitalist' uncle, which finally occurs when he is about to poison the animals, comes about spontaneously. He has never been subjected to any real criticism or pressure.

We cannot leave *A Chiangnan in the North* without remarking on one of its most important themes: the contrast between town and country. The town is a seductive vision on the horizon, the place where the real progress is being made and where the individual can enjoy a fuller, but less worthy, life. The uncle's smart daughter, perfumed and coiffeured, is an important influence on Little Wang after he visits her luxurious flat in the city. To the hard-working villagers, the town is obviously a refuge for weak characters and a solvent of personal standards, though it is true that one character does point out to Wang that hard work is done there too. This theme is especially relevant in the light of the regime's emphasis on agriculture and the consequent exodus from the cities in 1961.

The question of 'unacceptable works' on the socialist countryside could be pursued at great length. Here we can only mention one other film on a rural theme, *Two Families*, by 'Lin Mo-ch'en', which was criticised in 1966.[41] Based on a novel (*Bridge*) of the 1950s, it depicts the ultimate failure of an old poor peasant's attempt to stay out of the collective in the 1950s and to plan his own family's fortunes through the traditional means of thrift, hard work and piecemeal accumulation. The story of the failure of 'private planning' was presumably regarded as particularly relevant when the film was made in 1963, but the more subtle method used—essentially the 'middle-character' approach—was censured. A more particular reason for denouncing the film was that the 'poor and lower-middle peasants' have been built up since 1963 as the very source of revolution, and the film is therefore held to contradict historical fact and to constitute a malicious attack.

The last two films which will be discussed here bring up the question of comedy and humour. This was the subject of controversy about 1961 and 1962. Were such indirect methods of education (not much practised hitherto) valid in a socialist society? Humour is admittedly a difficult weapon for, though it can reflect the happiness of the new society and be used against survivals of the old, its use may blunt, distort, or even dissipate altogether, the contradictions which are the proper subject of socialist literature. Mao Tun himself, then Minister of Culture, held in 1961 that comedy and satire were permissible on the basis of the artistic criterion; literature must 'strike blows on the head' but they must be telling blows. Since 1964, it has been claimed that cultural leaders had at that time (i.e., *circa* 1959–64) put their weight behind the wider use of comedy and satire, and this can be confirmed to some extent from the work then produced.[42]

Humour has certainly been a feature of works on rural themes, yet it is curious that the two humorous films most prominently attacked in the summer of 1966 both deal with industrial society. *Big Li, Young Li and Old Li* appeared in 1962. A story about athletics in a factory community written by Yü Ling and others, it is a remarkably sharp satire on certain aspects of contemporary Chinese society.[43] Big Li, the chairman of the trade union and an outstanding worker, becomes responsible for physical training—something that had never interested him before—as a result of the conflict between his father, Old Li, who thinks that it is a waste of time, and his son, Young Li, who is an enthusiast. The boy is a cheerful clown, the old man testy and devious, and Big Li makes himself ridiculous by falling under the spell of physical training. The comedy is held by its critics to have besmirched the image of worker activists and to have undermined the party's policy on physical training. The other film, *Football Fans*, shows workers scrambling for tickets for a match.[44] The comedy arises out of the ridiculous and sometimes underhand stratagems used in the effort to get into the stadium and the exaggerated behaviour of the fans who ignore any interests but their own. 'The scene has basically nothing in common with a socialist city. The confusion on the screen looks more like the portrayal of New York in the United States.'[45] One cannot help feeling that, given the narrow framework of cultural theory in contemporary China, these works could only be acceptable during a period of unusual relaxation.[46]

Very many other works were criticised between 1964 and 1966, but a qualitative change took place in November 1965 with the criticism of Wu Han's *Dismissal of Hai Jui*, the new Peking opera mentioned earlier.[47] This opera, and a similar work (*Hsieh Yao-huan*)[48] written in 1961 by T'ien Han and criticised early in 1966, are two of a number of historical plays and operas written in the early 1960s and dealing with courageous and determined figures of the past. Several works deal with Hai Jui, a bold and upright statesman of the sixteenth century who acquired legendary fame. In *The Dismissal of Hai Jui*, the family of a powerful retired statesman, Hsu Chieh, has been annexing the common people's property, abducting their womenfolk and perpetrating other crimes. No legal redress is to be had, for the magistrate is in Hsu's pocket. Hai arrives as governor; having gained a clear picture of the general situation on arrival while moving among the people incognito, he decides to press the cause of justice against the Hsus and their accomplices. He refuses to be deterred by his obligation to Hsu Chieh, who had once saved his life in the capital. When dispensing justice in the case of a wronged peasant girl, a replacement for him arrives from the capital, procured by Hsu's intrigues at court. However, Hai manages to get his sentences of execution carried out on the two chief culprits, one of whom is Hsu Chieh's son, by the device of keeping hold of the seals of office for a short time after his replacement has been announced. He then leaves the area.

Hsieh Yao-huan, by T'ien Han, the most eminent modern playwright and chairman (until 1961) of the Union of Dramatists, is named after its heroine, a fictitious courtier of the historical Empress Wu Tse-t'ien of the seventh century. At the empress's command, she tries to break up an aristocratic clique which is abusing its position and misrepresenting facts at court in order to tyrannise over Chiang-nan. The people, though essentially loyal, are being driven to rebellion through the loss of their land and their equipment. Intrigues at court interrupt Hsieh's mission at the crucial juncture. On the strength of a surreptitiously altered imperial command, she is tortured to death, staunchly refusing to provide the miscreants with a confession of collusion with the 'rebels'. The empress arrives on the scene a few minutes too late.

Both operas sustained significant alterations in treatment. Wu Han, being a historian not a playwright and lacking in ideological experience, found it necessary to improve several times the drafts of *The Dismissal of Hai Jui*. The conflict between the peasants and the officials was strengthened, both in dramatic and political terms. More important was a shift in content: the return to the people of land taken from them by tyrannical appropriators was replaced, as Hai Jui's main aim, by the more general theme of 'eradication of tyrants'. This change was made after it had been pointed out to Wu Han that the retrocession of land had not really been a solution of the land problem at all and should therefore not be the subject of a positive treatment. Finally, the ending was made less negative. In the early drafts, Hai Jui merely engaged in a verbal dual with Hsu Chieh and his replacement, and though these two slunk off the stage to avoid the people's anger, Hai also left, having won nothing more than a verbal, moral victory. It went against the grain for Wu Han, an expert on Ming history, to manufacture, at others' advice, the present unhistorical ending. Nevertheless, the reader is bound to be struck by certain remaining features: only a stratagem saves the day; Hai is, in fact, dismissed; and his brief appearance in the area has probably made very little difference to the situation.

The ending is also a significant feature of *Hsieh Yao-huan*. The local opera from which T'ien Han developed his work had had a happy ending, with Hsieh escaping from her enemies. T'ien Han, however, considered that his tragic dénouement had a 'deeper educational significance'. (Some companies actually insisted on playing it with a happy ending.) Whereas the original had shown the empress in a bad light, T'ien Han's version rehabilitates her in accordance with the re-evaluation then going forward in the field of academic history. According to this theory, directly embodied in the opera, the empress is essentially sympathetic to the plight of the people, but the growth of aristocratic court cliques perverts her intentions. Hsieh Yao-huan's mission is seen as reasserting her true intentions and as turning the tables against her bad counsellors.

It can be seen that these new operas present the 'good official' theory in a literary form, and to this extent the criticisms levelled by Yao Wen-yüan and other critics merely ran over familiar ground. Wu Han, moreover, instead of making an irritated rejoinder as he had in 1964, now virtually abandoned his position on the substantive issues at stake and published self-criticisms in the Peking press in December 1965 and January 1966. The new element was the explicit political accusation made by Yao and later levelled against many other authors, including all those criticised in 1964 and 1965. Yao alleged that *The Dismissal of Hai Jui* had served to aid and abet the reactionaries and revisionists who had been trying to destroy the Communes and restore individual farming, and to secure the rehabilitation of the rightists and weaken the party's control between 1959 and 1962. He pointed to the themes of the 'restoration of the people's land', 'the eradication of tyrants' and 'the straightening out of misjudged cases' as evidence for the view that the play was really directed at the current situation. Wu Han denied this accusation, though he conceded that he had shown a lamentable unawareness of the connections between politics and literature. Very similar accusations were made against T'ien Han.

Yao's keynote article was published in a Shanghai newspaper on November 10, 1965. It was reprinted on November 29 in the army newspaper *Liberation Army Daily* (*Chieh-fang-chün Pao*) and on the following day in the *People's Daily* (*Jen-min Jih-pao*). The latter paper also printed a small preface to the article, indicating that it considered the question to be academic and literary but not political. Wu Han's first article of self-criticism appeared on December 30, 1965, in the *People's Daily* itself, and the second on January 12, 1966, but only in the local Peking press. These were interpreted by his critics as self-defensive rather than as self-critical, and he was subjected to further attacks. Articles continued to appear in Wu Han's support, however, asserting that there was no political problem and that his historical views were not entirely groundless.[49] The attack on T'ien Han, the most renowned of the revolutionary playwrights of the older generation, began in February 1966, the critical article in this case appearing first in the *People's Daily*.[50] Hsia Yen also was the target of renewed criticism, on account of his interest in the 1930s; and his famous play about the Boxer Rising, *Sai Chin-hua* (written in 1936), was denounced as a work of national betrayal.[51]

The next stage came on April 16, 1966, when two local organs in the capital, the *Peking Daily* (*Pei-ching Jih-pao* and *Front Line* (*Ch'ien Hsien*, a fortnightly), criticised articles written in 1961 and 1962 by three of the important cultural figures in the city. The first series of articles, appearing under the title of *The Three-Family Village*, had been written by Wu Han, Teng T'o and Liao Mo-sha.[52] Teng was a secretary of the municipal branch of the party, editor of *Front Line* and a former editor of the *People's Daily*; and Liao was the director of the party's United Front Department: a vulnerable position in the new anti-bourgeois climate. The second series, by Teng T'o alone, had appeared under the title of *Evening Chats at Yenshan,* and a selection from it had been published in five small volumes.[53] Given Teng's standing in the Peking party branch and press, this criticism in *Front Line* and the *Peking Daily* amounted to self-criticism, but the matter was not allowed to drop with an admission of political and ideological shortcomings. On May 8, the *Liberation Army Daily* launched a full attack on the three writers; this paper, and the *Kuangming Daily* (*Kuang-ming Jih-pao*), singled out Teng T'o for the strongest condemnation, using his writings of 1961–62 as material. The *People's Daily*, which had lagged behind ever since the criticism of Wu Han in November, reprinted this attack on May 9.[54] From that date, Teng T'o and his colleagues became the target of an intensive campaign of criticism. It was alleged that their writings of 1961–62 had been a vicious, covert attack on the party's leadership and on the Great Leap Forward.

Soon after the publication of the full indictment in the *Liberation Army Daily* on May 8, there appeared signs that a more eminent target was about to be identified and aimed at. On June 3, P'eng Chen himself, First Secretary of the Peking branch of the party and an outstanding figure in the national leadership, was removed from his post. There followed a purge of the Peking branch, the university, the city's Youth League and the organisation for party publications. Not long afterwards, on July 1, a major press campaign developed against Chou Yang, the virtual arbiter of cultural life since Yenan days. He was now described as an out-and-out villain, with a record of twenty-four years of political sabotage and treachery. Chou Yang was especially criticised for having fostered cultural revisionism after 1961.[55] By this time, the Cultural Rectification movement had broadened to embrace all kinds of targets, large and small, and similar attacks, covering a wide range, continued to appear throughout 1966.[56]

The Maoist case against Wu Han, T'ien Han and Teng T'o, though obscured by the exaggeration, dramatisation and falsification characteristic of such campaigns, has been put with enough detail and sufficient reference to the offending texts to convince most Western commentators that it is essentially well-based. Chinese precedents for oblique comment on current politics are regarded as virtually confirming the Maoist view. The problems—for there are two problems involved here—are far from solved, however. The first problem concerns the nature of the writings of 1959–62. The second and more important problem is the meaning of this campaign against these particular writers at this particular time.

The substantive and general issues of history, ethics and so forth, which were rehearsed once again in the campaigns of 1965–66 (except in the case of Teng T'o's articles, where the issues were entirely political), have been discussed already. The political accusations were different in that they changed and grew more serious with the passage of time. Wu Han was first of all accused of making veiled criticisms of the Commune system and of making a plea for the rightists. T'ien Han was accused of suggesting that the regime was unstable because the party, below the leader himself, was dominated by bad men, and because of the injustice of its agrarian policies. Teng T'o was accused of making malicious and satirical attacks on the party and on Mao Tse-tung himself. By mid-1966, the criticisms had become more violent—Wu Han, for example, being accused of having written his opera to champion the fallen P'eng Teh-huai.

Under a system in which expression is controlled, literature is apt to be used by some writers as a means for the subtle conveyance of dissenting social comment and also for actual political criticism. There were outstanding examples of this in the occupied countries of Western Europe during the last war, and it has certainly been a characteristic feature of Russian literature under both Tsarist and

Soviet regimes. In China, there was an even longer tradition of subtle comment and dissent 'between the lines', and the frontier between literature and politics was often crossed by the *literati*. In modern China, there have been many famous cases of the presentation of oblique political comment in historical drama. Kuo Mo-jo's wartime drama *Ch'ü Yüan*, about a patriotic but tragically misused statesman of ancient China, was related to the New Fourth Army Incident of January 1941 (see page 10). Hsia Yen's play *Sai Chin-hua* (1936) used a story of the Boxer Rising to criticise the Kuomintang's claim to be acting in the national interest while giving way to Japan. A rather different example of the same use of literature is *Stories about not being afraid of Ghosts*, a booklet compiled by the Peking literary authorities in 1961. This collection of traditional tales seeks to convey the message that the people should not be afraid of imperialism; the 'paper tiger', though frightening at first sight, turns out to have no substance.

In contemporary China, moreover, it is essential for every writer on every occasion to state a political motive for his work. It is not possible for an author to justify his writing a work if it does not have a current political significance. The writer, therefore, needs to keep in mind all the time the political significance of his work, and any defence against the charge of negligence in this respect is bound to be a weak one. T'ien Han, Wu Han and Teng T'o were certainly conscious of their educational and political role.

The question of the true nature of these texts is not unimportant; but unfortunately, a reading of the texts at present available (that is, of the whole texts and not only of those parts excerpted by critics) is not sufficient for their interpretation. Despite the suggestive passages and phrases, we need to know much more about the cultural and political scene in 1959–62 and about the men attacked before we can decide what is innuendo and what is not, and what the meaning of it was. We need to find out whether this kind of criticism, if criticism it was, was more widespread in those years or if it was confined to the writers named in 1966, and whether there is any evidence from that period, or even from 1966, of the reception of such political messages by the public. Again, how influential were these works? Wu Han's opera appears to have been performed only a few times. Neither this work nor *Hsieh Yao-huan* seems to have attracted much comment during the three year's discussion of the 'good official' question. Teng T'o, who occupied an important position in the capital's press and propaganda circles, was presumably very much more influential.

The relative unimportance of these targets, however, stands out clearly when seen in the light of what was to follow; and the question is therefore why these particular figures were chosen to inaugurate the Cultural Revolution of 1966. The answer undoubtedly lies in the fact that they were prominent figures in Peking, where the local party apparatus was dominated by the powerful figure of P'eng Chen. The attack itself was launched from Shanghai and the army's cultural and political establishment played a key role. The *Jen-min Jih-pao*, a national organ but published in Peking, was noticeably slow and cool in its handling of the Wu Han controversy; and, by April 1966, the press and propaganda organs of P'eng Chen's organisation probably were (as the Maoists asserted) engaged in a rearguard action against further and more serious pressure. The course of events between November 1965 and June 1966 strongly suggests that the party in Peking was unhappy about the trend of the campaigns and also that those pushing the movement forward were really in pursuit of more important quarries from the beginning. This has since been strongly implied in Maoist accounts of the early stages of the Great Proletarian Cultural Revolution in which November 10, 1965 (the date of Yao Wen-yüan's article) is presented as the opening shot in the great events which followed. Wu Han and Teng T'o, in particular, were mainly stalking-horses for use during the campaign against P'eng Chen's Peking organisation, though criticism of Wu Han could also be used to publicise general points which had been discussed for the previous two years.

On the other hand, the campaign against Chou Yang—the figure who had presided for so long over the sector of Chinese life discussed in this chapter—is more difficult to link with these developments. His fall was accompanied by a very widespread purge of the propaganda, press and university circles in many different parts of the country. The case put against him is shot through with many difficulties, and it is difficult to decide whether some factional 'power' consideration (such as opposition to the growing cultural role of the army) or questions of cultural policy were involved. Was his removal a necessary part of the break-up of the cultural 'bureaucracies' which had grown up over the years, and of the effective

promotion of the more radical policies coming to the fore since 1963?
Problems of faction and policy were very likely closely interwoven.

We have now passed the point at which the 'cultural' revolution
becomes more of a political than a cultural movement, to use the
convenient Western categories which clearly have some meaning in
China, too. These political developments will be discussed in the
next chapter. Before leaving the cultural theme, however, something
must be said about the culture approved by the Maoists, for we have
hitherto concentrated exclusively on the objects of criticism and
passed by those works which have been singled out for praise.

MAOIST CULTURE, 1963–67

The foundation of the Maoist cultural theory is, of course, the Mao
cult itself, which took on new life from 1963. Mao Tse-tung's works
have been distributed in ever-increasing numbers, particularly since
mid-1966, and the mass movement for their study has been at the
centre of official cultural policy ever since then.[57]
The most striking feature of the militant culture promoted since
the end of 1964 has been the return to the great days of Yenan. The
emphasis on the struggle ethos, on the mass line, on distinctively
national forms and on rural and army culture, all this is an indication of the desire to return to the source of the militant tradition of
Chinese Communism. The eclipse of the Western-influenced cultural
tradition of Shanghai by a 'native' and rural trend early in the war
period has been repeated in the undermining of the old guard in
'revolutionary' culture—the May Fourth generation—and in the
increasingly nativist trend on official culture, as is reflected, for
example, in the criticism of Stalin for his uncritical tolerance of
'Russian and European' bourgeois classics.[58] War themes—though
already a leading feature of contemporary Chinese literature—
have been given increasing prominence. In 1964 and 1965, many
works dealing with socialist society after 1950 were still being
commended and publicised by critics, but thereafter most attention
has been given to works dealing with the wars of 1937–49. Two-
thirds of the works put on in 1964 dealt with the period after 1950,
but all save two of the works described as 'the eight revolutionary
exemplary works' in May 1967 dealt with the period between 1927
and 1949.[59]

The vital difference between the literature of the war years and that of the most recent period is the contemporary emphasis on class divisions and on the poor and lower-middle peasants, rather than on the United Front. As we have seen from the criticism of films, there has, indeed, been a tendency to deny the historical fact of the United Front. It is, of course, an important indication of the Maoist ethos that current problems should be increasingly expressed through war themes.

The literary forms promoted includes reportage, story-telling, oral literature and songs; and short forms—one-act plays, 'revolutionary tales', duologues for chanting, and so forth—have been promoted. The key form is reportage which, in the inevitable military metaphor, has been called the 'patrol of literature': the form which seeks out the ground. It is regarded as having a major function in the search for mass creative talent and as providing a basis for larger and more mature works to be written at a later stage. The revival of reportage and other short forms can be traced—as a policy, if not as an established trend—to the end of 1962. In 1963 and 1964, the fostering of non-professional talent was re-established, though it is not clear on what scale. This development was very closely linked with the Socialist Education movement.[60]

A novel feature of the recent literary scene is the extraordinary publicity given to the 'revolutionary Peking opera on new themes'. The 'revolution in opera' can be formally traced back to a national theatrical conference held in August 1963, but it effectively began in Shanghai late in that year with the East China Modern Drama Festival. It was launched on a grander scale at a national festival held in Peking in the summer of 1964. This development was hailed in 1966 as 'the outstanding example of the great socialist cultural revolution of 1963–66', and also as its 'prologue'.[61] Chiang Ch'ing is now credited with an important role in the movement. Adapting this uniquely Chinese art-form is, of course, a classic instance of the promotion of distinctively national art forms. Its advocates claim that the very strength of stylisation and convention and the shallowness of characterisation in the opera make it an excellent vehicle for the conveyance of simple heroic themes. Most of the operas have undergone several revisions designed to stress two points: the importance of armed struggle, and the importance of party leadership. In the original version of *Shachiapang*, for example, which deals with the struggle between the party and anti-Communist troops in southern Kiangsu, the leading character was the courageous young underground Communist who continued to run her tea-house and consort with the enemy while all the time giving succour to wounded Red soldiers and acting as liaison. In later versions, the role of the partisan commander was given more prominence.[62]

In the visual arts, pride of place has been given to the exhibition of life-size clay figures, the *Rent Collection Court*. Originally designed as a group of 114 figures in five tableaux, it was created in Szechwan by a group of artists working in collaboration. It depicted the collection of rent in Kuomintang days and was designed to arouse class hatred and bitter memories, being essentially a visual aid to the Socialist Education movement. The cheapness and speed of the work were especially noted. Towards the end of 1965, replicas were made in Peking and elsewhere. In the autumn of 1966, as the activities of the Red Guard intensified, the ideological content of the exhibition in Peking was improved. A sixth tableau, entitled *Resistance*, was added showing the peasants turning on their oppressors, and various figures in the rest of the exhibition were made more defiant. More recently, pictures of another large exhibit, very similar in style, have been published. This is the *New Foolish Old Men of Tashu*, produced in Szechwan in 1965. This exhibit is entirely on the theme of man's struggle with nature.[63]

Ballet and symphonic music are also represented among the 'Eight Revolutionary Exemplary Works' named in May 1967, and both exemplify the reaction against Western and Soviet influences. It is doubtful, however, whether either form, being of recent import, is very influential in China. *The Red Detachment of Women*, staged in October 1964, was the first revolutionary ballet; but *The White-haired Girl*, created by the Shanghai City School of Dance in 1964–65, is more interesting.[64] Adapted from the famous wartime opera of the same title, it shows typical modifications of the original story. In the ballet, the People's Liberation Army take a more positive role in arousing the people of the village against the land-lord, and the heroine, Hsi Erh, finally joins the army and goes off to war. The tragic subtlety of the original opera-play has entirely disappeared for the sake of drawing more sharply the lines dividing the classes and emphasising the distinctions between good and bad more clearly. Hsi Erh now remains fearless in face of the landlord who takes her into his house, and her will to resist gradually gets stronger, though in the original she is a bewildered figure and only flees after realising that the landlord will not marry her. In the old version, her father allows himself to be brow-beaten into consenting to let the landlord take her away, in order to avoid imprisonment for debt. Full of remorse and unable to tell her or his friends, he takes his own life. In the ballet, he becomes a courageous poor peasant who is beaten to death resisting the landlord's scheme. Justifying these changes, one critic observed that it all hinged 'on how to treat the personality of the poor peasant masses in the period of the democratic revolution and on the question of what model type of the poor peasant should be established on the socialist stage'. The work is a good example of the direct application of class analysis to the depiction of human character and of the close links between this approach and current politics. It is clearly entirely different from the play of 1944, which in its day was much renowned in Communist circles.

"Shachiapang", a 'symphonic composition' based on the opera, is a revolutionary oratorio. Like *The White-haired Girl*, it is alleged to have been worked up in the thick of an anti-revisionist struggle within the old Central Philharmonic Society, declared to have been 'in the hands of a handful of party people taking the capitalist road and . . . becoming an orchestra similar to those in the United States, Britain or Italy, or in the ussr or Czechoslovakia. The society's work leaned heavily on eighteenth- and nineteenth-century works from the West.' This project for a new revolutionary and 'national' symphonic work was reported to have been promoted by Chiang Ch'ing early in 1964. The opponents of the project are supposed to have objected to the mixing of Chinese and Western musical styles, the use of realistic costume and other eclectic innovations. Eclecticism, an obvious feature both of this work and the *The White-haired Girl*, represents in these cases an endeavour to break out of the Soviet-dominated past.) The innovators added song and Chinese dances to the old 'unregenerated ballet', and their critics are said to have protested that ballet is 'a tiger's backside which you can't touch.'[65]

It has been pointed out earlier that a conflict exists between the 'short-form' approach to creation and the production of larger works. The Cultural Revolution has, however, produced one large work so far, the novel *The Song of Ouyang Hai,* written by Chin Ching-mai in 1964–65 and published in 1965–66 in an unusually large edition. Vice-premier Ch'en Yi praised it highly in February 1966, describing it as 'the first full-length novel depicting heroes in the socialiast era that has attained a high artistic level'.[66] Its great merit is held to be its tracing of the development of a socialist hero from birth onwards. It is based on the life of an authentic character, the eponymous hero of the title: a young soldier of poor-peasant background who sacrificed his life in 1963, at the age of twenty-one, in saving a train from derailment. The novel was written under party guidance within the army's cultural establishment.[67]

The Song of Ouyang Hai is perhaps the most notable example, in novel form, of the cult of martyrs which has been a marked feature of Chinese literature since 1963. There is now a whole library of stories in this 'heroic biography' genre. The most extensively publicised is the story of Lei Feng, a young soldier from a poor background who died at the age of twenty in 1962. Lei's death did not come from seeking to preserve state property or to save the lives of others, but it did occur in an accident in the course of routine duties, and he has been singled out for his devotion to the state's service and to his fellows, and for his diligent study of Mao's works. His diary was the mainstay of a publicity campaign which began in February 1963. Wang Chieh, another young soldier, threw himself over an explosive in the summer of 1965 to save his comrades. Ts'ai Yung-hsiang was only eighteen in October 1966 when he saved a trainload of Red Guards from derailment by a log placed across the track by saboteurs. Lu Hsiang-pi and Liu Ying-chün, less important figures, had something in common with many of the others whose deeds are now given special treatment in 'revolutionary literature'. Liu's gun-horse was frightened by the whistle of a train in March 1966; to save the people on a busy road, he held on to the reins of the bolting animal, and was killed. Lu performed a very similar deed in March 1967 on an army farm. The literature records a number of such figures, and the similarity of their stories is striking. But the question of their authenticity, though interesting, is not really important in the context of this discussion. The lauding of young martyrs—whose example is clearly held up to young people for emulation—is merely the furthest extension of the policy of presenting 'advanced characters' as exemplars. It is also necessary to qualify the account just given by observing that not all heroes are young soldiers; they are also exemplary young secretaries of party branches, like Chiao Yü-lu who died of illness after making great efforts to revive a poor country district.[68]

These hero stories serve above all as a vehicle for the cult of Mao, whose works are declared to be the chief influence on these exemplary young Communists. Their diaries turn out to be simple paraphrases and amplifications of Mao's thought. The message for the young soldier—and by extension for the young person in general —is very simple.

The Maoist approach to academic concerns, especially in the humanities, consists in the application of the mass line; the mass of the people are organised to 'master' history and philosophy, to take two examples. Historical work became involved in the Socialist Education movement in 1964 and 1965. 'Historical workers' (researchers) began to spend periods in the countryside and to apply themselves to organising the mass study of the 'four histories': histories of villages, old poor and lower-middle peasant families, Communes, and factories. These were to be written up from discussions among the people and village story-tellers, and the literate young seem to have played an important part in this. The term 'five histories' was also used to include either 'histories of class struggles' or the history of military units. The army units in Canton were engaged in this task in 1964–65.[69] These popular histories embody the recall of past miseries and conflicts. It is tempting to compare them with the 'autobiography' which was the centre of the thought-reform process for intellectuals. By June 1966, in the opening phase of the Cultural Revolution, the historical establishment came under general attack and by October the leading academic journal *Historical Studies (Li-shih Yen-chiu)* was denounced for its past record. Li Shu, Hou Wai-lu, Chien Po-ts'an and other leading historians of the older generation were denounced. Those who had expressed reservations about the revolutionary nature of peasant wars were picked out for special condemnation. Ch'i Pen-yü emerged as the leading light of the new school.[70]

Philosophy, as a mass study, means the discussion and study of Mao's philosophical works, namely: *On Practice* and *On Contradiction* (officially dated 1937), *On the Correct Handling of Contradictions Among the People* (1957), and a short passage entitled *Where Do Correct Ideas*

Come From? (dated May 1963). The first two and the fourth of these works set out the Marxist view of the inter-relationship of reality, knowledge and action, and the essentials of dialectical materialism, while the third is an application of Mao's approach to the problems of socialist society.[71] Since 1964, the widespread discussion of the 'one into two' material has dominated mass philosophical study.

In addition to the conversion of academic subjects into mass political movements, another important fruit of Maoist policy is the drastic reform of the educational system, which had previously been regarded with suspicion, as the begetter of elites, old and new. From 1964, the work-study movement and the policy of sending the educated down to the countryside were revived. These policies had first been implemented in 1958 but had lost their momentum in the interim. On June 13, 1966, while a full-scale purge of universities was taking place, the Central Committee decided to make a thorough reform of all higher education and to suspend entrance examinations for six months.[72] Shortly afterwards the functioning of the school system as a whole was interrupted by the Red Guard movement. By the early months of 1967, attempts were being made to reactivate the educational system. One document circulating in Peking in March gave details of a Central Committee decision that higher educational institutions should restart by the twentieth of that month.[73] The content of the educational reform, however, is still not clear, apart from the scrapping of the existing examination system.

The educational reform, like the criticism of Wu Han and Teng T'o, brings us face to face with the political events of 1966 and 1967 which are the subject of the next chapter.

V

THE CRISIS, 1966–67

THE FALL OF P'eng Chen in June 1966 marked the escalation of the Cultural Revolution into a political crisis.[1] His removal from office after a bitter struggle in the Central Committee, and the employment of troops to forestall the coup he was alleged to be planning, put the whole movement on a different footing. This becomes very obvious when the issue at stake in the position of P'eng Chen is isolated. The correspondent in China of the Yugoslav newsagency Tanjug was the first to appreciate the real issue: P'eng Chen, he said, had insisted that the cultural-revolution teams should, at each level, be subject (as all other work-teams of any sort invariably had been) to the party committee as a whole, at the level above; that is, for example, that the cultural-revolution team engaged in examining the record of a district party branch and government organ should be responsible, not to its provincial equivalent, but to the provincial party committee. In this way, the Cultural Revolution would have been kept under firm control by the existing party hierarchy.[2]

Some months before, the Maoists had insisted that the relationship between the cultural-revolution committee and the higher level party committee would not be one of subordination, but merely of 'liaison'. This clearly opened the way for a most destructive attack upon the whole existing party apparatus; and, in general terms, it was predictable that there would be a stubborn opposition from those most closely associated with the party apparatus and with the organisation of the state, which was so closely bound up with the apparatus. The history of the later stages of the movement shows very clearly what was at stake between Mao and the party, and confirms the Yugoslavian correspondent's theory. The cardinal error of which President Liu Shao-ch'i and Party Secretary Teng Hsiao-p'ing were to be accused was that, during June and July 1966, having failed to keep a grip of the conventional kind upon the cultural purge, they fell back upon a second line of defence whereby, although conceding the Maoist point on paper, they still sought, by the manipulation of the cultural work-teams sent out from Peking, to keep the Cultural Revolution within bounds and under the control and supervision of the apparatus. This is the only specific and relevant charge brought against them.

The crisis has many aspects, but it can be divided with some plausibility into five stages, in terms of the issue of party control. 1. The period of resistance symbolised by P'eng Chen and the maintenance of normal hierarchical control over the movement. 2. The period June-July 1966 when Liu Shao-ch'i and Teng Hsiao-p'ing sought to control the cultural-revolution teams from the centre. 3. The defeat of Liu and Teng at the Central Committee meeting at the end of July or the beginning of August, the removal of party control and the full uninhibited development of a 'mass movement' led by the Red Guards. 4. The beginning of the attempt, at the end of the year and in January 1967, to use these 'popular' forces, not simply for the purging of the administration, but for a revolutionary take-over, explicitly Paris–Commune in style. 5. The reimposition, as a result of ensuing chaos and the threat of civil strife, of a degree of control through a 'three-way alliance' of revolutionary forces, the army, and 'revolutionary cadres'—the third category representing the existing party and state apparatus, the vast majority of whose members were now affirmed to be loyal and trustworthy. This is accompanied by the promulgation of rules for the conduct of the Cultural Revolution which bear an uncanny resemblance to the conventional controls which P'eng Chen, Liu Shao-ch'i and Teng Hsiao-p'ing had sought to maintain.

The issue of who was to control the movement overshadowed all else, and obscured for the time being the basic, long-term issues of policy. The urgent issue was the integrity of the existing party apparatus, but even this was all but obscured by the confused, emotional and ideological tone of what was published in the press, over the radio and on the walls of Peking—those much be-postered walls that by this time became a palimpsest from which, if it could be read, the whole history of this extraordinary movement could be reconstructed.

Three closely related struggles were going on at the same time: the struggle in the streets, led by the Red Guards and other similar bodies; the struggle in the provinces; and the struggle in the Central Committee and the other central organs of party and state. There were organisational links between the three. The Red Guards included groups which enjoyed the patronage of members of the leadership on both sides of the struggle, and thus played a part in the struggles within the central organisations. The provincial Red Guard groups, brought to Peking for exposure to the movement there and then sent back to their own areas, were strengthened by commissions despatched to the provinces to represent the leading Peking groups, thus extending the struggle throughout China. The existing party and state apparatus maintained, with or without an effective system of organisation and communication, a degree of nation-wide solidarity in the face of the Maoist attack. The whole situation was complicated by the ambiguous role of the army under the Minister of Defence, Marshal Lin Piao.

Accompanying this is an escalation of targets. Before the fall of P'eng Chen, the targets were primarily literary figures, and perhaps had it not been for the stubborn protection offered to the heads of the Peking newspapers by P'eng and his colleagues, the movement might have stopped short at a literary reform. After the fall of P'eng, the target area widens to include the whole apparatus of education and propaganda throughout China; the characteristic victims are university administrators, propaganda chiefs and newspaper men. With the defeat, at the end of July, of Liu Shao-ch'i and Teng Hsiao-p'ing, the objects of attack change; they are now directed against manifestations of bourgeois values and those who support them. By the 'January revolution' of 1967, the movement has become an attempt to seize China for Maoism and to carry through profound but predictable institutional changes on the basis of the wholesale supersession of the existing administration.

This escalation cannot be entirely accounted for by the Cultural

Revolution in its narrow sense; it is the consequence of other campaigns distinct from, but overlapping with, the Cultural Revolution itself. The first of these was the campaign which began as early as 1960 for the indoctrination of the army in preparation for a guerrilla role in the event of invasion. The second was the Socialist Education movement, directed primarily at the peasants in the hope of creating a climate in the villages favourable to the recovery of collectivist forms of enterprise. The third was the 'Four Clean-Ups', also primarily a rural movement, directed against lax, apathetic and corrupt cadres at village level. The fourth was the movement for the study of the thought of Mao Tse-tung, in principle directed to the whole population, but with army conscripts, cadres in both civil and military life, and the young as the main points of concentration. Finally, in the background, stalled firmly since the withering away of the Commune movement, was the question of educational changes, closely related to the Cultural Revolution but having played little part in it—presumably because of the solid support in high places in the party throughout China (revealed in the purges of June and July 1966) for academic norms in the universities and other institutions of higher education.

None of these campaigns had been very successful, except (with some qualifications) those which affected the army. These latter were relatively productive partly because of the fact that recruits, although formally conscripts, were, in substance, a privileged group chosen in the first place for their political reliability. More generally, they were productive because of the advantages which propaganda of the sort put out is bound to enjoy in an army that brings such recruits together in vast numbers—under discipline and living a collective life as soldiers—whose loyalties must, in the nature of things, be more developed and intense than those of a scattered and backward peasant population.

Mao's own statements as recorded circumstantially and plausibly on Red Guard posters at the height of the crisis show that dissatisfaction with the progress of these campaigns was as important as the cultural issues which touched off the crisis. To Mao, indeed, the cultural issues were important only in relation to the whole question of further revolutionary advance. The escalation of the crisis into a general and unlimited revolutionary movement was thus natural, although not inevitable, once the institutional obstacles to change had been weakened, and a force capable of launching the new revolution had been found and organised.

This is not to say that Mao planned a revolutionary take-over; but there is no doubt that he willed it, hoped for it, and exploited the situation in order to make it possible.

CULTURAL PURGES AND PARTY STRUGGLE, JUNE 1—AUGUST 8, 1966

As soon as P'eng Chen was removed from power, the cultural apparatus in Peking was purged. P'eng himself was replaced by Li Hsüeh-feng. His propaganda chief, Li Chi, was dismissed. The secretary of the party committee of Peking University, Lu P'ing, and his deputy were driven from office after a campaign of accusations concerning their academic policies by students, and with them went Sung Shih, deputy director of the University Scientific Work Committee of the municipal party.

The pattern was immediately repeated throughout the country, and in province after province, major figures were removed from office in the fields of education and propaganda.[3] There were denunciations and dismissals in fifteen of China's twenty-three provinces. The results, however, varied. In some places there were immediate results; in others, six weeks of agitation and perhaps pressure from the leaders of the Cultural Revolution in Peking were necessary. In five provinces (Yunnan, Kweichow, Tsinghai, Kwangtung and Sinkiang) the only victim during this phase (up to the publication on August 8 of the Sixteen-Point Directive of the Central Committee, which opened a new phase) was the editor, or deputy-editor, of the respective provincial newspaper; and, with the exception of Kwangtung, these are all fringe provinces. In Szechwan, the only official whose denunciation was given publicity was no longer in high office; formerly a member of the administrative office of the South-West Region Bureau of the Central Committee, he was currently vice-secretary of the party committee of Mientang Special District. In the universities, the only substantial results of the agitation were the dismissal of the party secretaries of the universities of Nanking and Chungking, and the dismissal of Ho Ting-hua of Wuhan University. In a few other institutions, such as Anhui Normal College and the universities in Sian and Kiangsi, the results were more ambiguous. The vagueness of reports of the

Cultural Revolution in many of these institutions suggests that little was achieved. In Tientsin, six universities and institutions of higher education joined in an agitation which produced only the dismissal of one assistant professor of history; later Nankai University was reported to have been purged, but no details were given. In the field of propaganda, the deputy directors of propaganda of three provinces (Kiangsu, Kiangsi and Anhui) were dismissed. There is a very notable absence of any reference to the Manchurian provinces at this stage.

Nowhere, in fact, did anything comparable with the Peking purge occur, and the results in the provinces could hardly have satisfied the leaders of the Cultural Revolution in the capital.

The purge was carried out by work-teams sent from provincial party headquarters. In Yunnan, for example, a work-team moved in and 'took over the rights and functions of the editorial board' of the provincial daily newspaper in order 'to exercise leadership over the great cultural revolution there''. They condemned one member of the staff for having run a column, "Extra-editorial Chat" which opposed Lin Piao's instruction on the study of Mao's thought, and slandered the Great Leap Forward. The information upon which the actions of the work-teams were based came from organised students, poor-peasant associations and other socio-political groups, but little is said of these sources of information.

The charges against those denounced varied. In a number of cases given at length in provincial radio broadcasts between June 1 and August 7 (the eve of the Sixteen-Point Directive), a total of twenty-one specific accusations are made. Of these, four concern opposition to the Communes and the Great Leap Forward, and two relate specifically to the advocacy of individual, as opposed to collective, farming. Three concern obstruction of the Cultural Revolution; two involve general strictures on the party's leadership. Other charges made in individual cases concern opposition to the study of Mao's thought and criticism of China's foreign policy; and, in one case, there is reference to an attempt to redress injustice done to 'rightists' attacked in 1957. Two accusations concern education, and two are directed against literary works. One accusation deals with the denial of class struggle, and another with the accused's attitude to the 1957 rectification. The last concerns a book written on the literature of the thirties, respect for which was under attack in the Cultural

Revolution. This small number of cases can hardly be treated as a statistical sample, but, for what the information is worth, it suggests that the accusations were by no means concerned only with cultural matters, even if those accused were all men holding positions in the cultural field. The most repeated accusations concern, not literature or education, but the attitudes of those in a position to influence public opinion to the Commune organisation and ideology. It is probable, however, that most or all of those attacked were, whether it is so stated or not, obstructing in some manner the course of the Cultural Revolution by defending attitudes which were anti-Maoist but which they had expressed in a variety of criticisms, whether of the Communes, the party leadership, policy towards right-wing dissidents, or any other feature of Maoist policy which irritated them into indiscretions.

The relatively meagre results of the Cultural Revolution in the provinces at this stage were partly the result of the limits set to it by forces later to be identified with Liu Shao-ch'i and Teng Hsiao-p'ing. In Fukien, those engaged in the cultural movement were warned, even as late as July 19, that: 'The stronghold of the Great Cultural Revolution lies in the cities, in the cultural etc. circles, and also in the party and government leading organs above the level of special districts.'[4] Little or nothing is said about the participation of the masses; and, indeed, by this definition of the scope of the movement, their part was automatically minimised and the movement was made into an exchange between provincial administrations represented by work-teams, chosen by the administrations themselves, and their immediate subordinates in the special district offices. It is worth adding that one provincial leader later denounced had apparently made the point to his colleagues at this time: 'It is the provincial leaders who are the target.' In these circumstances, the provincial administrations were bound to protect themselves from mass criticism of the kind which the Maoists were seeking to organise, and limit their actions to making a few scapegoats in the cultural field.

Meanwhile an obscure struggle was going on in Peking. Marshal Lin Piao moved troops up to the city in July; later he justified this as a move to forestall a movement from Shansi of troops under the orders of Lo Jui-ch'ing, chief-of-staff, in defence of P'eng Chen.[5] Whatever the truth, Lo Jui-ch'ing was promptly dismissed.

Mao Tse-tung, according to statements attributed to him later in Red Guard publications, had been forced to remain in Shanghai because P'eng Chen held the capital as a 'fortress' against him.[6] With the city safely in Lin Piao's hands, a meeting of the Central Committee was held; it is said to have been packed by the Maoist faction, but even so, apparently, there was only a narrow majority in favour of Mao. Red Guard sources suggest that even this narrow majority for him was won only because Teng Hsiao-p'ing hesitated to oppose him, while Chou En-lai gave him support.

The Central Committee then issued on August 8 a Sixteen-Point Directive defining the aims and the methods of the Cultural Revolution.

The Directive alludes first to the tenth session of the Eighth Central Committee of 1962, at which the new line, 'production struggle, scientific experiment and class struggle' had first been put forward—the origin of the whole movement—and at which Mao had emphasised the necessity for moulding public opinion. It goes on to sanction a mass movement led by youth, and excuses in advance their excesses and mistakes as an inevitable part of their self-education by participation in revolution 'The masses must liberate themselves' and 'it is necessary to have confidence in them.' The aim of the leadership should be to discover and encourage left-wing elements, and to create a situation in which 95 per cent of the population are united against the extreme right-wing 5 per cent.

The Directive, in this respect, advocates care in distinguishing this handful of 'rightist' people from those who have merely expressed certain erroneous views or made mistakes, and from those who, while having had a bourgeois education, are not proponents of a bourgeois line. Having reminded the public of the difference between contradictions among the people and antagonistic contradictions 'between the enemy and us', it goes on to insist on free debate, the use of persuasion, the exercise of patience and the avoidance of quarrels. It warns against instigating students to struggle against students or the masses against the masses. It insists that the majority of cadres are good, or relatively good, and that the number of 'anti-party, anti-socialist, rightist elements' is very small. The cultural-revolution teams, committees and congresses formed in schools and elsewhere are indicated as the organs of the new revolution; these, stipulated as 'long-term, permanent organisations', are also held to be 'basically suitable for factory and mining enterprises, neighbourhoods and the countryside'. The Paris-Commune system of direct, mass election should be used in these, and the electors will have the right of recall. Arrangements are then suggested for linking up the cultural movement with the Socialist Education movement in the towns and the countryside. The Directive then deals with the opinion that the Cultural Revolution and the development of production may conflict, and points out that the aim of the movement is precisely to free the forces of production by 'revolutionising the people's ideology'; it puts forward the slogan, 'Grasp revolution to promote production'. It emphasises that, in the army, the revolution must be carried on under the Military Affairs Committee of the Central Committee and by the General Political Department of the People's Liberation Army.

Finally, the importance of the thought of Mao Tse-tung in the Cultural Revolution is emphasised, and a number of texts are recommended for study: *New Democracy*, the *Yenan Talks on Literature and Art*, the two rectification essays of 1957, *Some Questions on Methods of the Leadership* and *The Working Method of Party Committees*. In affirming authority of these writings, the Directive ends with renewed emphasis on the most basic Maoist text of all: 'From the masses and to the masses . . . be pupils of the masses before becoming their teachers.'

Red Flag immediately commented on the Directive.[7] Throughout it emphasised that the Directive called for the subordination of party members to the mass movement, and criticised those members and units that had resisted it or tried to redirect it against left-wing critics. The theme of leaving the masses to educate themselves and let them make their own mistakes is the main subject of the article; their experiences, wishes and criticisms must be listened to and studied, and summed up to ascertain what they want. On the methods of criticism, *Red Flag* said:

> The masses fully understand that strenuous efforts must be made to win over the middle-of-the-road elements. . . . Their names may be mentioned in the big-character posters issued by their own units after the masses are mobilised, but this is inevitable. So long as their names are not openly published in the newspapers and they are allowed in the meantime to issue posters to defend themselves, they will not be affected at all. . . .

It is striking that even Liu Shao-ch'i, Teng Hsiao-p'ing and T'ao Chu—the most important targets of the later stage of the movement —were not at this stage (nor for some time to come) officially attacked by name, although on the posters they were subjected to enormous abuse. The press and radio referred to them only as 'top people who have taken the capitalist road'.

Perhaps the most significant passage in the article is the paragraph concerned with the organisation of the movement; it reaffirms the rule against which P'eng Chen had fought:

> Experience has shown that each unit must carry out the work of the Cultural Revolution by relying on its own masses and should not depend on arrangements made by upper-level organs. . . . Each unit should carry out its work without the help of work-teams dispatched by upper-level organs.

Thus, after an eight-month struggle, Mao Tse-tung won the freedom of manœuvre which he sought, although at the expense of alienating some of the most important elements in the party.

However, before we conclude that, in the achieving and exploiting of this victory ever since the publication of the Directive, the Cultural Revolution has been the work of a single lonely and ageing fanatic, we should remember that Mao has not been without important support in the leadership. While unable to take the heads of the party apparatus with him (after all, it was the party apparatus against which he made his main attack; the primary aim of the movement, as defined in the Directive, is 'to strike down those powerful figures in the party who have taken the capitalist road'), he has carried with him, so far, two men who cannot, on their records (or their age) be regarded as unrealistic dreamers: Lin Piao and Chou En-lai.

Marshal Lin Piao believes that China can best defend itself by guerrilla methods. Preparation for such a defence has important political implications, and these Lin Piao is prepared to accept, in company with Mao. It is worth noting, as we have already pointed out, that Lin Piao, alone of all the major military figures of China, has experience of both guerrilla warfare and of a modern positional war (against the Americans in Korea). Consequently, his support for the guerrilla defence strategy, and his acceptance of its political and economic implications, have a better basis in experience than the opinions of any of his colleagues in China—except, perhaps, for P'eng Teh-huai who, however, had been dismissed in 1959.

Chou En-lai is universally regarded (though on rather flimsy evidence) as a moderate. He is, at any rate, a statesman of some reputation for realism and for administrative ability, and is seen as a man who can talk in language that the outside world can understand. Moreover, he has had since 1949 the responsibility for the smooth running of the administration and the economy of China. Yet, he, as well as Mao, is willing at this stage to back a potentially disruptive mass revolution, led by irresponsible youngsters. It has been argued that Chou may have made a bargain: to support Mao provided the economy be not tampered with. If so, it is a poor bargain, for the whole Maoist programme is obviously prejudicial to the good order and discipline with which Chou En-lai is identified abroad. It has also been suggested that Chou has joined Mao in the Cultural Revolution in order to try to control events. This may be true, but what is meant by controlling events is still obscure, for at the mass rally on August 18 to celebrate the Sixteen-Point Directive, at which the Red Guard movement was launched, it was Chou En-lai, and not Lin Piao, who went out of his way to emphasise the mass-movement nature of the policy which the Directive put forward:

> Chairman Mao has taught us [as citizens] that, to make revolution by ourselves, we must rely on ourselves. We will educate ourselves, liberate ourselves, and carry out the revolution by ourselves.... We should set ourselves [as party and government cadres] firmly against monopolising every undertaking, acting as high-and-mighty bureaucrats, and standing above the masses, blindly ordering them about.[8]

THE RED GUARD CAMPAIGN, AUGUST 1966– JANUARY 1967

The Red Guards first appeared in public with official approval at this rally on August 18 in Peking. They had grown (spontaneously or not it is impossible to say) out of the school organisations in the Cultural Revolution. In a radio report on the rally, they were defined:

The Red Guard is an organisation set up by middle-school pupils

124

from the families of workers, poor and lower-middle peasants, revolutionary cadres and revolutionary soldiers.[9]

The red armband which they wore was the insignia of the peasant militia of the Kiangsi and Yenan soviets. One contingent at the rally turned out in the tattered uniforms of their fathers who had followed the Red Army in the Long March. The red armband symbolised an appeal to the emotions of the revolutionary past, which was to form a major element in the whole movement.

To Western observers, it is incredible that a revolution which is meant to have the most profound consequences throughout a great country should be put in the hands of schoolchildren, and by a group of men who have forty years' experience of politics and of administration. There are two points to make. First, there is the position and history of intellectual youth in China. When the Chinese radio says 'it is an objective law of the Chinese revolution that in every mass movement students and schoolchildren have taken the lead, and the masses of workers and peasants have followed', this is an exaggeration, but it is not entirely untrue. Further, in a country where the vast majority is illiterate, the young people, as literacy spreads and they gain education, are bound to have an enormous influence. They may not always be able to convince their elders, but they are an essential and important means of communicating new ideas. This role of theirs is strengthened by the Chinese tradition of student participation in politics and even, long before the twentieth century, of students as martyrs to political oppression.

[margin note: but this contradicts the mass line !!]

Secondly, in present circumstances, all the Chinese leaders (and one probably need not distinguish among them as far as this opinion is concerned) appreciate that—with the expansion of modern science and technology, education and administration, and with the age-structure heavily weighted to youth (half of the population is under eighteen)—there is going to be, and already is, a very rapid absorption of young people into positions of responsibility and influence, for which they must be prepared. It is certain that no less unanimous within the leadership is the opinion that this preparation must involve 'political' preparation in the Chinese Communist sense of the word: that is, the inculcation of the appropriate social ethics. Nor need it be supposed that this 'political' conditioning is entirely concerned with indoctrination in specifically Communist ideology; it is as much, if not more, concerned with the inculcation of modern

[handwritten note at bottom: (true) - preponderance of students in Red Guard is simply a contradiction of the mass line]

attitudes which are no more Communist than they are Western.[10] The question of 'revolutionary successors' must be considered against this background.

Before we condemn the principle (apart from the practice) of the use of youth as the spearhead of the Cultural Revolution, we must ask ourselves, what other group, in a country in which an entrenched party bureaucracy faces an ignorant and apathetic peasant population, is likely to have the motive and the mobility and the knowledge to break the deadlock? Only the intellectual class can do this; and it is only here that we come to the beginnings of divergence among the Chinese leaders. Which intellectuals? The Maoists believe that the group among the intellectuals who are most likely to succeed are the educated sons and daughters of the poor majority, rather than those of the middle class.

It must also be remembered that the youth movement's role in the intended revolution is more limited and more specific than it seems at first sight. As the quotation from the radio report cited above implies, its role is to give a lead to workers and peasants, to be the yeast which will leaven the whole lump by public debate and demonstration; it is to communicate the ideas of the Cultural Revolution to the less sophisticated. By its courage, it is to set an example of criticism of the party machine, of which the masses, who are probably in their less articulate (and less privileged) way, already very critical. It is to provide the skeleton of a new and more democratic form of political organisation upon which the mass of the population will then put the flesh. The young activists will, in fact, play the part which their grandfathers played against the warlords and the imperialists in the May Fourth movement. If one wants to know why senior statesmen can put such faith in, and take such risks with, a force of millions of schoolchildren and young students, this is the answer: they did it themselves, in 1919 and in the years that followed. As Chou En-Lai stated at a later rally: "The Red Guards must build themselves up into a highly organised and disciplined militant army with high political consciousness. . . . Our Red Guards will certainly mature in the course of struggle and become pathfinders who display both intelligence and courage."[11]

The main task of the Red Guards, however, was in the summer of 1966 the reform of education in their own institution, school or college; the rest of their activities were less clearly adumbrated in the documents of the time, and there was some ambiguity as to what were to be their relations with the other mass movements among workers, peasants and soldiers. The Sixteen-Point Directive, explicit on all else, hedges on this. As far as the schools were concerned, their revolutionary work was already done by August 1966, and the schools and colleges were closed for six months while a new education system, ostensibly designed to meet the demands of the students themselves, was worked out.

The most important question about the Red Guards, however, is how far their activities were spontaneous, how far they really represented a mass-movement, a freeing of popular youthful initiative (in the terms emphasised by the Directive) by Mao Tse-tung and by Chou En-lai. To this, on present information, no answer can be given. It has been pointed out that the Red Guards who came to Peking to mix with and consult those of the capital, and the Red Guards of the capital who went as delegates elsewhere in China, were fed, housed and transported by the authorities, mainly by the army, and that there were always adults with these groups (assumed to be soldiers but probably more often teachers who had been permitted to accept invitation into their ranks from the beginning). It is probable that the peripatetic student groups, although they loomed very large in the capital for a brief period, and even larger in the foreign press, were only a minority of the total force, the vast majority of which were active in their own districts only. As far as the Peking groups themselves are concerned, their activities, and not least their rivalries and brawls, have given every appearance of spontaneity, and the Chinese press, at the height of the Red Guard phase and subsequently has been less concerned to goad them on to new heights of revolution than to plead for discipline and restraint.

On the other hand, by the end of 1966, it became obvious that rivalries between groups of Red Guards were not all evidence of freedom abused, and that some groups were quite clearly being patronised, and perhaps even manipulated, by members of the leadership. The activities of the Red Guards grew in scope from the changing of street names and expostulation with barbers providing 'bourgeois' hair styles, to the invasion of factories, the theft of state documents, the painful humiliation of aged veteran leaders of the party, and (at the end of the year) pitched battles with units of the army. Was this escalation directed or not? In the nature of the case we cannot tell. We can say that the Maoist group (a shrinking one throughout) welcomed this escalation, and that the Red Guard groups which seem to have led it (those of the Peking Aviation Institute and the Third Red Guard HQ) appear to have had a close relationship with Ch'en Po-ta and Mme Mao. Japanese observers even claimed that, at the stage of the maximum isolation of Mao and his few supporters, it was the funds and the power of political mobilisation represented by these two groups which kept Mao in power. But, in fact, we know too little of this relationship to be able to base an argument upon it.[12]

It is certain that the Red Guards had considerable freedom, even if in some important cases they received hints and inside information from above as to what they might do or publicise. Mao Tse-tung, at least, seems to have been sincere in his belief in allowing them the freedom to make mistakes; several times he is reported as having justified their more excessive activities by quoting his own report on the peasant movement in Hunan—i.e., that 'a mess' is to be expected when the masses rise, and that it does no harm. His only public intervention in the direction of moderation during this phase was of the most oblique and gentle kind: he allowed publication of a report of a conversation with his niece in which he deplored neglect and contempt for traditional Chinese literature, praised *The Dream of the Red Chamber* in particular, and indirectly defended foreign literature by urging his niece, a student of English, to translate the Bible. In this way he let it be known that he deplored the excessive iconoclasm which had already led to the sacking in August, 1966 of the Central Institute of Arts—an event described with approval by the New China News Agency—in spite of warnings against the destruction of works of art and historical relics by the *People's Daily* a few days before.[13]

The destruction of works of art, the defacing of buildings decorated in a bourgeois or imperialist manner, the hustling of people dressed in middle-class or foreign style, the interference with religious ceremonies, and the attacks on foreign churches—activities like these are not of much political significance. The poster wars over the denunciation of individuals in the units to which the Red Guards belong are of more importance, although they have received

128

very little publicity. Gradually, however, one can detect a change in the targets of the poster war, and out of the ritual denunciations of those already condemned, such as P'eng Chen, there developed the attack upon the major leaders. At the height of the Red Guard campaign (from August 1966 to January 1967), no one, except Mao Tse-tung and Marshal Lin Piao, was left unscathed. Even Mme Mao (Chiang Ch'ing), who emerged into the political arena at this point, was criticised. More than half of the 200-strong Central Committee, including virtually every member of any significance, was attacked. Most of them were defended on other posters, some so overwhelmingly that it seems probable that the defence was ordered. Whether the attacks were ordered is something we shall probably never know for certain.

The opening of a sustained campaign against President Liu Shao-ch'i and Party Secretary Teng Hsiao-p'ing seems to have begun with a rally on January 4, 1967 at which P'eng Chen and his associates in the Peking resistance to Mao Tse-tung in the spring of 1966 were treated to public humiliations. This rally was immediately followed by an article in *Red Flag* which issued a stern warning to 'the handful of persons in power who had taken the capitalist path'. Liu Shao-ch'i and Teng Hsiao-ping had made no public appearances for over a month; and their last appearance had been as participants in a very ambiguous exercise, in November, when a vast Red Guard rally in Tienanmen Square was treated only to a hurried appearance of the leaders, in a procession of three open cars, with Mao Tse-tung and Lin Piao in the first, Chou En-lai and Chu Teh in the second, and Liu Shao-ch'i and Teng Hsiao-p'ing in the third. Up to the end of 1966, both Liu and Teng were still listed among the top leaders present at public occasions, but much lower in the hierarchy: Teng listed as sixth, and Liu as eighth.

The rally of January 4 seems to have opened the flood-gates of mutual criticism. In the ensuing two or three weeks, scarcely one Chinese leader was not criticised or denounced in Red Guard posters; only Mao Tse-tung and Lin Piao escaped, and as the weeks wore on it was obvious that Lin Piao in some quarters was being damned with faint praise. Even the nucleus of the cultural-revolution group was not free from criticism. Mme Mao, Kang Sheng, and Ch'en Po-ta were attacked, although they were all immediately defended in a rash of rival posters; throughout, it is the strength or weakness, or the absence, of defending posters which gives the measure of the attitude of the nuclear group to the criticisms which were made. There is also evidence from some posters that certain criticisms were directly inspired by the Maoist leadership; Ch'en Po-ta and Mme Mao were frequently given on the posters as authorities for denunciations. Posters and Red Guard leaflets and newspapers also suggest that criticisms made in posters (besides the obvious cases of Liu Shao-ch'i and Teng Hsiao-p'ing) were taken up by Mao himself (if they had not been inspired by Mao or his associates originally) and made an issue in top-level consultations of the Politburo and other organs.

The confused information from Red Guard sources, representing rival attitudes, partial information and rumour, makes it very difficult to find a pattern in the accusations; and the fact that only a very small fraction of the Red Guard output could be reported by the few foreign correspondents (mostly Japanese) who could read them, makes any attempt at a strict chronology of events quite impossible. One cannot give with certainty the date at which a man was first criticised, but only the date at which the correspondent found and reported the criticism. In general, however, the date at which a criticism became general, signified by a rash of posters in the most favoured public places, probably coincided with the date when the criticism could be reported.

Attacks on the economic ministries went on with varying degrees of intensity throughout. The men who headed these ministries were obvious targets for the Maoists who believed in the ideology and strategy of the Great Leap Forward; they were bureaucratism incarnate. But, in the critical power struggle of January 1967, this was not an urgent issue, and on the whole Chou En-lai, by strenuous efforts through publication in posters and personal interviews with Red Guard groups, was able to keep his ministries intact. The real targets were elsewhere.

At the very beginning of 1966, T'ao Chu—the vigorous and successful ruler of south China who, in September, had been brought to Peking to take over the Central Committee's propaganda organs —was denounced for having acted on his own without consulting the Maoist leaders. He was replaced as head of propaganda, hauled before a hostile rally, and his name linked thereafter with Liu and

Teng. He had not been rehabilitated up to the time of writing. Of his close associates appointed to positions in the Maoist group, several were denounced soon after, and the Maoists lost the very great advantage of having the powerful and vital central-south region directly represented in Peking. The accusation later directed against T'ao Chu—namely, that he had advocated that 'the south must be free'—may reflect the hostility which his disgrace was bound to cause, to a degree which we can only guess at, in the party hierarchy of the central-south region, which comprises most of the rice-surplus lands of China. The fact that T'ao Chu was also a life-long associate of Lin Piao, who was very probably responsible for bringing him to Peking, may also be significant. The outbreak of violence in Nanking shortly after, which Red Guard sources linked with T'ao Chu, seems to have been the first signs of a hardening hostility in central China to the Maoist group in Peking. This hostility was to manifest itself clearly, after a history of stubborn resistance in the city of Wuhan from the beginning of 1967, in the detention there, in July, of Hsüeh Fu-chin (Maoist Minister of Security) and Wang Li (Maoist head of party propaganda in succession to T'ao Chu) by Ch'en Tsai-tao, provincial commander of Hupeh. The disgrace of the provincially powerful T'ao Chu, a convinced but practical Maoist, may have been a decisive point in the weakening of the Maoist cause.

The attack on T'ao Chu in early January was the first split in the ranks of the Maoist leadership, and it was followed within a week by evidence of further divisions. Red Guard posters turned their attacks against members of the Cultural Revolution Committee itself. Three members of the committee were accused of trying to set up a separate controlling body for the movement: Lu Chih-chien, deputy head of the Political Department of the People's Liberation Army, and Chang P'ing-huan and Wang Jen-chung of the Central Committee's Propaganda Department. One of the charges against Lu was that he sent out work-teams to carry on the Cultural Revolution in the army: the familiar issue once more. Ch'en Yi the Minister of Foreign Affairs, was accused at the same time of having 'maximised the excesses of the revolutionary forces, and minimised the mistakes of the work-teams'.[14] On January 12, Hsieh Fu-chih, the new Maoist Minister of Public Security, was accused (and Mme Mao quoted as the authority) for having 'set himself above the party and the people'.[15] What this meant in practice is not known, but it may have reflected an attempt to stabilise the situation in Peking by strengthening the authority of the police force, which must have been in utter chaos, judging by the frequency of attacks on the Ministry of Public Security itself and on police stations throughout Peking. (The first really bloody clashes reported between rival Red Guard groups were over control of police stations.) Hsiao Hua, appointed as the supreme head of the army's political affairs, was also criticised.

CIVIL STRIFE AND RESTABILISATION

On January 13, a new military commission was formed to direct the Cultural Revolution. It consisted of Mme Mao, Ch'en Po-ta, Hsü Hsiang-chen (the former commander of the First Field Army, brought out of retirement) and Yang Chen-wu, who was acting chief-of-staff in place of the dismissed Lo Jui-ch'ing. The significance of this new organisation is not known. It could not have been set up without Politburo authority, and so may have represented an attempt at compromise. At any rate, the following day Mme Mao publicly asked for the rehabilitation of some of those recently attacked; these included several economic ministers (T'an Chen-lin, Li Fu-chün and Li Hsien-nien), and indicated perhaps the resistance of Chou En-lai who was present and took the principal part at the rally at which this rehabilitation took place. But the significant rehabilitions were those of Hsieh Fu-chih and Hsiao Hua. At the same time, Hsieh Fu-chih issued regulations for the maintenance of public order, and although these specifically included as offences the insulting of Mao Tse-tung and Lin Piao, it can be assumed that their main purpose was to try to put limits to the excesses of the Red Guards, which in Peking and throughout China were already threatening to cause serious civil strife. It seems likely that the question of exercising this degree of control had been the issue between Hsieh and the Maoist leadership in the preceding few days.

This was not the end of strife, however. In the following few days, the question of the Cultural Revolution and the army loomed largest, if one can judge from the rostrum of those denounced. These included Hsiao Hsiang-jung of the Ministry of Defence; Liang Pi-yeh of the army's Political Department; Liao Hang-sheng,

Deputy Minister of Defence; Shao Chin-kuang, Deputy Minister of Defence; Hsü Hsiang-chen, who on January 13 had been appointed to the new military commission; and Marshal Ho Lung, whom Mme Mao had publicly named on January 16 as one of the six of China's nine marshals who supported Mao Tse-tung. Throughout this whole period, Lin Piao was silent. Two of the three members of the new propaganda commission were also denounced, but the question of divisions over the position of the army was primary. On January 21, it was reported that Mao had appealed personally to Lin Piao for the intervention of the People's Liberation Army, using the argument that his non-intervention was a form of intervention[16]—the first specific evidence that Lin had been reluctant to commit the army wholly on the Maoist side, or perhaps that divisions in the army were such that he could not do so without fear of civil war.

That there had been growing violence is indisputable, but its significance is doubtful. Moscow radio poured out a spate of stories of massive armed resistance by the majority of workers and peasants to the Cultural Revolution; but Japanese reports were more cautious, and so, for several weeks, were those of the East European agencies. Tanjug at first dismissed the sensational details of strife published in Red Guard posters as a gimmick to gain public sympathy,[17] and it is true that the reports on the posters all had the same form: they gave casualties among the revolutionary groups, seldom saying anything about victory or defeat; they did not always identify the enemy, and in general represented the victims as innocent martyrs. The Maoist strategy depended partly, after all, on the reluctance of those in authority to handle schoolchildren and students roughly, and naturally every instance of rough handling would be made the most of. In contrast to these gory agency reports are those of travellers in China, who reported 'a festival, not a violent atmosphere', and no signs of fighting.[18] It would be pointless to try to reproduce the endless, conflicting reports for which we have little or no corroborating evidence; but some developments are clear.

First, the most substantial resistance came from the north-west and Tibet. This is to be expected, and does not necessarily indicate that there were serious disagreements between the far west of China and Peking over basic policies or over the Cultural Revolution in general. In these areas of national minorities, even the most trivial of Red Guard activities, relatively harmless in Peking, were politically explosive. The 'destruction of the old' in the form of an attack on old habits and the symbols of the older way of life would be, at worst, saddening to the fellow citizens of the Red Guards in Peking; but they would constitute an attack upon the very characteristics which marked the distinction of the minority races in Sinkiang, Mongolia and Tibet; and their respective rulers—Wang En-mao, Ulanfu and Chang Kuo-hua—reacted very quickly. The only reports of military battles in the real sense, up to the end of January, came from these areas.

Secondly, the vast majority of stories of civil strife concern brief and limited clashes, without organised military force on either side, over key points in the cultural struggle, very often the offices of the provincial newspaper. The clashes reported as the most serious of all in Peking itself (though more in terms of bloody heads than of deaths) were battles for control of the Peking University printing press and the Peking Radio building.[19] Similar stories came from the provinces.

Thirdly, there was one area in which, even at this early stage, there were reports of organised army resistance directed from high places, and that was the city of Wuhan in southern Hupeh, where Ch'en Tsai-tao was already being accused of military suppression of the revolution. This may be more significant than simply the personal resistance of one provincial commander. The Wuhan area on the middle Yangtse is the strategic heart of China, the cockpit of civil war, the strategic pass between north and south. If the party hierarchs have to defend themselves by force, they must hold Wuhan at all costs, and it is possible to suppose that Ch'en's prompt resistance to the Maoist revolution there indicates that the party is prepared to carry resistance to the point of civil war. It may also be significant that it is only from Wuhan that we have rumours of the creation of a rival political party, in the reported creation of a central committee of the 'Chinese Workers' Party'.

Other straws in the wind suggest the 'smell of gunpowder'. Rumours of the setting up of an opposition military headquarters in Shansi may have been inspired by anticipation rather than fact; but they were followed by a strenuous and, for the time being, successful Maoist campaign to take the province over. This again reflects a commonplace of Chinese strategic geography. If the Maoists have to expect military resistance in south and central China, the automatic move—as for any government in Peking—is to secure their flank in Shansi, from which (if Lin Piao's justification of his military coup in Peking in July is true), they had already been threatened through the intrigues of Lo Jui-ch'ing.

The other dimension of resistance is in terms of groups of the population and their interests. While the Soviet picture of massive popular loyalty to the party hierarchy against Mao is neither probable nor provable, there are ample indications that some industrial workers at least have been prepared to fight against the authority of the Red Guards. We need not depend wholly on confused rumours of rioting to show this. The constant appeals of the Maoists against what they describe as the bribing of workers by additional incentives in order to win them from Maoism, make it plain that, for whatever reason, they had lost the support of a significant section of the urban working class. But the disagreement was deeper than this. One of the few specific acts of policy of the Maoists had been to abolish the incentive bonuses paid to workers during the years of relaxation; the 'bribing' of workers may simply have been the restoration of these bonuses. The existence of hostility had, in fact, been suggested at an earlier stage, when the All-China Federation of Trade Unions had been abolished (not necessarily the unions themselves) and the *Workers' Daily* (*Kung-jen Jih-pao*) closed by early January 1967.[20] But, without further information, we cannot make much of this. The abolition of the Federation is explicable, in a way consistent with the spirit of the Cultural Revolution, on the supposition that this step was meant to remove inhibitions to the free expression of opinion by the workers. The short-lived Shanghai Commune, established in early February, set up a committee to prepare for elections of the Paris-Commune type. The workers had as full a representation as would be expected (five out of eleven) on this committee, which had to include representatives of the army (two), the students (one), the party (one) and the peasants of Shanghai's very considerable rural suburbs (two). Clearly, the workers must have controlled this body.[21]

Of peasant opinion during the crisis we know even less. The peasants were, on the whole, shielded from the Cultural Revolution at this stage, although not wholly so. Ostensibly the Cultural

Revolution did not concern specific policies but merely aimed, in theory at least, to remove all institutional obstacles to free expression of the opinions of the poor majority. Two comments on this are necessary, however. First, the poor majority was itself profoundly divided into the skilled workers of the cities who, although their absolute standard of living was still fairly low, were in a position of privilege *vis-à-vis* the peasants. Secondly, the background of the Cultural Revolution and its concomitants, in the form of the Socialist Education movement and other such campaigns, included a stress on renewed collectivisation and adumbrated a return to the spirit of the Communes and the Great Leap Forward. The central committee or the party in Kwangtung province spelled out what they saw as the implications of the Sixteen-Point Directive, and in doing so probably expressed what the Chinese public anticipated from the movement, whether they hoped for or feared its success: 'A magnificent blueprint of Communism . . . points out the concrete road to the elimination of the Three Great Differences . . . a programme for the thorough completion of the socialist revolution and the transition to Communism. . . .' The Kwangtung central committee then put forward specific policies with a strongly Commune-collectivist basis in order to achieve these ends: policies which, whatever long-term advantages they might offer, would certainly involve the mass of the population in drastic alterations in their way of life. (See Documentary Appendix, page 207, for text.)

On January 25, the army responded to the appeal which Mao Tse-tung had made five days earlier to Lin Piao, and took action to restore order in local situations in Kirin and Anhui provinces.[22] Shortly after this, as a result of army action, the position was improved in Sinkiang, where it had been reported that the opposition held all approaches to the town of Shihotzu and that seven out of eight divisions were anti-Maoist. The restoration of order must therefore have been by agreement and, as one would expect, the price of the restoration of order was the end of the Cultural Revolution in its more anarchic forms in the provinces. Whether these and subsequent actions of the People's Liberation Army represent a decision on the part of its commanders and Lin Piao to come out on the Maoist side, or whether, as some commentators immediately declared, they signify the militarisation of China, it is too soon to say. The Maoists, after all, were still acting with the support, however agonised, of the rump of the Central Committee of the party. In the absence of contrary orders from the beleaguered President of the Republic, there was no other authority for them to obey except the Prime Minister, Chou En-lai; and from February 27 they were acting under his express orders. Their intervention was not clearly one-sided; reports are confused and suggest that they sought to make peace on the basis of the strength of local political forces. This, too, has been represented by commentators as intervention *against* the Maoists; but Red Guard reports of discussions among the leaders of the Cultural Revolution at this time suggest that a more flexible approach was being worked out; and this, conveyed to the army, as it no doubt was, could account for the actions of the armed forces without the necessity of assuming that the People's Liberation Army had adopted an independent political role.

The background of the new situation was that the Cultural Revolution had been both intensified and streamlined. The new aim of the Maoists was the seizure of power by the revolutionary groups. Power was seized in Shanghai and a Shanghai Commune proclaimed on January 6. A week later a Commune was proclaimed in Taiyuan, capital of Shansi province, and then in Peking with Hsieh Fu-chih as director. Peking was formally seized by the Red Guards on January 18, although their control was far from complete and their ranks far from unified. At the same time, Chou En-lai called for an end to the struggle against the members of the original cultural-revolution work-teams, and the Peking offices of national Red Guard organisations and of provincial organisations were closed. There was a call for the concentration of targets 'in the literary field'—a rather ambiguous definition—and only six men were named as the objects of continued struggle: the four principals in the opposition to Mao in Peking in the spring of 1966 (P'eng Chen, Lo Jui-ch'ing, Lu Ting-yi and Wang Shang-kun, the Politburo secretary accused of 'bugging' Mao's conversations), along with Chou Yang and Hsia Yen. The errors of others were said to be temporary. Chou En-lai, while calling in January for the seizure of power throughout the country, deplored the excessive humiliation of P'eng Chen, ordered an end to attacks on the ministries of Petroleum, Machine-Building and Commerce, and stipulated that the consent of the Central Committee must be obtained for

K

the seizure of ministries in the capital. He made these statements at a 'unity congress' at which the Red Guards and their adult successors, 'the Red Revolutionary Rebels,' were urged to form a single organisation.

This policy was perfectly consistent with a statement reported to have been made by Chou En-lai at a much earlier stage in events, when he said that there were two different problems: on the one hand, control of the provinces; and on the other hand, a very limited but powerful opposition in Peking. He had now succeeded in limiting the targets in the capital and concentrating effort on the reform of the party hierarchy in the provinces.

As far as present information is concerned, therefore, the actions of the People's Liberation Army seem to have been consistent with the orders and the policy of the Prime Minister.

Some further details of the policy upon which Chou En-lai and Mao Tse-tung seem to have agreed by the end of January were reported in Red Guard materials. It was reported that Chou, in discussion with Mao, had suggested that the opposition could be divided into five groups: 'villains'; 'those in power taking the capitalist road'; stubbornly bourgeois elements; those who have admitted mistakes but continue in error; and those guilty only of minor errors to which they have confessed.[23] The 'villains' were probably the P'eng Chen group.'Those taking the capitalist road' referred primarily to Liu Shao-ch'i and Teng Hsiao-p'ing. The stubbornly bourgeois elements probably were certain of Chou's own vice-premiers whom he did not, for reasons unknown, choose to protect (notably the Minister of Railways and the Minister of Agriculture, and perhaps Po Yi-po, who seems on his poster record to have been the most unpopular of all). Beyond this point, the reports of the posters are confused, but the following factors seem clear. First, Chou En-lai was concerned to lay down a system of treatment for members of the opposition, distinguishing among those who should be dismissed, those who should be suspended, and those who should be put under the supervision of the revolutionary forces; and he insisted that, for each category, there should be a period during which the sentence was suspended to give time for self-criticism. Mao in turn appears to have agreed that 'total reorganisation', as in Shanghai, was not the only possible method of taking power, and that elsewhere it would be possible to use the existing administration

under surveillance by revolutionary organs. He added, character-
istically, that dismissed or suspended cadres should then in most
cases be given an opportunity to participate in the work of the
Cultural Revolution. In this way the 'villains' and 'persons in
authority taking the capitalist road' would be isolated. Chou is
reported to have added that the young activists would have to be
trained before the old leaders were replaced. It is worth notice that
Mao mentioned retirement of leaders as well as dismissal: a timely
reminder that part of the problem is the high average age of those in
high power throughout China, and that the Cultural Revolution is,
as much as anything else, an attempt to break up the new Communist gerontocracy which has replaced the old Confucian one.
Finally, Chou En-lai stressed that 'take-over' did not mean that the
revolutionary youth would immediately replace the superseded
cadres in their duties, but that they should supervise their conduct.
This conversation seems to have taken place on or about January 25.

Throughout February, the process of the restoration of order and
control in Peking went on. A new cultural-revolution commission,
this time for the party and the government, was formed, with Chou
En-lai as adviser and Mme Mao as chairman. The army took over
the security offices in Peking. Undesirable (not necessarily right-
wing) revolutionary organisations were banned, and when there
was renewed criticism of Ch'en Yi, Chou named ten organisations
permitted to take part. He called for an end to demonstrations
against the Soviet Union. On February 27, he issued his first direct
orders to the People's Liberation Army, sending troops to Honan to
take over the disputed offices of the provincial newspaper and induce
the warring factions to send delegates to Peking. Other stipulations
were made in the name of the Central Committee, which does not
appear to have issued any directives or instructions after the Sixteen-
Point Directive of August 8, 1966. The Committee now forbad the
expulsion of members of the party under mass pressure. A letter was
also published assuring rural cadres that they would not suffer
indiscriminate criticism and disgrace.

On March 2, the formation of a 'three-way alliance' was
announced in Heilunchiang, between the People's Liberation Army,
the revolutionary forces, and the 'revolutionary cadres' representing
the trustworthy members of the existing party and administrative
hierarchies. This was in line with the policy discussed by Mao and

Chou, and was promptly taken up.[24] On March 3, posters quoted Mao Tse-tung as having condemned as reactionary the attitude of 'being suspicious of everybody', described Shanghai demands for the abolition of cabinet ministers as 'extreme anarchism', and condemned the Communes as premature. He then stressed the idea of the three-way alliance. This, it was reported, was in the course of discussions with the two Maoist leaders in Shanghai, Chang Chün-chao and Yao Wen-yüan.

"more Maoist than Mao" ✓

There was still a revolutionary head of steam in Peking, however. The Red Guards of the Aviation Institute, whose strictures on Liu Shao-ch'i and Teng Hsiao-p'ing became even shriller now, protested strongly at the attempts to bring the revolutionary forces under a single joint command. But the process of bringing the Cultural Revolution under the authority of the state and of the party's Central Committee went inexorably on. One of its results was the unification of the Red Guards. Denunciations continued: the Deputy Minister of Finance was condemned, but only after Chou En-lai had interviewed his Red Guard accusers; and meanwhile there was an increasing number of rehabilitations. On March 1, the schools and colleges were reopened. The leader of the Third Red Guard HQ, in a reported speech, said: 'We are in the lull before the decisive battle.'[25]

In the provinces, however, there was no lull. The forces of the Cultural Revolution held only Heilunchiang, Shansi, Kweichow, Shanghai and Peking itself, according to their own claims, and in mid-March fighting was reported in Kirin, Kansu, Hupeh, Anhui, and even in Kweichow.

There were widespread reports of the taking over of factories and public security offices by the army in Kwantung, Shansi, Sinkiang and Mongolia, and a report that the army had taken over the offices of the Kwangtung provincial committee. Reports of military government in Tibet seemed to indicate that Chang Kuo-Lua, in spite of having been accused of organising 'white terror' against the revolutionaries, had been permitted to restore order under his own authority.

In April, a poster announced the formation of a new central government said to include Chou En-lai as Prime Minister, Li Hsien-nien (Finance and Trade), Ch'en Po-ta (Foreign Affairs), and the retired general Liu Po-cheng (Defence), while Ch'en Yi, the former Foreign Minister, was in the government without specified responsibilities. This, if it is true, represents a middle-of-the road government. It should be noted, however, that even at this late date, when he had undoubtedly become the most powerful man in Peking, Chou En-lai is reported to have given the casting vote, out of eleven votes on the Politburo, in favour of the condemnation of Liu Shao-ch'i, and at a rally in April 1967 accused him of having followed an anti-party policy for twenty-two years.

OUTCOME AND SIGNIFICANCE OF THE CRISIS

Between July 1967, when the foregoing sections of this chapter were written, and the end of the year, it has become obvious that a clear-cut Maoist victory is unlikely, and that the process of revolution since the failure of the Paris-Commune movement of January 1967 has become at best a kind of erosion, a whittling away of the centres of bureaucratic power in the provinces, the final results of which are bound to vary from place to place. The purpose is still to take over the administration of China at all levels; but this clear-cut aim is confused by the 'three-way alliance' which is supposed to include the trustworthy members of the existing administration, and by the widespread confusion as to which of the innumerable splinter groups of militants with their high-sounding revolutionary titles actually represent the Cultural Revolution; of this, local army commanders are often, *faut de mieux*, the judges in the first instance.

It seems clear that much of this confusion was, as the Maoists protested, the result of the use of the rebel name by the party apparatus in an effort to smother the Cultural Revolution, or bring it under control—an attempt to do, through 'false' mass organisations, what the work-teams of June and July 1966 had failed to achieve. While the Maoists have the advantage of control over the mass media in most of China, the apparatus has the advantage of its powerful grip upon all organisations in public life. It can turn out the vote (a vote with the feet) far more effectively. In Canton, in July, the Maoist forces reckoned their own numbers at 7,000, but estimated those controlled by the provincial party committee and directed against them at 300,000, and similar figures were given or implied for other provinces. (These relative numbers, of course, represent organisational strength rather than public support.) In these circumstances at least, one can take Maoist injunctions against the use of force as being sincere, especially when the forces of the party apparatus came to be armed with automatic weapons, machine guns and artillery (as in August 1967 in Canton).

Given the disparity in armed force, what has to be explained is why, in the provinces where this situation prevailed (possibly representing four-fifths of China), the Maoist groups were not very summarily dealt with and the movement brought to an end. The answer is that both sides were acting under a degree of restraint which the wildness of their propaganda statements would not readily suggest. The Maoist groups were in constant touch with Peking, and Chou En-lai on behalf of Mao and the Central Committee had the last word as to which of the local organisations were truly 'leftist'. The reversal by Chou En-lai of the previous condemnation of an organisation by the local party chiefs represented one of the most telling blows which the local party apparatus could suffer in the course of the conflict, and this inhibited drastic action.

There is another side to this. The Maoists, at the time of writing, very effectively control the central state apparatus, the Central Committee and the cities of Peking and Shanghai. They are in a position, probably, to carry through a normal purge from the top by bureaucratic methods, if this was what they have been seeking. But it is not. Chou En-lai made this clear when he addressed the Academy of Sciences. Listing by name the members of the organisation who were said to represent the 'capitalist line', he added that, of course, there had been nothing to prevent the Central Committee from simply dismissing the offenders, and that this would have been easier, especially for him; but, he went on to argue, that was not the point. It was up to the members of the Academy to find out who the offenders were for themselves, and to subject them to their own criticism, not criticism from the top. In this, Chou En-lai took the same line as he had taken at the first Red Guard rally a year before: that the process of the Cultural Revolution was one of self-education through political action. Through the confusion of the whole revolution one can see that, essentially, the purpose of the Red Guard demonstrations was to outflank an entrenched bureaucracy by a dramatic publication of grievances in the streets—an Aldermaston March on a vastly greater scale. The object of this was to 'induce ferment', to use an old Maoist phrase. The youthful Red

Guards were in this way to leaven the lump of popular opinion and gradually, by revealing the real political issues, to create a majority on Mao's side by a 'mass criticism'. How far this has or can be successful is still in doubt.

Our attempts to estimate this, however, are prejudiced, in a very familiar way, by the fact that the proximity of Kwangtung to Hong Kong results in our having far better information about events there (and also an infinitely greater volume of naïve and extravagant rumour) than we have about any other part of China. This has been true especially since the summer of 1967, when wall posters gave way to pamphleteering, and copies of some of these pamphlets began to trickle into Hong Kong. We must guard against assuming that the situation thus revealed in Canton was typical of the whole of China. Probably it was not. Perhaps the only comparable part of China is Wuhan, the other great city of the central-south region, the bailiwick of the disgraced T'ao Chu. The first reports of armed clashes came immediately after his disgrace at the end of 1966, and violence escalated thereafter in Wuhan and Canton. It was suggested above (page 131) that the disgrace of T'ao Chu might cost the Maoists dear, and it has; it may have been the principal factor in depriving them so far of victory.

T'ao Chu is a key

T'ao Chu may well stand as the type of the convinced but moderate Maoist. His career has not yet been studied, but the charges made against him, and such of his own writings as are readily available, suggest a man who was convinced of the overwhelming advantages of the policies symbolised by the Communes, but showed himself willing in 1961 to make drastic and positive concessions in the crisis of that time: not merely, as elsewhere, to let the Communes slip, but to put all his considerable energies into creating for the time being a freer system of agricultural enterprise and to acknowledge frankly that he was taking a calculated risk. He is even accused (with a mass of circumstantial detail) of having opened the frontier for the mass efflux of Cantonese to Hong Kong in May 1961, on the grounds that Canton was economically 'a suburb of Hong Kong' and that a free flow between the two cities was a necessity in the conditions of the time. The reasons for his disgrace are not yet clear; if we could solve this problem, we would understand much better the present political configuration of China.

There is little sign elsewhere in China, except in Kwantang, of a

provincial movement of resistance inspired by comparable sentiments. The pattern of Maoist power at present seems to be a random
one. A year ago, it seemed as if the great centres of eastern China
would be Maoist, and the western centres would resist, at least for
some time. This is no longer so. While the anti-Maoists are still
strongly entrenched in Canton and possibly in Wuhan and Anhui,
representing important enclaves in the Maoist east, the Maoists
now claim decisive victories in Ch'inghai, Kansu and Kweichow,
in the west; and Ulanfu, the ruler of Inner Mongolia, has fallen.
Szechwan, however, as always has gone its own way, and Maoist
reports of local victories there are among the least convincing of
their claims.

In terms of class, political allegiances are even more obscure.
The Maoist press is full of stories of 'deluded masses', who often
play a part in bloody attacks upon the Maoist groups; but, as has
already been suggested, the apparent unpopularity of the Maoist
activist minority may be the result of the apparat's power of organisation rather than an expression of popular attitudes. Maoist groups
in Canton, analysing the situation in autumn 1967, claimed that
they had successfully revolutionised institutions of education and
culture, had been partly successful in organs of government and
controlled much of industry, but had failed to make an impression
on the provincial party apparatus itself and on the largest and the
older-established factories of the Ho-nan (Canton) area. This makes
sense, and is what one might have predicted; it represents, not public
opinion, but the strength of the apparatus in different walks of life.
The position of the peasants is even less easy to discuss. One of the
most active 'conservative' groups in Canton was the Association of
Suburban Poor and Middle Peasants. This might suggest that
peasant opinion was anti-Maoist, and perhaps it is, or part of it;
but the allegiance of the peasants probably depends in the short
term upon who got to them to organise them first. Here again the
apparat has the advantage, especially as the Maoist forces were dis-
couraged, though not with complete success or complete consistency,
from activism in the villages. Also, the economic interests of suburban cultivators around great cities, as opposed to rural farmers,
are very much bound up with private cultivation and marketing of
vegetables and other non-staple foods. However, the role of the
peasants in the Cultural Revolution has been a constant cause for

144

anxiety. Both Maoists and anti-Maoists appear to have encouraged peasants into the cities in order to swell their own forces; and Mao had to state that his old slogan, 'use the countryside to encircle the towns', was in this situation reactionary. This does not suggest a pro-Maoist peasant movement.

The issues of the Cultural Revolution, as they affect the life of the majority, are now much clearer than they were in mid-1967. There has been a steady escalation of revelations about the past attitudes of the principal figures under attack. We can, as a result, piece together a story of controversies within the Chinese Communist Party since 1950, and even before, which were only suspected previously, although the truth of this story remains to be proved.

The burden of the accusations which lay this story bare concern attitudes to collectivism in its various forms. Liu Shao-ch'i and many others are accused of having encouraged, in 1950–53, the protection of the rich-peasant economy to the detriment of thorough land reform and of subsequent collectivisation; of having opposed, in 1955, the progress of the co-operativisation of farming; of having supported P'eng Teh-huai's attacks on the Commune system in 1959; and of having encouraged the dismantling of Commune institutions in 1961 and 1962. With a wealth of details—some significant and convincing, some irrelevant and scurrilous—a picture of Chinese politics consonant with what has been suggested in chapter II has been built up since mid-1967. That the fate of the Commune and all it stands for, in economic, social, political and military terms, is the essential issue of the Cultural Revolution is thus put beyond doubt. The surprise is that the opposition to it is now identified with Liu Shao-ch'i, and that Liu should now appear, not in the role in which the West has always cast him, of a Maoist inclined to out-Herod Herod, but as a man of sometimes genial, sometimes withering common sense, standing in contrast to the humourless and uncompromising purism of the Maoists. Liu Shao-ch'i and Chou En-lai seem to have exchanged hats.

Whatever the final balance of opinion in future may be, this apparent confusion of roles offers a salutary lesson for those who tend to see Chinese politics in oversimplified terms, as the working out of a situation set in its main lines at least as far back as 1949. In fact, China has been in flux, as the whole Communist world has been in flux. China's leaders have been changing their minds, with a great deal of inevitable inconsistency and a realignment of loyalties. Mao, too, has changed his mind and developed; whether he has developed more or less than his colleagues is a question of opinion, and one's answer depends upon how one judges the particular solution to the accepted evil of bureaucracy with which he has so clearly identified himself.

The fate of that solution—in a situation in which, for all the lack of formal democratic machinery, Mao has appealed to public opinion and must abide by its final ruling—depends upon the impact of the revolution upon 700 million individuals whose temperaments and interests vary as much as those of any other human population, and whose articulateness in politics is already a matter of common observation.

The policies for which the Cultural Revolution stands run counter to the interests of many groups of Chinese. The skilled urban workers have already been deprived of their incentive bonuses, and must know that their privileged position among manual workers generally is under attack. Those peasants who are prosperous enough to gain from the private sector of agriculture and the private rural fairs (on average a minority, but possibly a majority in some important places) must see very clearly what is intended for them. The professional classes are to be flooded with graduates from shortened courses and with depressed qualifications, as a result of the forcible circumvention of the disadvantages from which the children of illiterate parents inevitably suffer in competition (IQ for IQ) with the children from intellectual or middle-class households; and, under pressure to go and serve in the countryside, such 'bourgeois' students and trainees face the bitter loss of their urban amenities. The members of the party apparatus face criticism, interrogation, humiliation, demotion, or worse, and suffer the traumatic loss of the security provided by the hierarchy of which they have been a part. It might be argued that few, apart from the poorer peasants, have anything very obvious to gain except the Red Guard students themselves, children of poor parents, suffering from grievous educational disadvantages and limited opportunities, but now promised a privileged place in the universities and rapid promotion in the party and the state.

146

pp. 146-149: Discussion of what C.R. means for various groups in China:

Interests alone, however, are not necessarily the decisive factors in the situation. Mao Tse-tung has raised the struggle to a moral plane. He has appealed to public opinion on uncompromising moral grounds, through the young intellectuals who are, no doubt, the class most receptive to such uncompromising moral appeals, and he has launched a campaign of great dramatic effectiveness on this basis. This may in the end be the decisive factor. The appeal to the basic (in China almost platitudinous) moral premises of collectivism, which no one dares gainsay, the dramatic externalisation of the moral conflicts in individual Chinese hearts, the impossibility of admitting to being less fervent than one's fellows on behalf of these moral assumptions—all this makes resistance very difficult. Assuming that collectivism plays the same psychological part in China as patriotism plays elsewhere in wartime (and remembering how closely tied up nationalism and egalitarian collectivism are in modern China), the situation is understandable. With Mao's prestige behind it and with the PLA (despite some local falling from grace) holding the ring and preventing a decision by force, the Red Guards and the Red Revolutionary Rebels may well win out and force a situation in which the ungainsayable morality is institutionalised before the interest groups can find another moral rationalisation upon which they can take a stand.

Looking at the situation in terms of both interests and moral aspirations, what does it mean to individuals?

For the student hampered by the poverty of a peasant background, it means increased opportunities of education and employment. For the academically minded student probably, from a middle-class home, it may mean the disruption of what he regards as a normal education by participation in manual labour; although we tend to forget that his annual period of manual labour will be shorter than the long vacation during which the majority of our own students take a job. For some of these, labour service may mean an inspiring opportunity to learn at first hand how the other half of his own people lives; and this spirit cannot be wholly lacking in China.

After graduation, it means for vast numbers the acceptance of serving in the countryside with its almost medievally low level of amenities, its risks to health and its poor opportunities of advancement. Some will face this with dismay, others as a challenge; it is

147

impossible for anyone outside China to surmise how many will fall into each category, but some at least must be inspired by the prospect of forming, perhaps, part of a pioneering mobile medical team; or perhaps of setting up alone and by their own enterprise and capacity to handle other human beings, the first modern school in a remote village.

To their professors, it means the relinquishment of cherished academic and scientific standards; but it is hard to believe that all are opposed to a policy of shorter courses and less rigid examinations if this may lead to a more rapid raising of the general level of Chinese life and to the more rapid exploitation of untapped talent. In science and technology, Mao's call to 'overthrow conventions', and to reject the idea that China must in all things painfully retrace every step of Western technological development, cannot go unheard by all China's technical experts. Many scientists must have thought hard about the economics of scientific work in a poor country, and have arrived at conclusions little different from those of Mao.

To the writer and the film-maker, the Cultural Revolution cannot but represent a severe limitation of their creative opportunities; and these limitations, many must feel, are such as force them to misrepresent Chinese society, especially by the insistence on cutting out 'middle characters' who, one can be sure, make up a large part of the population. This must be the more difficult to accept in that—until this present time, when Mao seems to believe that a wartime, heroic, 'black and white' literature is what is needed—the Chinese leader has himself been the greatest exemplar of attention to middle characters; the strength of his political strategy has always, until now, lain in his careful calculations of the psychology of the uncommitted. However, as is stressed in chapter IV), we must not interpret the discontents of Chinese writers as if they were Western writers. Few of them aspire to be apolitical or uncommitted; the great majority seek to be good socialist writers, and their position is therefore one difficult to defend against Mao's demands. Nor should we forget the possibility that some writers and film-makers may find inspiration in the Cultural Revolution itself.

To those in China who hoped for a liberalisation of Chinese life on the lines of the thaw in Eastern Europe and the USSR, and who believed that such a liberalisation was well under way by 1962, the

148

Cultural Revolution is a severe blow. It is perhaps easier for out-
siders, in spite of imperfect information, to see the positive side of
Mao's aims, his determination to subject the bureaucracy to constant
mass criticism; and easier to relate this to the policy implications of
the movement, with their heavy stress upon the destruction of 'the
Three Great Differences'. To Chinese liberalisers, what is likely to
be more obvious is that this whole movement has involved a partial
rehabilitation of Stalin; and that whatever it produces, if it is
successful, will offer little place for the strengthening of the powers
of the National People's Congress, of civil freedoms or of the rule of
law in any sense familiar to those with a Western education. The
anti-bureaucratic aspect of the movement is indeed, in one sense,
a reversion to the primitive anarchism which has always characterised Chinese lower-class political protest, and in which the Paris
Commune rather than the Constituent Assembly is the classical case
of revolutionary organisation. This has no attractions for those of
Western education.

The attitudes of all of these groups, however, must be more or
less conditioned by the effects of the moral, collective, nationalist
appeal. Much depends upon how much conviction Mao's insistence
on the imminent danger of war carries at various levels of sophistica-
tion in China. P'eng Teh-huai discounted it, and millions more of
informed people may do the same. But the great majority of
Chinese undoubtedly believe that their country is gravely imperilled
by outside forces. With China and America in hostile confrontation,
it is hardly surprising that Chinese, of all political persuasions short of
outright loyalty to Taiwan, should regard the disposition of American bases in the Far East as a direct threat to mainland China,
particularly at a time when in some Western quarters it is believed
that an American invasion of North Vietnam is a real possibility.
The breach with the Soviet Union, moreover, and the ensuing
tension along wide sections of the Sino-Russian frontier have added
to the sense of national insecurity. As long as the belief in external
threat remains, Mao's cry of 'the Republic in danger' is bound to
carry a great deal of conviction and to complicate Chinese reactions
by inhibiting opposition to his whole political position, which can be
represented as based upon the economic and political demands of
guerrilla organisation: the only means of defence open to China
without the renewal of dependence upon the Soviet Union.

DOCUMENTARY APPENDIX

A.

LITERARY TEXTS

1. *The Dismissal of Hai Jui*

A Peking Opera by Wu Han*

Scene IX: Dismissal

Place: The great hall of the Governor's court in Soochow.

Characters:

HAI JUI, aged fifty-four, Governor of Ying-t'ien.

TAI FENG-HSIANG, aged fifty, the newly appointed successor to the governorship.

HSU CHIEH, aged seventy-five, a retired statesman, wealthy and powerful, living in the district.

HSU YING, his son, aged about forty; perpetrator of many evil deeds and now under a death-sentence imposed by Hai Jui.

WANG MING-YU, aged about forty, the corrupt former magistrate of Hua-t'ing district; an accomplice of Hsu Ying's, and also under sentence of death.

Heralds, soldiers, etc.

> *Enter* TAI FENG-HSIANG *in official dress, gauze hat and red gown, with attendants.*

TAI (*sings*): I press forward into Kiangnan to take up my post.

* For a brief outline of the story, see page 100 above. The translation is literal and no attempt has been made to render the songs in verse, though the alternation of prose and verse is indicated. Details of the *dramatis personae* are amplified from earlier scenes. This excerpt makes a slightly strange impression in a bald prose translation. It is also difficult to appreciate the opera without the music, the colourful costumes and the stylised gestures of this old and highly formalised type of drama.

L

Accumulating a huge fortune will not be hard.
Through hypocrisy I shall avoid offending the great families.
If I follow the stream I shall have a trouble-free time.
(*spoken voice*): I am Tai Feng-hsiang, the new Governor of
Ying-t'ien. I have come as quickly as possible for His Excellency Hsu wrote to me not long ago asking me to do so.

Exit TAI *and attendants. Enter* HSU CHIEH.

HSU CHIEH (*sings*): I am riding fast to meet the new Governor,
Anxious to save my son.
(*spoken voice*): An official in the Governor's penal department
has let me know that the decisions of the autumn judicial
review will be out very shortly. The new Governor, Tai Feng-
hsiang, set out some time ago, and in order to save my son's
life I am hurrying to meet him.

He rides off. Enter HERALD.

HERALD: His Excellency orders that the court be in session.

Enter officials, soldiers and court servants. Enter HAI JUI *in gauze hat
and red gown.*

HAI JUI (*sings*): I have been commissioned by the Emperor to
administer the penal statutes,
To eradicate wrongdoers and improve morals.
(*spoken voice*): Attendants, bring on Hsu Ying and Wang
Ming-yu, who have been condemned to death, that their
sentences may be carried out forthwith.

Enter soldiers with HSU YING *and* WANG MING-YU, *both bound.*

HAI JUI: Hsu Ying and Wang Ming-yu, the autumn judicial review
has been made and you are both to be executed at once.
(*sings*) By breaking the laws of the state, you have enmeshed
yourselves in the toils of the law.
This will be a warning to the covetous and the cruel, and will
make it more widely known that they must mend their ways.

HSU YING:⎱ Spare our lives, Your Excellency. (*They kowtow.*)
WANG: ⎰

HAI JUI: Take them away and execute them at the appointed time.

Soldiers lead them off. Enter TAI FENG-HSIANG's *herald.*

HERALD: An important edict has arrived!

Appendix A. 1. The Dismissal of Hai Jui

Gongs sound. Enter TAI FENG-HSIANG *and* HSU CHIEH *together.*

TAI: I bear an important edict. 'Hai Jui, Governor of Ying-t'ien, has been dismissed and banished to the countryside. Tai Feng-hsiang has been appointed in his stead. This is an order!'

HAI JUI: Long live the Emperor! May I ask Your Excellency for what offence I have merited dismissal and banishment?

TAI: An official at court has accused you to the throne of inciting the people to violence and greed and of tyranny over the local officials.

HAI JUI: Ha!
(*sings*)
Local officials oppress the poor people
Like wolves and tigers, and the fields are empty.
'Tyranny over the local officials' is nonsense.
My dismissal is quite unjustified.
(*spoken voice*): May I ask Your Excellency when the new Governor will arrive?

TAI: I myself am he. I am honoured to make your acquaintance.

HAI JUI: I too am honoured. Now that you have arrived to take up the post, I have a word to say.

TAI: Please speak then.

HAI JUI (*sings*): The local officials are the great bane in Kiangnan.
They appropriate the people's land by force and make farming difficult.
Many, many wrongful judgements need to be straightened out or reversed.
And only if the land is returned to the people will they be at peace.

TAI: Stop! It is just because you compelled the local officials to restore land, incited the people and tyrannised over the local officials that the Emperor has dismissed you!　　　(*sings*)
Honour and lowly status, riches and poverty are decided by fate.
That the simple people suffer is just as things should be.
Those who work with their minds are good and those who work with their hands are bad.
I have read the books of the sages,
And incitement of the people to the injury of others
And tyranny over the local officials are extremely wrong.

HAI JUI: Who has done wrong?

TAI: You have!

HAI JUI: Enough!
(*sings*)
You say the common people are violent and covetous,
But do you know that the local officials have been injuring the people?
With all this clamour about tyranny over the local officials,
Do you know that the people are living off swill?
You pretend to hold that the people are the foundation of the state;
Masquerading as a good person, you deceive the Emperor.
Walking by day you must be ashamed of your shadow, and by night you must lie ashamed in your bed.

TAI: Your curses will kill me with anger!

HSU CHIEH: Your Excellencies, do not drive away good feelings! I once warned you, Hai, that the anger of a multitude should never be provoked and that local officials should not be cheated. But you would not listen and persisted in your errors. Now that you have been dismissed, I have a word of advice.
(*sings*)
In the middle age your choler has increased and your temperament has hardened.
And you have experienced many decades of hardship.
Administering the law, you have corrected abuses but with excessive severity.
Too much one-sidedness and extremism can do people harm.
Last time I spoke to you my words did not carry.
But this time you have stumbled and the whole situation has changed.
I exhort you hereafter to make greater efforts to improve yourself.
As an official, never more show such zeal!

HAI JUI: Your Honour Hsu!
(*sings*)
Your words are ill-considered.
Though dismissed, my name is good.
A man's inner character and his external image ought to be consistent with each other;
And plotting and injuring others is wrong.

HSU CHIEH: Who has plotted and injured others?

HAI JUI: You have!
(*sings*)
At court you once used to harmonise the dual powers of Yin and Yang;

Appendix A. *1. The Dismissal of Hai Jui*

In discussing studies you spoke of Confucius and Mencius and
  discoursed on the rulers of yore.
But you allowed your younger relatives at home to seize land
  by force.
Abducting daughters of the people and making bribes, they lost
  all conscience.
And though you devise treacherous schemes to deceive your
  sovereign,
Slandering the common people as tigers and wolves,
And saying that the local officials are being oppressed and
  denied a hearing,
Where will you hide from the hatred of the populace?
Though I lose my office, my heart is light,
For I will hold office some other day and will reform the conduct
  of the law.

HSU CHIEH: If you persist in your errors there is nothing more to be
  said.

HERALD: The hour has come. Please issue the official warrant for
  the carrying out of the sentences.

TAI:
HSU CHIEH:} What sentences?

HAI JUI: The order has already been given for the immediate
  execution of Hsu Ying and Wang Ming-yu.

HSU CHIEH (*blanches with alarm and trembles*): Ah!

TAI: Send the order to stop the executions!

HAI JUI: Send the order to carry them out!

TAI: The newly appointed Governer orders their suspension!

HAI JUI: The present incumbent orders that they be carried out!

TAI: Your Excellency Hai, they must not be killed!

HAI JUI: And why not?

TAI: I personally received the command of Minister Li and Chancellor Feng to the effect that Hsu Chieh was advanced in years
  and had served the state with distinction. Hsu Ying's sentence
  is to be suspended and further orders awaited.

HAI JUI: Where are these further orders?

TAI: They are on their way behind me.

HAI JUI: And what happens in the meantime?

TAI: I am now ordering the suspension of the execution in accordance with the orders of the Minister and the Chancellor.

HAI JUI: But you cannot give orders!

TAI: Why not?

HAI JUI: I have not handed over the seal and the warrant, which
  are still in my hand. How can you give orders?

TAI: Hand them over then.

HAI JUI: Never! I have made the orders of the autumn review, and I will hand them over after I have carried out the executions.

TAI: Oh, Your Excellency!

(*sings*)

It is no light crime to resist an imperial edict.

The ruin of yourself and your family lie before you.

Hsu Chieh's advanced age must be taken into consideration.

Remorse for impetuous anger will be hard to bear.

HAI JUI: Ha, ha!

(*sings*)

With an imperial commission I deal with crime.

Immediate execution is right and proper.

How can an official take personal considerations into account?

The guilty ones are being disposed of as I wish.

TAI: Do you not fear your own death?

HAI JUI: A courageous man, self-reliant and standing alone, how can he fear death? To bend the law for personal reasons, on the other hand, that is to become a dishonest and shameless man.

He holds the warrant.

Herald, order the executions!

HERALD (*takes the warrant*): Yes!

Exit HERALD. *Three cannon shots sound.* HSU CHIEH *collapses on the ground.* TAI *is confounded.* HAI JUI *lifts up the great seal.*

HAI JUI: Your Excellency Tai, I hereby hand over the great seal and announce my departure.

TAI FENG-HSIANG *stands rooted to the spot while* HAI JUI *still holds the seal. Curtain.*

CHORUS: The heavens and the earth are cold and the winds blow.

Millions of hearts regret his departure.

Our father Hai came back to the South but could not stay.

Incense is burned for a good official, the Living Buddha of 10,000 families.

End

2. *Hai Jui's Place in History*

By Wu Han*

In his own time, Hai Jui was loved, respected and praised by the people. He opposed greed and corruption, waste and extravagance, and stood for frugality. He attacked powerful families and protected the poor. He upheld the accurate survey of land, made the law universally applicable to all, abolished customary practices and promoted water conservancy work. In these respects, he benefited the peasantry, particularly the poor and middle peasants, and the peasants' love, respect and praise for him are very natural. For the town dwellers, especially the merchants, he reduced the burdens of the taxation system, forbad the supply of goods without payment, and so forth. These moves were beneficial in reducing the burdens on manufacturers and commerce in the towns. The love, respect and praise of the town dwellers were also natural. In addition, he paid much attention to judicial and especially to capital cases, giving great weight to investigation. When he was a district magistrate and when a provincial governor, he always dispensed justice in person, cleared up the backlog of unresolved cases and straightened out many wrong judgements. In lawsuits involving peasants and landlords he stood on the peasants' side. As magistrate and governor, Hai was the saviour of the oppressed, cheated and wronged people of that time. He was lauded by the broad mass of the people, his portrait was worshipped and his praises spread abroad in song; a great crowd followed his funeral. He was remembered mainly in stories about the cases he tried, and his memory is preserved among the broad masses of the people up to the present day.

Though in his own day he was attacked, rejected, disgraced, imprisoned and dismissed, yet he was praised and commended even by a section of the feudal ruling class itself. It was not only some of the younger men who admired him and regarded him as the great man of the age; even some of his opponents, such representatives of the big landlord class as Kao Kung, Chang Chü-cheng and Ho liang-chün, could not but speak well of him. After his death he was accorded the posthumous title Chung-chieh (Loyal and Steadfast)

* This is the concluding section of Wu Han's article "On Hai Jui", published in *Jen-min Jih-pao*, Peking, September 19, 1959. The article itsel is dated September 17.

and the emperor sent an official to offer ritual sacrifice. The funeral address was full of praise and commendation. The contemporary historians Ho Ch'iao-yuan and Li Chih both wrote laudatory biographies. When the Ch'ing came to compile the *History of the Ming Dynasty*, he was included in the "Main Biographies" section; and although it said that he was somewhat one-sided and impetuous in carrying out his duties, it also said that in his handling of affairs from his magistracy right up to his governorship he had made the interests of the people his chief concern, and that this was to be commended.

Hai Jui has a place in history. From the point of view of the present day, of the new age in which socialism is being built up, should this kind of historical figure be approved and commended? My answer is, yes, he should be.

The evaluation of historical figures should start out from the conditions existing in the given time and place, from the question whether their function was of benefit to the people and from the development of production at the time. By our analysis, the people living from the period of Chia Ching to early Wan Li* in Kiangsu, Anhwei, Chekiang, Kiangsi and Fukien, the areas where Hai Jui served as an official, and in a wider area, loved and respected him. He did have opponents but they were just a tiny minority of big landlords and big bureaucrats. His policies and actions benefited the people of his time and the (economic) production of his time. But they did not benefit the evil actions of the landlords, their land-grabbing and their shifting of tax burdens on to the impoverished populace.

Surely anyone who is loved, respected and praised by the broad mass of the people, but is attacked and opposed by a minority of large landowners and bureaucrats, must be commended and praised by us?

We praise and commend his lifelong opposition to bad men and bad deeds, his lifelong opposition to greed and corruption, waste, extravagance and hypocrisy. We praise and commend his lifelong concern for the people and his promotion of their interests in every place and in all matters. We praise and commend his lifelong fortitude in adversity and his indomitable fighting spirit, the lifelong consistency of his words and deeds and his consistent spirit of practice. These traits are ones that we must learn from and promote;

* Hai Jui (1515–87) was born in Chiungchow, Hainan Island. He served as magistrate in various places and as Governor of Ying-t'ien (Kiangsu and Anhwei) in 1569–70. The period 'Chia Ching to early Wan Li' indicates approximately 1522–80.

and, moreover, it is only in the age of socialism that they can enjoy full expression, though the Hai Jui we need today and the Hai Jui of feudal society are fundamentally different in social character.

Today in this age of building socialism we need Hai Juis who take the standpoint of the people and the working class, who carry on an unyielding struggle for the building of socialism, who oppose the hypocrisy of the old days and the bureacratism of today, who enter deeply into the masses and lead them, who make tremendous efforts and who force themselves against the stream. The Hai Jui of the feudal epoch, therefore, is still worthy of study today.

It is, however, absolutely wrong to twist (the true) Hai Jui by falsely claiming to follow him. Hai Jui stood on the side of the people and all his life opposed bad men and bad deeds; he never opposed good men and good deeds. In his stuggles with Hsu Chieh and Kao Kung he did not get things quite clear; he saw only Hsu Chieh's good side, not his bad side, and only realised Kao Kung's deficiencies and not the good side of his political behaviour, and thus gave support and attacked mistakenly. Despite this, however, he gained a clearer understanding after a few years, examined himself and recognised his mistakes and in his actions rectified his error.

There are those who call themselves Hai Juis and call themselves the 'opposition' but, in absolute contrast to Hai Jui, they do not stand on the people's side and on the side of the tasks of the people today—the tasks of socialism; they do not oppose bad men and bad acts but devote themselves to opposing good men and good deeds saying 'this is premature, it's too fast, that's been made a mess of, it's excessive, this is too direct, that's too one-sided, this is defective, that is faulty'. They seek out spots on the sun, they search for any faults and magnify them as much as possible, they pour cold water over the heads of the masses and sap their morale. This kind of person, the single-minded opponent of the people's tasks and of the tasks of socialism, not only has nothing whatever in common with Hai Jui, but is in fact exactly like the representatives of the big landlords whom Hai Jui opposed and who opposed him. The masses must certainly weed out such people and place them under the bright daylight and shout out loud: 'You are not allowed to masquerade!', so that the masses will see clearly that their true right-opportunist features are nothing like those of a Hai Jui! Thus learning from Hai Jui and research upon him, and opposition to the twisting of Hai Jui, are profitable, necessary and practical.

3 *On the new historical drama,* The Dismissal of Hai
Jui

By Yao Wen-yüan*

. . . What does *The Dismissal of Hai Jui* extol? Let us see what the
author extols through this spurious Hai Jui character.

We know that the state is the instrument of class struggle and a
mechanism whereby one class oppresses another. There is no non-
class or supra-class state. This is the basic viewpoint of Marxism-
Leninism on the question of the state. Starting out from this we
have to admit that the feudal state is an instrument for the enforcement of dictatorship over the peasants by the landlords. The laws
and the courts of the feudal state and the officials who rule over the
people—including 'honest officials' and 'good officials'—can only
be the instruments of the dictatorship of the landlord class and can
never transcend class, nor can they serve the ruled as well as the
ruling class. Of course, because there are different strata and groups
within the landlord class and because of changes in circumstance
in the class struggle, they may differ and come into conflict over this
or that problem, over the attitude adopted towards the interests
of the big landlords, the middle and small landowners and the rich
peasants, and over the degree and method of oppression to which the
peasants should be subjected. Essentially, however, the substance
of such conflicts can never transcend support for the dictatorship
of the landlord class. We can never twist the conflict within the
landlord class into a class struggle between the peasants and the
landlords. To take for example the struggle between 'honest officials'
and 'corrupt officials', there really have been honest officials who
punished 'corrupt officials' in the courts under provisions of the
law of the landlord class. There have also been cases in which an
individual peasant 'won' his case against a member of a faction
because the case was tried by an 'honest official' who happened to
be an opponent of the faction to which the defendant belonged.
Such phenomena have misled many peasants without experience

* Published in *Wen-hui Pao*, Shanghai, November 1965, and in *Jen-min
Jih-pao*, Peking, November 30, 1965. A full translation is given in *Current
Background*, Hong Kong, no. 783. This excerpt follows a section in which
Yao has challenged the historical accuracy of the Hai Jui presented by
Wu Han.

in class struggle and made them lose sight of the class features of the 'honest officials' and the class essence of the feudal state and the feudal courts. The landlord class also made constant use of such phenomena to numb the peasants' consciousness and used the 'honest officials' as a means of covering up the essence of class rule and as an important means of carrying out the class struggle against the peasants in coordination with armed suppression. In the *History of the Ming Dynasty*, there are records of the appointment of 'honest officials' by the landlord class—the strategy of delaying the approach of the enemy—before action was taken to destroy rebellious peasants with one blow. Basically, however, no matter how 'honest' or 'good' the 'honest' or 'good officials' are, they can only be 'honest' or 'good officials' for the implementation of the dictatorship of the landlord class over the peasants, and can never take the opposite course.

The Dismissal of Hai Jui, however, tells us: no! The 'honest officials' are not the instruments of the landlord class but are in the service of the peasant class. The Hai Jui in the play, you see, is an envoy of the feudal dynasty, but he wages a fierce struggle against Hsu Chieh and represents the interests of the poor peasants. In this struggle the 'honest official' Hai Jui, for his part, is portrayed as a great hero who safeguards the interests of the tenants of the Hsü family and all poor peasants. He is opposed to other officials who implement the dictatorship of the landlord class and the contradiction between the 'honest' officials and the 'corrupt officials' is portrayed as the contradiction between the protection and the oppression of the peasants as well as the contradiction between the return of land to the peasants and the seizure of land from them. We can see nothing of the role of the 'honest officials' in consolidating the dictatorship of the landlord class. On the other hand, all the peasants are portrayed as a passive lot devoid of any spirit of revolutionary struggle. Their sole role is to kneel before 'The Honourable Hai', beseech him to redress their grievances and to regard the 'honest official' as their saviour. Clearly, in the view of the author of *The Dismissal of Hai Jui*, the motive force propelling history forward is not the class struggle but is the 'honest officials'. There is no need for the masses to rise and liberate themselves for, with the blessings of an 'honest official', they can soon lead a 'good life'.

4. *Write mass history, and write history for the masses*
By Hsia Hsiang*

Between October 1964 and June 1965, some of the comrades at the Institute for Research on the Teaching of Chinese History in the Department of History, Chinese People's University, participated in the rural Socialist Education Movement in Lichiachuang Brigade, Yangpai Commune, Wutai District, Shansi. We learned something about cultural life in the villages and the historical knowledge and conceptions circulating among the peasants. We gained some understanding of the problems of making historical science penetrate the rural areas and making it serve the peasant masses. We invite readers to correct the account which follows.

The Cultural needs of the villages. The working people are the masters and the true makers of history. In class society the peasants created the material and the spiritual and cultural wealth of society with their sweat and blood, but they were the oppressed and the exploited and had no right to culture. Chairman Mao has said: 'In China only the landlords ever had culture; the peasants were denied it. But the landlords' culture was created by the peasants for what made it was nothing but the sweat and blood extracted from the peasants' (*Selected Works of Mao Tse-tung*, Vol. 1, p. 41). Since the Liberation the peasants have turned around and become the masters in politics and in the economy, and at the same time are urgently demanding that they become the masters of culture also. In the past very few people in the countryside were literate but now a new generation of educated youth is rapidly growing up in the villages, a large number of demobilised soldiers and industrial workers who have returned home to the countryside are participating in agricultural production, and many peasants who were previously completely illiterate have become literate through effort and study. The number of educated people in the countryside has increased a great deal. In Lichiachuang, for example, out of a total of 160 households or over 550 people in the brigade, there are nearly a hundred educated young folk of both sexes (of fourth year primary standard or above). There are more than twenty demobilised soldiers and returned workers, and if the literate peasants of middle or advanced age are added in, there are about 150 persons who have some kind of cultural level, and these amount to 28 per cent of the population of the entire village.

* Published in *Li-shih Yen-chiu*, no. 5, October 1965; SCMM, no. 511.

Appendix A. 4. Write Mass History . . .

Since the Liberation we have done a great deal of work in cultural construction in the rural areas, but it is still very far from adequate to satisfy the rapidly growing demands of the peasant masses. Before the Socialist Education movement, Lichiachuang had only a four-year junior primary school; there was no cultural room, club or medical clinic. The few copies of the newspapers in the brigade office or in the primary school were often avidly read by many people; there were also very few books and they were in the possession of individuals and did not circulate much, and there were, besides, quite a number of pre-Liberation books. In recent years film projection work in the villages has been stepped up, but the number of peasants who see films is still small. When there is spare time from farming or every evening a number of people regularly used to crowd into a small cave and listen to an old poor peasant playing the *so-na* [a kind of flute] and telling stories. This old poor peasant was the voluntary musician of the village and his 'concerts' were given nearly every evening, rain or shine. Unfortunately the only instrument he had was his *so-na*.

After a day of labour the peasants yearned for some cultural life, but they lacked organisation and leadership and did not have the requisite books and equipment. During the Socialist Education movement we helped the peasants to get organised and to study Chairman Mao's works. With much zest they methodically examined their thought, their work, and their production in the light of the Chairman's words. They said: 'After studying the Chairman's writings our direction is clear and our methods improved.' Together with the peasants we also set up a cultural room to which we contributed over 500 books. We got a lecture hall and story meetings going, which were welcomed by the peasant masses. Within forty days the cultural room made 1,200 book loans with an average borrowing of two books per person. After supper the youths had no worry about having nowhere to go; they would make arrangements among themselves: 'Come on! Let's go and listen to Old Li and Old Yin talking about the current situation or telling stories.'

The peasants keenly desire to study politics and culture, and the countryside is now going through a profound socialist cultural revolution. The spirit of the 500 million peasants is up and with a hundred times more confidence they are struggling to uproot thoroughly the cultural backwardness left to them by history. In such a situation and in face of such requirements can we workers in historical science contribute something to the cultural revolution and cultural construction in the rural areas? Should the science of history go to the countryside and how can it serve the broad peasant masses?

The Peasants like learning history. Before answering the question whether historical science should go to the countryside, we ought to see how much historical knowledge and what kind of historical ideas are circulating among the peasantry. Do they need and like history? What part can history play in their life?

Many historical stories and traditions are circulating in the countryside and the peasants are very fond of listening to them. Historical knowledge has in fact always been an important component of the traditional culture of the village. In the villages there are many *hsiu-ts'ai** who can write and calculate and are good speakers. They are very often the village story-tellers. . . . Among their stories a very large proportion are historical.

The history of the contemporary revolution in their own area, as told by the peasants is very authentic and valuable. In Lichiachuang and neighbouring villages there were several heroic figures like Hu Lan and the brave men of Langya mountain. Their glorious and stirring deeds are very moving and are worth special treatment by workers in historical science. But beyond the limits of local and contemporary history and in the sphere of more ancient history, the peasants have fragmentary, blurred and inaccurate impressions. Apart from the few rural *hsiu-ts'ai*, the majority of peasants have little historical knowledge, this applies particularly to women and to the illiterate. We talked to four educated girls—they were all graduates of primary school. They knew about Kuan Kung, Ts'ao Ts'ao, Pao Ch'ing-t'ien, Yang Wu-lang and Mu Kuei-ying, but not about the Emperor Wu of the Han Dynasty, Li Tzu-ch'eng, Lin Tse-hsu or Hung-Hsiu-ch'üan. Some replied: 'We've only heard the names and studied them in the textbook, but we've forgotten all about them.' Some did not even know who Sun Yat-sen was. Asked when the Communist Party was established, they first of all answered in unison '1949'. When asked a second time one replied: 'Probably in 1937.'

5. *Evening Chats at Yenshan: Teng T'o and his Critics*

The following selection begins with the first item cited by Lin Chieh and his collaborators:† an excerpt from Teng T'o's

---

* A *hsiu-ts'ai* was a graduate of the old Imperial state examinations. The term is figurative in the present context.

† "Teng T'o's *Evening Chats at Yenshan* is anti-party and anti-socialist double-talk", published in *Chieh-fang-chün Pao* and *Kuang-ming Jih-pao*, May 8, 1966, translated in *The Great Socialist Cultural Revolution in China* (2), pp. 12–49.

Appendix A. 5. Evening Chats at Yenshan

article, "Great Empty Talk", with their comment on it.*

The second item is an integral translation of an article by Teng T'o,† followed by an indication of the passage cited by Teng's critics and by their comment.

(i) Criticism of Teng T'o's "Great Empty Talk" by Lin Chieh and collaborators.

Venomous attacks on our great party, viciously attacking the scientific thesis that 'the East Wind prevails over the West Wind' as 'Great Empty Talk' and a 'cliché'.

[Excerpt selected for censure.]

Some people have the gift of the gab. They can talk endlessly on any occasion, like water flowing from an undammed river. After listening to them, however, when you try to recall what they have said, you can remember nothing.

Making long speeches without really saying anything, making confusion worse confounded by explaining, or giving explanations which are not explanatory—these are the characteristics of great empty talk.

We cannot deny that in certain special situations such great empty talk is inevitable, and therefore in a certain sense is a necessity. Still, it will be quite awful if great empty talk should be made into a prevalent fashion indulged in on every occasion or even cultivated as a special skill. It would be still more disastrous if our children should be taught this skill and turned into hordes of experts in great empty talk.

As chance would have it, my neighbour's child has recently often imitated the style of some great poet and put into writing a lot of 'great empty talk'. . . .‡ Not long ago he wrote a poem entitled *Ode to Wild Grass* which is nothing but empty talk. The poem reads as follows:

> The venerable heaven is our father,
> The Great Earth is our mother
> And the sun is our nanny;
> The East Wind is our benefactor
> And the West Wind is our enemy.

* Teng's article was published in *Ch'ien-hsien*, Peking, 1961, no. 21. Though the original is not at present available for translation as a complete article, the excerpt and the comments are typical of the attack on Teng T'o.

† Teng T'o, "A fortune consisting of a single egg", *Yen-shan Yeh-hua*, Vol. I, pp. 76–8; first published in *Pei-ching Wan-pao*, Peking, June 18, 1961.

‡ The 'omission points' indicate a passage in Teng's article omitted by Lin Chieh.

Although such words as heaven, earth, father, mother, sun, nanny, the East Wind, the West Wind, benefactor and enemy catch our eye, they are used to no purpose here and have become mere clichés.

Recourse to even the finest words and phrases is futile, or rather, the more such clichés are uttered, the worse the situation will become. Therefore I would advise those friends given to great empty talk to read more, think more, say less and take a rest when the time comes for talking, so as to save their own as well as other people's time and energy.

Comment

"The East Wind prevails over the West Wind" is a scientific thesis advanced by Chairman Mao Tse-tung at the Meeting of Communist and Workers' Parties on November 18, 1957. It says by way of a vivid image that the international situation has reached a new turning point and that the forces of socialism are prevailing over the forces of imperialism. The East Wind symbolises the anti-imperialist revolutionary forces of the proletariat and of the oppressed peoples of Asia, Africa and Latin America. The West Wind symbolises the decadent forces of imperialism and reaction in all countries. It is entirely correct to praise the East Wind and to detest the West Wind. Why then should Teng T'o pick up the statement, 'the East Wind is our benefactor and the West Wind is our enemy', and malign it as great empty talk and a cliché? The Khrushchev revisionists have said inflammatorily that it is necessary to 'oppose the dogmatic theories concerning a mythical competition between 'the West and East Winds more boldly and more resolutely'''. Thus Teng T'o is singing the same tune as that of Khrushchev.

(ii) Teng T'o, "A fortune consisting of a single egg"*

... When we say that someone has a 'fortune', we are usually stating that he has a certain amount of wealth, but nobody would believe that one egg could be reckoned a fortune! Chuang Tzu, however, already spoke of one who 'saw an egg and sought riches', and for this reason we should not underestimate a fortune consisting of an egg.

In fact, any large amount of wealth very often begins with a small amount in the first stages of accumulation. This is on the same principle as 'collecting the pieces under the forelegs to make a fur garment' and 'drops making a river'. But this is not to say that in all

* The first paragraph of the article has been omitted from this translation. It deals with the meaning and the ways of writing the term *chia-tang*, translated here as 'fortune'.

circumstances all you need for a fortune is an egg. Things cannot be so simple and easy.

In the reign of Wan Li of the Ming dynasty (1573–1620), there was a writer of fiction called Chiang Ying-k'o. He wrote a work entitled *Tales of Hsueh-t'ao* and in it is the story which follows:

'There was once a townsman who was so poor that he could scarcely live through the day. One day he picked up an egg and joyfully told his wife: "I have a fortune here." "Where?" asked his wife. He held up the egg and showed it to her. "Here it is", said he, "but it will only be complete in ten years' time." He worked it out for his wife in this way: "I will put this egg of mine out to be hatched by a neighbour's hen. When the chicks are hatched I will select a female and it will produce eggs in its turn and in one month I will get fifteen chickens. Within two years these chickens will produce three hundred more chickens which can be sold for ten gold taels. With this money I will buy five cows, these cows will bear others and in three years I will have twenty-five beasts. In a further three years these cows will produce fifty beasts and these can be sold for three hundred taels. I will use this money to make loans and in another three years I will get five hundred."'

There followed further episodes in the second half of the story which are not very interesting, and we need not recount them. There is one point, however, which must be mentioned and that is that this man, obsessed with wealth, later on said that he was also planning to take a concubine. This provoked his wife's wrath 'and she broke the egg with her hand'. The fortune of a single egg was thereupon completely destroyed.

I'm sure you'll agree that this story explains a number of problems. Even this man, so keen on money, knew that the accumulation of a fortune required a good deal of time. For this reason he told his wife that ten years would be needed to build such a fortune. This seems to be quite reasonable. His plan, however, had absolutely no reliable basis but was completely derived from hypotheses: every step depended entirely on the outcome of the preceding hypothesis. With regard to the situation after ten years, he entirely substituted illusion for reality thus fully and clearly revealing the true nature of one obsessed with money, so much so that he provoked his wife's anger and she then, with one blow of her fist, completely smashed his fortune. More important still is the fact that his plan for the accumulation of riches did not start out from production; the pursuit of his goal of money-making was through tricks and devices.

Where, for example, did he get his egg? The answer is that he picked it up, really a rather inglorious fact. And his plan to have this egg which he had picked up hatched together with several others by a neighbour's hen was even more transparently a case of drawing an unearned benefit from others. When the chicks were hatched he was going to ignore the equally balanced odds and take a female chick. It is obvious that the first phase of this plan for making a fortune was a kind of fraud.

Thereafter, his suppositions that the hens would produce other hens, that these could be sold for money, that the money could be used for the purchase of a cow, that the cows would be very fertile, and that they could be sold and the proceeds put out on loan—this whole plan cannot be called a production plan. Almost every important phase depends for success on opportunistic trading and on exploiting others. This shows that this 'townsman' described by Chiang Ying-k'o, though 'very poor', was not one of the toiling populace but was probably one of the ruined urban tradesmen of the medieval period, preoccupied with ways of cheating and exploiting, and innocent of any idea of an honest effort at productive work. Even though such a person gathered a certain fortune he would not be able to organise a productive enterprise but would just think about getting a concubine or something of the kind. Ending up by provoking a quarrel with his wife and having his fortune dispersed—that was just the natural outcome.

Only the true and genuine workers have ever understood the truth that labour produces wealth, and only they have been able to eliminate unrealistic attitudes towards the making of wealth and have, in a firm and practical manner, used their own assiduous labour to create and accumulate wealth for themselves and society.

[*Lin Chieh's censure*]*

. . . When our Party set forward its plan for socialist economic construction, the Khrushchev revisionists shouted: 'We have to wait and see if there's any truth in it.' When we were in temporary difficulties, they attacked our great leap forward as having 'failed' and 'collapsed'. In the present piece, Ten T'o also makes talk of

* In section II of his article, subtitled "Opposing the General Line for Socialist Construction and the Great Leap Forward, and attacking the Dictatorship of the Proletariat" (see *The Great Socialist Cultural Revolution in China* (2), pp. 26–7), Lin Chieh includes an excerpt from Teng T'o's 'fortune' article, placing it under the subsidiary heading "Slandering our cause of socialist construction as being 'finished'". The excerpt begins with the second paragraph of our cited text ('In fact, any large amount . . .') and runs up to near the end of the sixth paragraph ('. . . she then, with one blow of her fist, completely smashed his fortune.')

indulging in fantasy, 'substituting illusion for reality', and 'the fortune consisting of a single egg' which is 'totally destroyed', etc. Are not these also attacks on our great leap forward as having 'failed'? Do they not chime in with the attacks of the Khrushchev revisionists?

B.

DOCTRINAL AND NATIONAL
POLICY TEXTS

---

*1. Communiqué of the Tenth Plenary Session of the Eighth
Central Committee of the Communist Party of China**

The Eighth Central Committee of the Communist Party of China
held its Tenth Plenary Session in Peking, September 24–27, 1962 . . .
presided over by Comrade Mao Tse-tung. Eighty-two Members and
88 Alternate Members of the Central Committee attended. Thirty-
three other comrades from the departments concerned of the
Central Committee and from the provincial, municipal and autonomous region Party committees were also present.

Consolidating the Collective Economy of the People's Communes. The Tenth
Plenary Session discussed and took decisions on the question of
further consolidating the collective economy of the people's communes and developing agricultural production and on the question
of commercial work. It made a decision on the planned inter-
change of important leading cadres of Party and government
organisations at various levels. It decided to strengthen the work of
the Party control commissions at all levels and elected additional
members to the Central Control Commission. It elected Comrades
Lu Ting-yi, Kang Sheng and Lo Jui-ch'ing as additional members
of the Secretariat of the Central Committee, and at the same time
decided to dismiss Comrades Huang Ke-cheng and Tan Cheng
from their posts as members of the Secretariat.

The Tenth Plenary Session discussed the international and
domestic situation.

* Translated text published in the *Peking Review*, September 28, 1962,
with minor adjustments.

Appendix B. 1. Central Committee Communiqué, Sept. 1962

The session points out that the international situation is developing in a direction even more favourable to the people of all countries. The struggle of the people of the world against the u.s. imperialist policies of aggression and war and against colonialism, old and new, is surging forward. The Cuban people, after winning victory in their revolution, have embarked on the road of socialism and have continually defeated the u.s. imperialists' aggressives schemes. The Algerian people have attained independence through protracted armed struggle. In Laos, armistice has been realised and provisional coalition government has been formed. The people in southern Viet Nam have won one victory after another in their patriotic armed struggle. The Indonesian people have waged a successful struggle for the recovery of West Irian. The Japanese people have conducted continued heroic struggles against u.s. imperialist aggression and oppression. All these are important landmarks in the vigorous development of the national and democratic movements of the peoples of Asia, Africa and Latin America. The struggles of the oppressed nations and peoples of the world for national independence, democracy and socialism are playing an ever greater role in the defence of world peace. The growing strength of the countries in the socialist camp and their unity based on Marxism-Leninism and internationalism constitute the decisive factor in defending world peace and give an extremely important encouragement and support to the liberation struggle of the people of various countries.

The u.s. imperialists are redoubling their efforts to push through their plans of aggression and war which are aimed at attaining world hegemony, the reactionaries of various countries are serving imperialism in a less disguised way, and the modern revisionists represented by the Tito clique have become more despicable in betraying the cause of communism and meeting the needs of imperialism. All this shows that the class struggle is raging in the international sphere.

The imperialists, the reactionaries of various countries and the modern revisionists have engaged in all kinds of criminal activities to oppose communism, oppose the people, oppose the mass struggle of all oppressed nations and oppose the People's Republic of China and all other independent countries in Asia, Africa, Latin America and elsewhere, which refuse to be slaves, but the result is contrary to their expectations. Their criminal activities have only served to further reveal their ugly features and land them in greater isolation. Although the struggle against the imperialists, the reactionaries of various countries and the modern revisionists is protracted, tortuous and complicated, the revolutionary cause of the people of all countries continues to develop, the international communist movement is growing daily in strength, and our friends have become more numerous.

The General Line of China's Foreign Policy. The Tenth Plenary Session holds that the development of the international situation has proved more convincingly that the general line of our country's foreign policy is entirely correct. This general line is: to develop relations of friendship, mutual assistance and co-operation with the Soviet Union and the other fraternal socialist countries in accordance with the principle of proletarian internationalism; to strive for peaceful coexistence on the basis of the Five Principles with countries having differing social systems and oppose the imperialist policies of aggression and war; to support the revolutionary struggles of the oppressed peoples and oppressed nations against imperialism and colonialism. We should continue to carry out this general line in international affairs in the future.

We should continue to hold high the banner of opposing imperialism and defending world peace and unite all the peace-loving countries and people of the world to form the broadest possible united front against U.S. and other imperialists and their running-dogs in various countries.

We should continue to hold high the banner of revolution and give active support to the liberation struggle of the peoples of various countries, especially the struggle of the Asian, African and Latin American peoples for winning and safeguarding their national independence.

We should continue to hold high the banner of proletarian internationalism and strive to safeguard and strengthen the unity of the socialist camp and the international communist movement.

Holding High the Banner of Marxism-Leninism. We should continue to hold high the revolutionary banner of Marxism-Leninism, uphold the revolutionary principles of the 1957 Moscow Declaration and the 1960 Moscow Statement and resolutely and thoroughly oppose modern revisionism—the main danger in the international communist movement. This is our main task at present and for a long time to come. At the same time we should resolutely and thoroughly oppose dogmatism, oppose sectarianism and oppose great-nation chauvinism and narrow nationalism. This is also a long-term task. The purpose of all this is to safeguard the purity of Marxism-Leninism.

The Tenth Plenary Session notes with satisfaction that since the Ninth Plenary Session held in 1961, and particularly since the beginning of this year, the work done by the whole Party in implementing the policy of readjustment, consolidation, filling out and raising standards in the national economy and in strengthening the agricultural front has yielded remarkable results. Despite the serious natural disasters for several consecutive years and the shortcomings and mistakes in the work, the condition of the national economy last year was slightly better than the year before, and this year it is again slightly better than that of last year.

In agriculture, the actual harvest of summer crops this year has shown a slight gain over that of last year, and the yield of autumn crops is also expected to register an increase. This is the result of carrying through the Party's series of policies concerning the rural people's communes and thus giving play to the advantages of the collective economy of the people's communes.

In industry, positive results have been achieved through the adoption of effective measures of readjustment. The output of means of production in support of agriculture, light industrial products using industrial products as raw materials, many handicrafts and some badly needed heavy industrial products has registered a considerable increase during the January-August period as compared with the corresponding period of last year. Many enterprises have improved their management, their products are of a higher quality and cover a greater range, their production costs have been cut down and their labour productivity has been raised.

In the field of commerce there are also new improvements and supply of commodities is slightly better than before.

All this shows that both in town and countryside, our economic conditions are getting better and better with each passing day.

It should be pointed out that some of our work is not well done. For instance, because of the incompetence of the leading cadres, some production teams, some factories and some business establishments have produced less or become unwelcome to the masses. We should endeavour to change this state of affairs and improve the work of those units without delay.

The people of our country have always united closely around the Central Committee of the Party and Comrade Mao Tse-tung. Even when confronted with serious difficulties at home and from abroad, the broadest masses and cadres of our country have always firmly believed in the correctness of the general line for socialist construction, the big leap forward and the people's commune—the three red banners. Giving full play to the glorious tradition of working hard and building the country with diligence and thrift, and to the militant spirit of relying on our own efforts and working with vigour for the country's prosperity, they have actively grappled with the difficulties and scored brilliant achievements under the leadership of the Party and the People's Government.

The Chinese People's Liberation Army and the Public Security Forces are strong and reliable armed forces of the people. Our country has also a heroic militia force of vast numbers. They have performed well their glorious task of defending the motherland, the people's labour and the socialist system. At all times they are vigilantly guarding the frontiers of our great motherland and protecting public order and stand ready to smash the aggressive and sabotage activities of any enemy.

Tested in Struggle. Tested in all these struggles, our country is worthy of being called a great country, our people a great people, our armed forces great armed forces, and our Party a great Party.

The imperialists, the reactionaries of various countries and the modern revisionists gloated over the temporary difficulties encountered by the Chinese people, and they wantonly vilified China's general line for socialist construction, the big leap forward and the people's commune, striking up an anti-Chinese chorus which was sensational for a time. U.S. imperialism instigated the Chiang Kai-shek gang entrenched in Taiwan to plot vainly an invasion of the coastal areas of the mainland. At home, those landlords, rich peasants and bourgeois rightists who have not reformed themselves and the remnant counter-revolutionaries also gloated over our difficulties and tried to take advantage of the situation. But the imperialists and their running-dogs in China and abroad completely miscalculated. All their criminal activities have not only further exposed their hideous features but have heightened the socialist and patriotic fervour of our people in working vigorously for the prosperity of our country. Our people have resolutely smashed and will continue to smash every one of their scheming activities, be it intrusion, provocation or aggression, or subversion within our state or our Party.

The Tenth Plenary Session of the Eighth Central Committee points out that throughout the historical period of proletarian revolution and proletarian dictatorship, throughout the historical period of transition from capitalism to communism (which will last scores of years or even longer), there is class struggle between the proletariat and the bourgeoisie and struggle between the socialist road and the capitalist road. The reactionary ruling classes which have been overthrown are not reconciled to their doom. They always attempt to stage a comeback. Meanwhile, there still exist in society bourgeois influence, the force of habit of old society and the spontaneous tendency towards capitalism among part of the small producers. Therefore, among the people, a small number of persons, making up only a tiny fraction of the total population, who have not yet undergone socialist remoulding, always attempt to depart from the socialist road and turn to the capitalist road whenever there is an opportunity. Class struggle is inevitable under these circumstances. This is a law of history which has long been elucidated by Marxism-Leninism. We must never forget it. This class struggle is complicated, tortuous, with ups and downs and sometimes it is very sharp. This class struggle inevitably finds expression within the Party. Pressure from foreign imperialism and the existence of bourgeois influence at home constitute the social source of revisionist ideas in the Party. While waging a struggle against the foreign and domestic class enemies, we must remain vigilant and resolutely oppose in good time various opportunist ideological tendencies in the Party. The great historic significance of the Eighth Plenary Session of the Eighth Central Committee held in Lushan in August 1959 lies in the fact that it victoriously smashed attacks by right opportunism, i.e., revisionism, and safeguarded the Party line and the unity of the Party. Both at present and in the future, our Party must sharpen its vigilance and correctly wage a struggle on two fronts, against revisionism and against dogmatism. Only thus can the purity of Marxism-Leninism be always preserved, the unity of the Party constantly strengthened and the fighting power of the Party continuously increased.

The Urgent Task. The Tenth Plenary Session holds that the urgent task facing the people of our country at present is to carry through the general policy of developing the national economy with agriculture as the foundation and industry the leading factor, as put forward by Comrade Mao Tse-tung, attach first importance to the development of agriculture, correctly handle the relationship between industry and agriculture and resolutely readjust the work of the industrial departments according to the policy of making agriculture the foundation of the national economy.

In the field of agriculture, it is necessary to continue to carry out the Central Committee's various policies concerning the people's communes, consolidate still further the collective economy, bring the peasants' enthusiasm for collective production into still greater play, give priority to the development of grain production and at the same time strive to develop cotton, oil-bearing and other industrial crops as well as livestock breeding, aquatic production, forestry and side-occupations. Meanwhile, it is necessary to mobilise and concentrate the strength of the whole Party and the whole nation in an active way to give agriculture and the collective economy of the people's communes every possible material, technical and financial aid as well as aid in the fields of leadership and personnel, and to bring about the technical transformation of agriculture, stage by stage and in a manner suited to local conditions.

In the field of industry, the first thing to do is, in accordance with the needs of the technical transformation of agriculture and the present availability of materials and manpower, to further carry out rational readjustment, strengthen the productive capacity of the weaker departments, energetically improve management, increase the variety and raise the quality of products.

In the field of commerce, it is necessary, in accordance with the principle of 'ensuring supplies by increasing production' and the policy of commerce serving agricultural and industrial production and the livelihood of the people and through the channels of state-run commerce, cooperative commerce and village fair trade, to make great efforts to arrange for the interflow of farm produce and manufactured goods between the rural and urban areas, so as to supply the rural areas with more means of production, supply industry with more materials, and supply the urban and rural people with more daily necessities.

In the fields of science, culture and education, it is necessary to strengthen scientific and technological research, and particularly to pay attention to the scientific and technological research in agriculture, vigorously train personnel in these fields, and at the same time strengthen the work of uniting with and educating the intellectuals so that they may fully play their role as they should.

Although we have produced more goods both last year and this year and the living conditions of the people have improved, the goods we produce are still insufficient to meet the needs of the urban and rural people. The whole Party and the whole nation must strive to expand production, ensure the supply of goods and so gradually improve the livelihood of the people. At the same time, the urban and rural inhabitants of the whole country must give attention to diligence and thrift in construction work and house-keeping, practise economy and lay up some savings so that we may gradually be better off and be prepared against the needs caused by natural disasters and other unforeseen events.

The Tenth Plenary Session is firmly convinced that, though certain difficulties still exist, it is entirely possible to overcome them. We have already made great achievements. Our future is bright. Provided the whole Party and the whole nation, united as one, strengthen democratic centralism, carry through the general policy of developing the national economy with agriculture as the foundation and industry as the leading factor, and further conscientiously carry out the work of readjustment, consolidation, filling out and raising standards in the national economy, we will certainly be able, after making efforts for a period of time, to usher in a new period of great upsurge in our country's socialist construction.

The Tenth Plenary Session calls on the workers, peasants, intellectuals, democratic parties and patriots of all the nationalities throughout the country to unite even more closely, hold still higher the glorious banners of the general line for socialist construction, the big leap forward and the people's commune under the leadership of the Party's Central Committee and Comrade Mao Tse-tung, go all out in their efforts to increase production and practise economy and strive for a bumper harvest next year, for the new growth of the national economy and for new victories in the socialist cause of our country.

2. *The People's Communes Are Making Progress*

A preliminary summary of the five years' experience of the rural people's communes in Kwangtung Province.*

By T'ao Chu

The national rural people's commune movement, started in 1958, has been a great event of epoch-making significance in Chinese history. . . . In the past five years, the rural people's communes in Kwangtung Province, like those in other parts of the country, have played an extremely important role in developing agricultural production, defeating natural calamities and consolidating the socialist position in the countryside. . . .

I

. . . The law of the planned and proportionate development of the national economy is an economic law of the socialist society, and the relations between agriculture and industry are the most important proportionate relations therein. In socialist construction, a country with the proletarian dictatorship must correctly handle these proportionate relations, so that the development of agriculture may be in keeping with the development of industry, and national economy as a whole, may rapidly progress forward.

* Original text published in *Hung-ch'i*, no. 4, February 26, 1964. English translation, abridged with minor adjustments, from SCMM, no. 410, 1964.

At the same time, it should be noted that, up to the present, the economic construction of all countries in the socialist camp is carried out under the conditions of the economic blockade and the threat of military aggression by imperialism. In order to consolidate the victories already won, and to increase their aid to the righteous cause of the people of all countries in the world, the countries in the socialist camp must resolutely implement the policy depending on their own efforts for revival, and achieve economic independence and sovereignty. . . .

It should be specially pointed out that the Central Committee of the Party and Comrade Mao Tse-tung, on the basis of the practical experience of socialist construction in China, have brought forward the general policy for the development of the national economy, with agriculture as the foundation and industry as the guiding factor. That is to say, China's socialist construction must stem from the development of agriculture, and make arrangements for the development of the national economy in the order of agriculture, light industry and heavy industry. The work of the industrial departments must be switched to the track of making agriculture the foundation, and on this foundation a complete industrial system should be established. . . .

What course should a socialist country pursue if it seeks to solve the agricultural problem basically so that agriculture may truly develop its role of being the foundation of the national economy? There is not the least doubt that the preservation of the small peasant economy will not do. Similarly, the road of capitalist big agriculture is even more at variance with socialism. The realisation of agricultural collectivisation is a common road all the socialist countries must follow. The Chinese Communist Party has strictly followed the teachings of Marxism-Leninism, and unswervingly kept to the road of carrying out a socialist transformation of agriculture and building a socialist big agriculture.

The fundamental line charted by the Party for agricultural transformation is: to realise agricultural collectivisation as the first step; and in the second step, on the basis of agricultural collectivisation, to attain irrigation for all the farmland which can be irrigated, adequate application of chemical fertiliser and insecticide, mechanisation and electrification in agriculture. . . .

In 1958, the Central Committee of the Party put forward the general line of going all out, aiming high, and building socialism with faster, better, greater and more economical results. This line greatly inspired the enthusiasm of the whole nation for socialist construction, thus bringing about a great leap forward in socialist construction in the farms, developing multiple economy and speedily putting an end to the backwardness of the country's agriculture.

This brought out all the more clearly the agricultural producer cooperative as a comparatively small-scale collective economic organisation, its limitations, and its existent contradictions. There was the contradiction between the need of large-scale farmland irrigation construction for mutual aid and co-operation on a greater scope, and that of small-scale farmland irrigation construction for the agricultural producer co-operative. This demanded the comprehensive utilisation of natural resources. There was the contradiction between the development of multiple economy, and the single-line operation of the agricultural producer co-operative. And there was the contradiction between the need for adequate co-operation in production among the agricultural producer co-operatives, and the scattered nature of the operation of these co-operatives. And so forth. The comparatively narrow scope of the original agricultural producer co-operatives had to be broken down.

To solve these various contradictions, in many localities the masses of peasants voluntarily merged and expanded their co-operatives. In some areas a further step was taken in the formation of federations of co-operatives. These federations already initially possessed the characteristics of the people's commune, and were actually the embryo of the commune. The Central Committee of the Party and Comrade Mao Tse-tung undertook a timely summation of the experiences and creations of the masses of the people, and made the resolution on the establishment of people's communes in the countryside. . . .

II

In the five years since the people's commune came into being, a tremendous change has taken place in the countryside. The situation in Kwangtung is also completely so. With reliance on the strength of the people's commune, agricultural production has greatly developed, the material and cultural life of the peasantry improved and the mentality of the people has shown a marked change.

Two extraordinary natural adversities hit Kwangtung Province in the past five years, a flood in 1959 and a severe dry spell in 1963. Nevertheless, thanks to the might of the people's commune, both natural calamities have been defeated. What may be specially pointed out is that, despite the 1963 dry spell lasting for eight to nine months, unknown in the recent sixty years, the province reaped a bumper harvest of grain topping the previous year's output by 1·1 billion catties.* In this year, there were 16 *hsien* and municipalities in Kwangtung where the per-unit area yield of paddy reached or exceeded the target of 800 catties per *mow* laid down in the *National Program for Agricultural Development, 1956–1967*. Output of industrial crops and the production of livestock breeding also showed a big margin of increase. Sugar cane and hemp output both showed an increase of more than 80 per cent compared with 1962. The number of live hogs remaining in the stockyards showed a increase of 34 per cent.

How did these miracles happen? It is because in the past five years, the superiority of the people's commune has been brought into full play and a large amount of work has been done.

First, large numbers of irrigation projects have been constructed and electrification and mechanisation have begun to operate in parts of the province. This has greatly improved the conditions of production. Statistics show that the province now has 90,515 units of water conservancy projects of varying sizes with an aggregate storage capacity of 30 billion cubic meters. Power generation and flood detention aside, the reservoirs capable of irrigating the farmland can store 14 billion cubic meters. Among them are 22 large reservoirs and 173 medium-size reservoirs. With the exception of one large reservoir and 18 medium-size reservoirs built before 1957, the rest were all constructed after the development of people's communes. The province has now 120,000 units of drainage projects of varying sizes, designed for the drainage volume of 1,900 second/cubic meters. Among them all the 36 large and medium-size projects have been built after development of communes. All the 246,700 horse power of electric pumps and over 80 per cent of the 135,900 horse power of engine-driven pumps now in use in the province have been installed since the people's communes were set up.

Water conservancy is the artery of agricultural production. With these water conservancy projects, the face of agricultural production has greatly changed. At the time of liberation, the greater part of the province's more than 30 million *mow* of paddy fields depended on rain water. Less than one-third had guaranteed irrigation (that is, capable of withstanding a two-month long dry spell or longer). By 1957, the area under guaranteed irrigation was extended to close to half the total. But by 1963, guaranteed irrigation had been extended to 24 million *mow*. If all the existing irrigation projects are coordinated in systems completely, and management is strengthened, with the raising of efficiency, then the guaranteed irrigation will

* Here billion = thousand million.

reach 30 million *mow*. That is to say, by that time, 90 per cent of the paddy fields will have guaranteed irrigation.

During these past years, apart from the large-scale electrification and mechanisation of water drainage and irrigation, the mechanisation of farming has also been partially started. There have been considerable increases in the numbers of tractors and other modern agricultural implements.

Second, technical renovations in farming techniques have been carried out in a planned way and on a large scale. The development of agricultural production through the technical reform of farming techniques has been the unversal demand of the broad masses of peasants, but during the time of individual economy in the past, it was hard to accomplish. After the formation of people's communes, along with the growth in collective strength and improvement in field irrigation, experiments in agro-technology have been conducted widely and actively, and good results have been achieved. Many *hsien* and people's communes have fostered a sizable force of agro-technicians and set up agricultural experimental stations. These stations have carried out fruitful work in experimentation in close planting with reasonable density, seed selection and breeding, soil improvement and reform in farming system and techniques.

Take, for instance, the work of fostering and popularising good paddy seeds, which has been very earnestly taken up in all areas after the building of communes, and very marked results have been achieved. In many *hsien* in the province, from the *hsien*, the people's commune, the production brigade, right down to the production team, there is organised the system of seed workers and seed plots. The selected cultivation and popularisation of good seeds has become a mass action. Originally, the early-crop rice seeds in Kwangtung had many defects. After several years of selected breeding and popularisation, in the majority of areas in the province, basically good seeds are entirely used for the early rice crop. The output of the early crop has been raised. There has been changed the former situation in paddy production of 'early four and late six' (from the same paddy plot, the early crop yields 40 per cent, and the late crop 60 per cent, of the total annual output) to become 'early five and late five'. The task in the future is to further carry out the selected breeding and popularisation of late crop seeds, to raise the output of the late crop.

The speed in the popularisation of good seeds has also been greatly accelerated. In the past, the popularisation of a new breed would take four to five years, but now two to three years are adequate. The reasonable close planting of paddy also was taken up in the days of the agricultural producer co-operative, but it could not be extensively popularised. After the building of communes, with the active leadership and push of the communes, with the example shown by the agricultural experimental stations, close planting specifications suited to different localities and different breeds were gradually found, and the reasonable close planting of paddy has become a habit of the masses. Today it is basically practised in the whole province.

Third, under the unified leadership and overall planning of the people's communes, it has been possible to achieve better and all-round exploitation of the resources, make better use of both manpower and land, develop multi-economy in accordance with specific local conditions, and make all-round development in agricultural and sideline production. This is an important hallmark of the fact that agriculture is gradually being rid of the limitations which were unavoidably imposed by small-scale operation. In recent years, many communes in the whole province have made rational arrangements for production by its subsidiary production teams. In the commodity grain areas, forces are concentrated for grain production in combination with the development of animal husbandry; in the industrial crop areas, in addition to the production of grain, appropriately more peanut, sugar cane and other industrial crops are cultivated; in areas near cities and towns more vegetables are grown, and poultry and ducks are bred in quantity, while surplus labour power is arranged for the operation of short distance transportation and other temporary sideline activities. In accordance with the production arrangements for the different production teams, the state has also correspondingly adjusted their tasks in the delivery and sales of agricultural and subsidiary products to the state. Such development of production with consideration of local expediency has fully unearthed production potentials and rapidly increased both output and income.

There is still another situation. In the days of the agricultural co-operatives, between different co-operatives, there were many land plots which were lying idle and this obstructed the rational utilisation of land, and obstructed the large-scale irrigation development and the promotion of mechanisation and electrification. At the time many areas had hoped for a rational solution of this problem, but due to the difficulty of reaching agreement among the co-operatives, it could not be achieved. After the organization of communes, farmland has been adjusted under unified plans, and the former contradictions can now be handled in a better manner.

Fourth, perseverance in the principle of distribution to each according to his work, promotion of the communist style of mutual assistance and active help to poorer production teams, have insured a common road to prosperity for all. As a result, the better-off teams with more favourable natural conditions have become still richer while those with worse natural conditions and lower income have gradually overcome their poverty and backwardness and caught up with the more advanced. When the communes were first formed, such poor production teams accounted for a quarter of the total. Over the past five years, the number of the poor teams has dropped by 30 to 40 per cent. They now account for about one-sixth of all teams. . . .

Fifth, the people's communes have improved the material well-being of their members and effected a profound change in the spiritual face of the masses of the peasants. During the five years since the development of communes, particularly during the past two years, the life of the broad masses of commune members has shown a marked improvement.

Data from Nan-hai *hsien* can clearly illustrate this problem. This *hsien* is situated in the network of water courses in the Pearl River Delta. Production conditions here are generally not bad. The life of peasants is not low for Kwangtung. However, before the building of communes, the water conservancy problem was not solved basically, floods occurred rather frequently. A portion of the higher fields, on the other hand, was constantly affected by drought. Production was not stable. After the building of communes, the people carried out large-scale farmland irrigation construction. After five years of efforts, in the whole *hsien* there has been built a comparatively complete electrical irrigation network. The natural conditions have been basically changed. Added to this has been the the active popularisation of good seeds and the reform of farming techniques, which enabled a big marginal growth of agricultural production. The total grain output of the *hsien* was 295 million catties in 1957, and in 1963 it was increased to 503 million catties, an increase of more than 70 per cent. In the year 1963 especially, there was an increase of 114 million catties of grain. On the 520,000 *mow* of farmland in the whole *hsien*, on the average each *mow* increased production by more than 200 catties. The restoration and development of industrial crops have been also rapid. In sideline production, there has been very great development in the numbers of hogs, poultry, ducks and geese fed. Due to the development of production, the collective income has increased greatly, and the collective distribution of income for commune members in 1963 nearly doubled that of 1957. The rationed grain level of the *hsien* has always been comparatively high, and that in 1963 also increased by nearly 20 per cent over that of 1957. The purchasing power of the commune members has also been greatly raised. The retail sales volume of social commodities in 1963 increased by 50 per cent over that of 1958. After the development of communes, the life of peasants in Nan-hai, on the foundation of its comparatively high level for the whole province of Kwantgung, continued to see such improvement. The broad masses of peasants are naturally very satisfied.

Social existence determines people's consciousness. The people's commune is a brand new system. Its birth must naturally lead to a new revolution in the ideology of the broad masses of the peasants. The people's communes have improved the material well-being of their members and effected a profound change in the spiritual face of the masses of the peasants. The destiny of the peasants is linked together with daily growing solidarity of the material foundation created by the people's communes. They are more determined to rely on the collective than ever before. Socialism has taken a deeper root in the countryside. . . .

Thus because the people's communes insure common prosperity for all their production teams, and a daily improving life of security for all the members, they have eliminated the possibility of bipolar differentiation which is otherwise unavoidable under small peasant economy.

All this, with the added practice by the people's communes of the 'integration of the government with the commune', and the strengthening of the political and ideological education of the members, powerful influence cannot but be exerted over the consciousness of the people. The socialist and patriotic consciousness of the broad masses of commune members is also greatly strengthened. Today, the tasks of delivering and selling to the state agricultural and sideline products are being fulfilled in time and of required quality. This has become the self-conscious action of the leadership of communes at all levels and the broad masses of commune members. Enthusiastic participation in the militia corps, assistance to the People's Liberation Army in the safeguarding of the frontiers have also been recognised as the sacred duty of the broad masses of young men and women. During these past few years, in the struggles against the disturbance of the coastal areas by u.s.-Chiang special agents, the militiamen of all localities have courageously thrown themselves in the fight and contributed laudable services. . . .

The period of five years is only a very short interval in the long course of history. But the people's commune system has initially manifested its incomparable superiority and achieved great results. It can be definitely stated that had it not been for reliance on the might of the people's commune, the accomplishment of any of the above tasks would have been difficult. It can also be definitely stated that in the future continued march forward, the people's commune will further fully develop its superiority, and create more brilliant achievements.

III

. . . The people's commune is an organisation which 'first, is big and, secondly, communal'. In comparison with the agricultural producer co-operative, the people's commune has many more new contents, is bigger in scale, and is on a higher level of collective ownership. . . . The advantage of the people's commune in being 'first, big and, secondly, communal', its practice of a more perfect system compared with the higher agricultural producer co-operative have led to more extensive manpower, material resources and financial resources for the collective economy, and greater strength of leadership forces. This breaks through the limitations of the higher agricultural producer co-operatives, and facilitates the unified planning of all kinds of production and construction projects on a larger scale, facilitates the raising of funds, the arrangement of labour power, the organisation of co-operation and the undertaking of enterprises beyond the capacity of the co-operative.

To take farmland water conservancy construction in the past years as an example. Had it not been for the comparatively extensive manpower, material resources and financial resources of the people's communes, the gigantic achievements as made would have been impossible. . . . In the construction of larger water conservancy projects, some areas receive greater benefits and others smaller. Some farmland also has to be inundated and requisitioned. This calls for unified planning. Without the unified leadership of the people's communes, and without organised co-operation within the scope of the communes and in accordance with the principles of voluntariness and mutual benefit, the contradictions between areas and between units will be hard of solution. As to the practice of the irrigation of all land which can be irrigated, the chemicalisation, electrification and mechanisation of agriculture, the promotion of technological reforms, the overall utilisation of resources for the development of multi-economy, the aid to poor production teams in the development of production, and so forth, marked achievements have also been possible because of the development of the superiority of the people's commune in being 'first, big, and secondly, communal'.

The people's commune at its present stage makes the production team the basic accounting unit, carrying out its independent accounting, and bearing its own profit and loss. Within the production team is practised the principle of distribution according to work. Within the commune, between different teams and between a team and the commune is practised the principle of exchange at equal values. This is completely in keeping with China's present level of agricultural productive forces, and the situation of the development of production in the various production teams.

The mechanisation of China's agriculture is only at its beginning, agricultural production at the moment is still dependent mainly on manpower and animal power, and the production team is still the unit directly organising production. Under such conditions, the practice of using the production team as the basic accounting unit will unify the unit directly organising production with the basic accounting unit. This benefits the mobilisation of the production activism of the production teams and the broad masses of commune members. At the same time, due to the objective existence of differences in levels of economic development among the various production teams, and under the situation in which the levels of development of the different production teams are not yet balanced, the practice of using the production team as the basic accounting unit will make it possible to recognise the differences and avoid egalitarianism.

In the days of the agricultural producer co-operative, because accounting at the co-operative level was practised, with the co-operative undertaking the unified distribution of products, the production team which directly organised production was only a unit underwriting production and not an accounting unit. This gave birth to the irrational phenomenon of the lack of proper unity between distribution and production. It in turn gave rise to the question that distribution could not properly take care of differences, and affected the activism of the production teams and co-operative members. ... In the past few years, the overwhelming majority of communes used the production team as the basic accounting unit. This developed to a high degree its activism and initiative for the development of collective production and the strengthening of collective economy, and effectively promoted the restoration and development of agricultural production. ...

In the overwhelming majority of cases, the two levels—the people's commune and the production team—today are still of the nature of partial ownership. But this system of partial ownership in the two levels has already developed an important role. On the role of the people's commune level, it can already be clearly seen in the great achievements during the five years of the people's commune movement, as discussed above.

Here, on the basis of the experiences of Kwangtung, we shall discuss the role of ownership of the level of the production brigade. At present, the scale of the production brigade is generally equal to the original higher agricultural producer co-operative. After the formation of the people's commune, it remained as an ownership level, an organisation of the level which is below the upper level and above the lower level, and also as the basic level organisation of the Party, the unit where the Party branch is located. It plays a very important role.

Because the scale of the production team is comparatively small, a commune has very many production teams. In a place like Kwangtung, without the production brigades, the communes will find it hard to exercise leadership. At the same time, due to the limitations in their strength, the production teams also need the level of production brigade regularly to strengthen leadership and give concrete assistance. The brigade is needed for the unified organisation of certain indispensable activities in production co-operation among different teams, and in the joint operation of undertakings and projects by several teams.

Today, the two levels—the production brigade and the people's commune—have in possession a definite brigade-operated economy or commune-operated economy. Though these two portions today still do not possess an extensive economy, yet an active role is being played, and in the long run there is a great future. With the consolidation and development of the economy at different levels of the people's commune, at the appropriate time, the accumulation at the two levels of the people's commune and the production brigade should also be gradually increased, and commune-operated and brigade-operated economy will also be gradually developed. Naturally, at the present moment the economy of the commune level and the brigade level cannot yet be developed excessively, particularly the method of weakening the economy of the production team cannot be used to develop the economy of the commune and the brigade. . . . In the future, after a comparatively long period, with the raising of the level of agricultural productive forces, and the further development of the economy of the commune and brigade levels, when the needed conditions are available, the people's commune will replace the system of using the production team as the basic accounting unit with the system of using the production brigade as the basic accounting unit. After a further period, a further step will be taken with the use of the commune as the basic accounting unit. The superiority of the people's commune which is 'first, big and, secondly, communal' will be more and more fully developed.

The people's commune is an organisation 'integrating the government with the commune'. Viewed from the practical conditions of different areas in Kwangtung, the coming into being of the people's commune 'integrating the government with the commune' has greatly strengthened the state's political leadership and economic leadership over collective economy. The cadres of the commune level and the principal cadres of some production brigades are both cadres of the collective economic organization and cadres of the state. . . .

IV

The whole history of the agricultural collectivisation movement in China has been a history of class struggles in the countryside. This was so in the early period of the organisation of mutual-aid teams and agricultural co-operatives, and it was also so in the later period of the organisation of people's communes. The five years since the coming into being of the people's communes have been a course full of class struggles, as well as a course of using proletarian ideology to educate and remould the peasantry.

The characteristics of the people's commune as being 'first, big and, secondly, communal', the colossal superiority it has initially revealed, and the great achievements it has registered have won it the enthusiastic support of the broad masses of poor peasants, lower-middle peasants, and other peasants in the countryside. They have enthusiastically taken the lead in joining the communes, and resolutely supported the interests of collective economy. They zealously eulogise the people's commune, treating it as the big road on which they will for ever rid themselves of poverty and backwardness.

However, for the overthrown feudal landlord class and the rich peasants, the people's commune movement implies the further smashing of their attempts to live again the life of parasites. They would not be resigned to their defeat, and among them some adopt all kinds of measures at sabotage activities, to undermine collective production, to fabricate rumours to confuse the masses, to carry out feudal religious activities, to corrode and hit the cadres, and even to usurp leadership, in the attempt to stage a restoration. Among the well-to-do middle peasants, a small number with serious capitalist trends also adopt various measures of encroaching upon the public for self-aggrandisement, to weaken and disintegrate the collective economy, in the attempt to take the road of capitalism.

The class struggles in the countryside thus objectively exist. They cannot be avoided, nor can they be reconciled. As pointed out by the 10th plenum of the 8th Central Committee of the Party: 'Throughout the historical period of proletarian revolution and proletarian dictatorship, throughout the historical period of transition from capitalism to communism (which will last scores of years or even longer), there is class struggle between the proletariat and the bourgeoisie and struggle between the capitalist road and the socialist road.' Innumerable facts have proved that this conclusion is an unbreakable truth. . . .

Today, with this weapon of the powerful people's commune, we can all the better strengthen the proletarian dictatorship in the rural areas, check the growth of the rural spontaneous trend towards capitalism. Over a long time in the future, in the continued prosecution of the struggle between the two roads to see 'who defeats whom', the victory of socialism, organisationally and as a system, will be better guaranteed. So long as we fully develop the superiority of the people's commune, our agricultural productive forces will have more and more rapid development, and the socialist ground in the rural areas will be more and more consolidated. Furthermore, with the people's commune system, our rural areas can be led in the future transition from socialism to communism. This is our far-reaching ideal and the direction for our march forward. . . . Accordingly, at all times, we must stress that politics comes first, that politics holds the command, and that politics is the soul. . . .

3. *Long Live the Victory of People's War!*

In Commemoration of the 20th Anniversary of Victory in the Chinese People's War of Resistance against Japan.*

By Lin Piao

Full twenty years have elapsed since our victory in the great War of Resistance against Japan. . . .

How was it possible for a weak country finally to defeat a strong country? How was it possible for a seemingly weak army to become the main force in the war?

The basic reasons were that the War of Resistance against Japan was a genuine people's war led by the Communist Party of China

* Translated text published in the *Peking Review*, August 4, 1965, abridged.

and Comrade Mao Tse-tung, a war in which the correct Marxist-Leninist political and military lines were put into effect, and that the Eighth Route and New Fourth Armies were genuine people's armies which applied the whole range of strategy and tactics of people's war as formulated by Comrade Mao Tse-tung. . . .

The Chinese people's victory in the War of Resistance paved the way for their seizure of state power throughout the country. When the Kuomintang reactionaries, backed by the u.s. imperialists, launched a nation-wide civil war in 1946, the Communist Party of China and Comrade Mao Tse-tung further developed the theory of people's war, led the Chinese people in waging a people's war on a still larger scale, and in the space of a little over three years the great victory of the People's Liberation War was won, the rule of imperialism, feudalism and bureaucrat-capitalism in our country ended and the People's Republic of China founded.

The victory of the Chinese people's revolutionary war breached the imperialist front in the East, wrought a great change in the world balance of forces, and accelerated the revolutionary movement among the people of all countries. From then on, the national liberation movement in Asia, Africa, and Latin America entered a new historical period. . . . The Communist Party of China and Comrade Mao Tse-tung were able to lead the Chinese people to victory in the War of Resistance against Japan primarily because they formulated and applied a Marxist-Leninist line. Basing himself on the fundamental tenets of Marxism-Leninism and applying the method of class analysis, Comrade Mao Tse-tung analysed, first, the mutual transformation of China's principal and non-principal contradictions following the invasion of China by Japanese imperialism; second, the consequent changes in class relations within China and in international relations; and, third, the balance of forces as between China and Japan. This analysis provided the scientific basis upon which the political and military lines of the War of Resistance were formulated. . . .

How was one to assess the changes in China's political situation, and what conclusion was to be drawn? This question had a direct bearing on the very survival of the Chinese nation.

For a period prior to the outbreak of the War of Resistance, the 'Left' opportunists, represented by Wang Ming within the Chinese Communist Party, were blind to the important changes in China's political situation caused by Japanese aggression since 1931 and denied the sharpening of the Sino-Japanese national contradiction and the demands of various social strata for a war of resistance; instead, they stressed that all the counter-revolutionary factions

192

and intermediate forces in China and all the imperialist countries were a monolithic bloc. They persisted in their line of 'closed-doorism' and continued to advocate, 'Down with the whole lot.' Comrade Mao Tse-tung resolutely fought the 'Left' opportunist errors and penetratingly analysed the new situation in the Chinese revolution. . . .

He pointed out that the Japanese imperialist attempt to reduce Chinese to a Japanese colony heightened the contradiction between China and Japan and made it the principal contradiction; that China's internal class contradictions—such as those between the masses of the people and feudalism, between the peasantry and the landlord class, between the proletariat and the bourgeoisie, and between the peasantry and urban petty bourgeoisie on the one hand and the bourgeoisie on the other—still remained, but that they had all been relegated to a secondary or subordinate position as a result of the war of aggression unleashed by Japan; and that throughout China opposition to Japanese imperialism had become the common demand of the people of all classes and strata, except for a handful of pro-Japanese traitors among the big landlords and the big bourgeoisie. . . .

In the face of Japanese imperialist aggression, was the Party to continue with the civil war and the Agrarian Revolution? Or was it to hold aloft the banner of national liberation, unite with all the forces that could be united to form a broad national united front and concentrate on fighting the Japanese aggressors? This was the problem sharply confronting our Party. . . . Could the War of Resistance be victorious? And how was victory to be won? These were the questions to which all the Chinese people demanded immediate answers. . . .

In his celebrated work *On Protracted War*, Comrade Mao Tse-tung pointed out the contrasting features of China and Japan, the two sides in the war. Japan was a powerful imperialist country. But Japanese imperialism was in its era of decline and doom. The war it had unleashed was a war of aggression, a war that was retrogressive and barbarous; it was deficient in manpower and material resources and could not stand a protracted war; it was engaged in an unjust cause and therefore had meagre support internationally. China, on the other hand, was a weak semi-colonial and semi-feudal country. But she was in her era of progress. She was fighting a war against aggression, a war that was progressive and just; she had sufficient manpower and material resources to sustain a protracted war; internationally, China enjoyed extensive sympathy and support. These comprised all the basic factors in the Sino-Japanese war.

He went on to show how these factors would influence the course of the war. Japan's advantage was temporary and would gradually diminish as a result of our efforts. Her disadvantages were fundamental; they could not be overcome and would gradually grow in the course of the war. China's disadvantage was temporary and could be gradually overcome. China's advantages were fundamental and would play an increasingly positive role in the course of the war. Japan's advantage and China's disadvantage determined the impossibility of quick victory for China. China's advantages and Japan's disadvantages determined the inevitability of Japan's defeat and China's ultimate victory. . . .

In order to turn the anti-Japanese war into a genuine people's war, our Party firmly relied on the broadest masses of the people, united with all the anti-Japanese forces that could be united, and consolidated and expanded the Anti-Japanese National United Front. The basic line of our Party was: boldly to arouse the masses of the people and expand the people's forces so that, under the leadership of the Party, they could defeat the aggressors and build a new China. . . .

The concrete analysis of concrete conditions and the concrete resolution of concrete contradictions are the living soul of Marxism-Leninism. Comrade Mao Tse-tung has invariably been able to single out the principal contradiction from among a complexity of contradictions, analyse the two aspects of this principal contradiction concretely and, 'pressing on irresistibly from this commanding height', successfully solve the problem of understanding and handling the various contradictions. . . .

In formulating the Party's line of the Anti-Japanese National United Front, Comrade Mao Tse-tung made the following class analysis of Chinese society.

The workers, the peasants and the urban petty bourgeoisie firmly demanded that the War of Resistance should be carried through to the end; they were the main force in the fight against Japanese aggression and constituted the basic masses who demanded unity and progress.

The bourgeoisie was divided into the national and the comprador bourgeoisie. The national bourgeoisie formed the majority of the bourgeoisie; it was rather flabby, often vacillated and had contradictions with the workers, but it also had a certain degree of readiness to oppose imperialism and was one of our allies in the War of Resistance. The comprador bourgeoisie was the bureaucrat-capitalist class, which was very small in number but occupied the ruling position in China. Its members attached themselves to different imperialist powers, some of them being pro-Japanese and others pro-British and pro-American. The pro-Japanese section of the comprador bourgeoisie were the capitulators, the overt and covert traitors. The pro-British and pro-American section of this class favoured resistance to Japan to a certain extent, but they were not firm in their resistance and very much wished to compromise with Japan, and by their nature they were opposed to the Communist Party and the people.

The landlords fell into different categories; there were the big, the middle and the small landlords. Some of the big landlords became traitors, while others favoured resistance but vacillated a great deal. Many of the middle and small landlords had the desire to resist, but there were contradictions between them and the peasants.

In the face of these complicated class relationships, our Party's policy regarding work within the united front was one of both alliance and struggle. That is to say, its policy was to unite with all the anti-Japanese classes and strata, try to win over even those who could be only vacillating and temporary allies, and adopt appropriate policies to adjust the relations among these classes and strata so that they all served the general cause of resisting Japan. At the same time, we had to maintain our Party's principle of independence and initiative, make the bold arousing of the masses and expansion of the people's forces the centre of gravity in our work, and wage the necessary struggles against all activities harmful to resistance, unity and progress. . . .

Our Party made a series of adjustments in its policies in order to unite all the anti-Japanese parties and groups, including the Kuomintang, and all the anti-Japanese strata in a joint fight against the foe. We pledged ourselves to fight for the complete realisation of Dr Sun Yat-sen's revolutionary Three People's Principles. . . . In our own base areas we carried out the 'three thirds system' in our organs of political power, drawing in those representatives of the petty bourgeoisie, the national bourgeoisie and the enlightened gentry and those members of the Kuomintang who stood for resistance to Japan and did not oppose the Communist Party. In accordance with the principles of the Anti-Japanese National United Front, we also made necessary and appropriate changes in our policies relating to the economy, taxation, labour and wages, anti-espionage, people's rights, culture and education, etc. While making these policy adjustments, we maintained the independence of the Communist Party, the people's army and the base areas. . . .

Comrade Mao Tse-tung constantly summed up the experience

gained by the whole Party in implementing the line of the Anti-Japanese National United Front and worked out a whole set of policies in good time. They were mainly as follows:

1. All people favouring resistance (that is, all the anti-Japanese workers, peasants, soldiers, students and intellectuals, and business-men) were to unite and form the Anti-Japanese National United Front.

2. Within the united front, our policy was to be one of indepen-dence and initiative, i.e. both unity and independence were neces-sary.

3. As far as military strategy was concerned, our policy was to be guerrilla warfare waged independently and with the initiative in our own hands, within the framework of a unified strategy; guerrilla warfare was to be basic, but no chance of waging mobile warfare was to be lost when the conditions were favourable.

4. In the struggle against the anti-Communist die-hards headed by Chiang Kai-shek, our policy was to make use of contradictions, win over the many, oppose the few and destroy our enemies one by one, and to wage struggles on just grounds, to our advantage, and with restraint.

5. In the Japanese-occupied and Kuomintang areas our policy was, on the one hand, to develop the united front to the greatest possible extent and, on the other, to have selected cadres working underground. With regard to the forms of organisation and struggle, our policy was to assign selected cadres to work under cover for a long period, so as to accumulate strength and bide our time.

6. As regards the alignment of the various classes within the country, our basic policy was to develop the progressive forces, win over the middle forces and isolate the anti-Communist die-hard forces.

7. As for the anti-Communist die-hards, we followed a revolu-tionary dual policy of uniting with them, in so far as they were still capable of bringing themselves to resist Japan, and of struggling against and isolating them, in so far as they were determined to oppose the Communist Party.

8. With respect to the landlords and the bourgeoisie—even the big landlords and big bourgeoisie—it was necessary to analyse each case and draw distinctions. On the basis of these distinctions we were to formulate different policies so as to achieve our aim of uniting with all the forces that could be united. . . .

Rely on the Peasants and Establish Rural Base Areas. The peasantry constituted more than 80 per cent of the entire population of semi-colonial and semi-feudal China. They were subjected to the three-fold oppression and exploitation of imperialism, feudalism and bureaucrat-capitalism, and they were eager for resistance against Japan and for revolution. It was essential to rely mainly on the peasants if the people's war was to be won.

But at the outset many comrades in our Party did not see this point. The history of our Party shows that in the period of the First Revolutionary Civil War, one of the major errors of the Right opportunists, represented by Ch'en Tu-hsiu, was their failure to recognise the importance of the peasant question and their opposition to arousing and arming the peasants. In the period of the Second Revolutionary Civil War, one of the major errors of the 'Left' opportunists, represented by Wang Ming, was likewise their failure to recognise the importance of the peasant question. They did not realise that it was essential to undertake long-term and painstaking work among the peasants and establish revolutionary base areas in the countryside; they were under the illusion that they could rapidly seize the big cities and quickly win nation-wide victory in the revolution. The errors of both the Right and the 'Left' opportunists brought serious setbacks and defeats to the Chinese revolution.

As far back as the period of the First Revolutionary Civil War, Comrade Mao Tse-tung had pointed out that the peasant question occupied an extremely important position in the Chinese revolution, that the bourgeois-democratic revolution against imperialism and feudalism was in essence a peasant revolution and that the basic task of the Chinese proletariat in the bourgeois-democratic revolution was to give leadership to the peasants' struggle.

In the period of the War of Resistance against Japan, Comrade Mao Tse-tung again stressed that the peasants were the most reliable and the most numerous ally of the proletariat and constituted the main force in the War of Resistance. The peasants were the main source of manpower for China's armies. The funds and the supplies needed for a protracted war came chiefly from the peasants. In the anti-Japanese war it was imperative to rely mainly on the peasants and to arouse them to participate in the war on the broadest scale. . . .

During the War of Resistance against Japan, the Japanese imperialist forces occupied many of China's big cities and the main lines of communication, but owing to the shortage of troops they were unable to occupy the vast countryside, which remained the vulnerable sector of the enemy's rule. . . .

In the anti-Japanese base areas, we carried out democratic reforms, improved the livelihood of the people, and mobilised and organised the peasant masses. Organs of anti-Japanese democratic political power were established on an extensive scale and the masses of the people enjoyed the democratic right to run their own affairs; at the same time we carried out the policies of 'a reasonable burden' and 'the reduction of rent and interest', which weakened the feudal system of exploitation and improved the people's livelihood. As a result, the enthusiasm of the peasant masses was deeply aroused. . . . In the enemy-occupied cities and villages, we combined legal with illegal struggle, united the basic masses and all patriots, and divided and disintegrated the political power of the enemy and his puppets so as to prepare ourselves to attack the enemy from within in co-ordination with operations from without when conditions were ripe. . . .

At the same time, the work of building the revolutionary base areas was a grand rehearsal in preparation for nation-wide victory. In these base areas, we built the Party, ran the organs of state power, built the people's armed forces and set up mass organisations; we engaged in industry and agriculture and operated cultural, educational and all other undertakings necessary for the independent existence of a separate region. Our base areas were in fact a state in miniature. And with the steady expansion of our work in the base areas, our Party established a powerful people's army, trained cadres for various kinds of work, accumulated experience in many fields and built up both the material and the moral strength that provided favourable conditions for nation-wide victory. . . .

Build a People's Army of a New Type. 'Without a people's army the people have nothing.' This is the conclusion drawn by Comrade Mao Tse-tung from the Chinese people's experience in their long years of revolutionary struggle, experience that was bought in blood. This is a universal truth of Marxism-Leninism.

The special feature of the Chinese revolution was armed revolution against armed counter-revolution. The main form of struggle was war and the main form of organisation was the army which was under the absolute leadership of the Chinese Communist Party, while all the other forms of organisation and struggle led by our Party were co-ordinated, directly or indirectly, with the war. . . .

Why were the Eighth Route and New Fourth Armies able to grow big and strong from being small and weak and to score such great victories in the War of Resistance against Japan? The fundamental reason was that the Eighth Route and New Fourth Armies were founded on Comrade Mao-Tse-tung's theory of army building. They were armies of a new type, a people's army which whole-heartedly serves the interests of the people. . . . The essence of

Comrade Mao Tse-tung's theory of army building is that in building a people's army prominence must be given to politics, i.e., the army must first and foremost be built on a political basis. Politics is the commander, politics is the soul of everything. Political work is the lifeline of our army. True, a people's army must pay attention to the constant improvement of its weapons and equipment and its military technique, but in its fighting it does not rely purely on weapons and technique, it relies mainly on politics, on the proletarian revolutionary consciousness and courage of the commanders and fighters, on the support and backing of the masses. . . .

All this makes the people's army led by the Chinese Communist Party fundamentally different from any bourgeois army, and from all the armies of the old type which served the exploiting classes and were driven and utilised by a handful of people. The experience of the people's war in China shows that a people's army created in accordance with Comrade Mao Tse-tung's theory of army building is incomparably strong and invincible.

Carry Out the Strategy and Tactics of People's War. Engels said: 'The emancipation of the proletariat, in its turn, will have its specific expression in military affairs and create its specific, new military method.' Engels' profound prediction has been fulfilled in the revolutionary wars waged by the Chinese people under the leadership of the Chinese Communist Party. In the course of protracted armed struggle, we have created a whole range of strategy and tactics of people's war by which we have been able to utilise our strong points to attack the enemy at his weak points.

During the War of Resistance against Japan, on the basis of his comprehensive analysis of the enemy and ourselves, Comrade Mao Tse-tung laid down the following strategic principle for the Communist-led Eighth Route and New Fourth Armies: 'Guerrilla warfare is basic, but lose no chance for mobile warfare under favourable conditions.' He raised guerrilla warfare to the level of strategy, because, if they are to defeat a formidable enemy, revolutionary armed forces should not fight with a reckless disregard for the consequences when there is a great disparity between their own strength and the enemy's. If they do, they will suffer serious losses and bring heavy setbacks to the revolution. Guerrilla warfare is the only way to mobilise and apply the whole strength of the people against the enemy, the only way to expand our forces in the course of the war, deplete and weaken the enemy, gradually change the balance of forces between the enemy and ourselves, switch from guerrilla to mobile warfare, and finally defeat the enemy. . . .

War of annihilation is the fundamental guiding principle of our military operations. . . . Comrade Mao Tse-tung has pointed out:

> A battle in which the enemy is routed is not basically decisive in a contest with a foe of great strength. A battle of annihilation, on the other hand, produces a great and immediate impact on any enemy. Injuring all of a man's ten fingers is not as effective as chopping off one, and routing ten enemy divisions is not as effective as annihilating one of them.

> . . . In order to annihilate the enemy, we must adopt the policy of luring him in deep and abandon some cities and districts of our own accord in a planned way, so as to let him in. It is only after letting the enemy in that the people can take part in the war in various ways and that the power of a people's war can be fully exerted. It is only after letting the enemy in that he can be compelled to divide up his forces, take on heavy burdens and commit mistakes. In other words, we must let the enemy become elated, stretch out all his ten fingers and become hopelessly bogged down. Thus, we can concentrate superior forces to destroy the enemy forces one by one, to eat them up mouthful by mouthful. . . .

Comrade Mao Tse-tung has provided a masterly summary of the strategy and tactics of people's war: You fight in your way and we fight in ours; we fight when we can win and move away when we can't. In other words, you rely on modern weapons and we rely on highly conscious revolutionary people; you give full play to your superiority and we give full play to ours; you have your way of fighting and we have ours. When you want to fight us, we don't let you and you can't even find us. But when we want to fight you, we make sure that you can't get away and we hit you squarely on the chin and wipe you out. When we are able to wipe you out, we do so with a vengeance; when we can't, we see to it that you don't wipe us out. . . .

Adhere to the Policy of Self-Reliance. The Chinese people's War of Resistance against Japan was an important part of the Anti-Fascist World War. The victory of the Anti-Fascist War as a whole was the result of the common struggle of the people of the world. . . . The common victory was won by all the peoples, who gave one another support and encouragement. Yet each country was, above all, liberated as a result of its own people's efforts.

The liberation of the masses is accomplished by the masses themselves—this is a basic principle of Marxism-Leninism. Revolution or people's war in any country is the business of the masses in that country and should be carried out primarily by their own efforts; there is no other way.

Appendix B. 3. Long Live the Victory of People's War

During the War of Resistance against Japan, our Party maintained that China should rely mainly on her own strength while at the same time trying to get as much foreign assistance as possible. We firmly opposed the Kuomintang ruling clique's policy of exclusive reliance on foreign aid. In the eyes of the Kuomintang and Chiang Kai-shek, China's industry and agriculture were no good, her weapons and equipment were no good, nothing in China was any good, so that if she wanted to defeat Japan, she had to depend on other countries, and particularly on the u.s.-British imperialists. This was completely slavish thinking. . . .

Self-reliance was especially important for the people's armed forces and the Liberated Areas led by our Party. The Kuomintang government gave the Eighth Route and New Fourth Armies some small allowances in the initial stage of the anti-Japanese war, but gave them not a single penny later. The Liberated Areas faced great difficulties as a result of the Japanese imperialists' savage attacks and brutal 'mopping-up' campaigns, of the Kuomintang's military encirclement and economic blockade and of natural calamities. The difficulties were particularly great in the years 1941 and 1942, when we were very short of food and clothing.

What were we to do? Comrade Mao Tse-tung asked: How has mankind managed to keep alive from time immemorial? Has it not been by men using their hands to provide for themselves? Why should we, their latter-day descendants, be devoid of this tiny bit of wisdom? Why can't we use our own hands?

The Central Committee of the Party and Comrade Mao Tse-tung put forward the policies of 'ample food and clothing through self-reliance' and 'develop the economy and ensure supplies', and the army and the people of the Liberated Areas accordingly launched an extensive production campaign, with the main emphasis on agriculture.

Difficulties are not invincible monsters. If everyone co-operates and fights them, they will be overcome. The Kuomintang reactionaries thought that they could starve us to death by cutting off allowances and imposing an economic blockade, but in fact they helped us by stimulating us to rely on our own efforts to surmount our difficulties. While launching the great campaign for production, we applied the policy of 'better troops and simpler administration' and economised in the use of manpower and material resources; thus we not only surmounted the severe material difficulties and successfully met the crisis, but lightened the people's burden, improved their livelihood and laid the material foundations for victory in the anti-Japanese war.

The problem of military equipment was solved mainly by relying on the capture of arms from the enemy, though we did turn out some weapons too. Chiang Kai-shek, the Japanese imperialists and the u.s. imperialists have all been our 'chiefs of transportation corps'. The arsenals of the imperialists always provide the oppressed peoples and nations with arms. . . .

The Chinese revolution is a continuation of the great October Revolution. The road of the October Revolution is the common road for all people's revolutions. The Chinese revolution and the October Revolution have in common the following basic characteristics: (1) Both were led by the working class with a Marxist-Leninist party as its nucleus. (2) Both were based on the worker-peasant alliance. (3) In both cases state power was seized through violent revolution and the dictatorship of the proletariat was established. (4) In both cases the socialist system was built after victory in the revolution. (5) Both were component parts of the proletarian world revolution.

Naturally, the Chinese revolution had its own peculiar characteristics. The October Revolution took place in imperialist Russia, but the Chinese revolution broke out in a semi-colonial and semi-feudal country. The former was a proletarian socialist revolution, while the latter developed into a socialist revolution after the complete victory of the new-democratic revolution. The October Revolution began with armed uprisings in the cities and then spread to the countryside, while the Chinese revolution won nation-wide victory through the encirclement of the cities from the rural areas and the final capture of the cities.

Comrade Mao Tse-tung's great merit lies in the fact that he has succeeded in integrating the universal truth of Marxism-Leninism with the concrete practice of the Chinese revolution and has enriched and developed Marxism-Leninism by his masterly generalisation and summation of the experience gained during the Chinese people's protracted revolutionary struggle.

Comrade Mao Tse-tung's theory of people's war has been proved by the long practice of the Chinese revolution to be in accord with the objective laws of such wars and to be invincible. It has not only been valid for China, it is a great contribution to the revolutionary struggles of the oppressed nations and peoples throughout the world.

The people's war led by the Chinese Communist Party, comprising the War of Resistance and the Revolutionary Civil Wars, lasted for twenty-two years. It constitutes the most drawn-out and most complex people's war led by the proletariat in modern history, and it has been the richest in experience. . . .

Appendix B. 3. Long Live the Victory of People's War

In the world today, all the imperialists headed by the United States and their lackeys, without exception, are strengthening their state machinery, and especially their armed forces. U.S. imperialism, in particular, is carrying out armed aggression and suppression everywhere.

What should the oppressed nations and the oppressed people do in the face of wars of aggression and armed suppression by the imperialists and their lackeys? Should they submit and remain slaves in perpetuity? Or should they rise in resistance and fight for their liberation?

Comrade Mao Tse-tung answered this question in vivid terms. . . . In view of the fact that some people were afflicted with the fear of the imperialists and reactionaries, Comrade Mao Tse-tung put forward his famous thesis that 'imperialism and all reactionaries are paper tigers'. He said,

> All reactionaries are paper tigers. In appearance, the reaction-aries are terrifying, but in reality they are not so powerful. From a long-term point of view, it is not the reactionaries but the people who are really powerful.

The history of people's war in China and other countries provides conclusive evidence that the growth of the people's revolutionary forces from weak and small beginnings into strong and large forces is a universal law of development of class struggle, a universal law of development of people's war. A people's war inevitably meets with many difficulties, with ups and downs and setbacks in the course of its development, but no force can alter its general trend towards inevitable triumph.

Comrade Mao Tse-tung points out that we must despise the enemy strategically and take full account of him tactically. . . . Dialectical and historical materialism teaches us that what is important primarily is not that which at the given moment seems to be durable and yet is already beginning to die away, but that which is arising and developing, even though at the given moment it may not appear to be durable, for only that which is arising and developing is invincible. . . .

Comrade Mao Tse-tung's theory of people's war solves not only the problem of daring to fight a people's war, but also that of how to wage it. . . . It must be emphasised that Comrade Mao Tse-tung's theory of the establishment of rural revolutionary base areas and the encirclement of the cities from the countryside is of outstanding and universal practical importance for the present revolutionary struggles of all the oppressed nations and peoples, and particularly for the revolutionary struggles of the oppressed nations and peoples in Asia, Africa and Latin America against imperialism and its lackeys. . . .

Taking the entire globe, if North America and Western Europe can be called 'the cities of the world', then Asia, Africa and Latin America constitute 'the rural areas of the world'. Since World War II, the proletarian revolutionary movement has for various reasons been temporarily held back in the North American and West European capitalist countries, while the people's revolutionary movement in Asia, Africa and Latin America has been growing vigorously. In a sense, the contemporary world revolution also presents a picture of the encirclement of cities by the rural areas. In the final analysis, the whole cause of world revolution hinges on the revolutionary struggles of the Asian, African and Latin American peoples who make up the overwhelming majority of the world's population. The socialist countries should regard it as their internationalist duty to support the people's revolutionary struggles in Asia, Africa and Latin America. . . .

Comrade Mao Tse-tung has pointed out that, in the epoch since the October Revolution, anti-imperialist revolution in any colonial or semi-colonial country is no longer part of the old bourgeois, or capitalist world revolution, but is part of the new world revolution, the proletarian-socialist world revolution. [He] has formulated a complete theory of the new-democratic revolution. He indicated that this revolution, which is different from all others, can only be, nay must be, a revolution against imperialism, feudalism and bureaucrat-capitalism waged by the broad masses of the people under the leadership of the proletariat. . . .

The new-democratic revolution leads to socialism, and not to capitalism. . . . The Chinese revolution provides a successful lesson for making a thoroughgoing national-democratic revolution under the leadership of the proletariat; it likewise provides a successful lesson for the timely transition from the national-democratic revolution to the socialist revolution under the leadership of the proletariat.

Mao Tse-tung's thought has been the guide to the victory of the Chinese revolution. It has integrated the universal truth of Marxism-Leninism with the concrete practice of the Chinese revolution and creatively developed Marxism-Leninism, thus adding new weapons to the arsenal of Marxism-Leninism. . . .

Since World War II, people's war has increasingly demonstrated its power in Asia, Africa and Latin America. The people's of China, Korea, Vietnam, Laos, Cuba, Indonesia, Algeria and other countries have waged people's wars against the imperialists and their lackeys and won great victories. The classes leading these people's wars may vary, and so may the breadth and depth of mass mobilisation and the extent of victory, but the victories in these people's wars have very much weakened and pinned down the forces of imperialism, upset the u.s. imperialist plan to launch a world war, and become mighty factors defending world peace.

Today, the conditions are more favourable than ever before for the waging of people's wars by the revolutionary peoples of Asia, Africa and Latin America against u.s. imperialism and its lackeys. . . u.s. imperialism is stronger, but also more vulnerable, than any imperialism of the past. It sets itself against the people of the whole world, including the people of the United States. Its human, military, material and financial resources are far from sufficient for the realisation of its ambition of dominating the whole world. u.s. imperialism has further weakened itself by occupying so many places in the world, over-reaching itself, stretching its fingers out wide and dispersing its strength, with its rear so far away and its supply lines so long. As Comrade Mao Tse-tung has said: 'Wherever it commits aggression, it puts a new noose around its neck'. . . . The people subjected to its aggression are having a trial of strength with u.s. imperialism neither in Washington nor New York, neither in Honolulu nor Florida, but are fighting for independence and freedom on their own soil. Once they are mobilised on a broad scale, they will have inexhaustible strength. Thus superiority will belong not to the United States but to the people subjected to its aggression. The latter, though apparently weak and small, are really more powerful than u.s. imperialism. . . .

Everything is divisible. And so is this colossus of u.s. imperialism. It can be split up and defeated. The people's of Asia, Africa, Latin America and other regions can destroy it piece by piece, some striking at its head and others at its feet. That is why the greatest fear of u.s. imperialism is that people's wars will be launched in different parts of the world, and particularly in Asia, Africa and Latin America, and why it regards people's war as a mortal danger.

u.s. imperialism relies solely on its nuclear weapons to intimidate people. But these weapons cannot save u.s. imperialism from its doom. Nuclear weapons cannot be used lightly. u.s. imperialism has been condemned by the people of the whole world for its towering crime of dropping two atom bombs on Japan. If it uses nuclear weapons again, it will become isolated in the extreme. Moreover, the u.s. monopoly of nuclear weapons has long been broken; u.s. imperialism has these weapons, but others have them too. If it threatens other countries with nuclear weapons, U.S. imperialism will expose its own country to the same threat. . . .

Vietnam is the most convincing current example of a victim of aggression defeating U.S. imperialism by a people's war. The United States has made south Vietnam a testing ground for the suppression of people's war. . . .

The Khrushchev revisionists have come to the rescue of U.S. imperialism just when it is most panic-stricken and helpless in its efforts to cope with people's war. Working hand in glove with the U.S. imperialists, they are doing their utmost to spread all kinds of arguments against people's war and, wherever they can, they are scheming to undermine it by overt or covert means.

The fundamental reason why the Khrushchev revisionists are opposed to people's war is that they have no faith in the masses and are afraid of U.S. imperialism, of war and of revolution. . . . . [They] insist that a nation without nuclear weapons is incapable of defeating an enemy with nuclear weapons, whatever methods of fighting it may adopt. This is tantamount to saying that anyone without nuclear weapons is destined to come to grief, destined to be bullied and annihilated, and must either capitulate to the enemy when confronted with his nuclear weapons or come under the 'protection' of some other nuclear power and submit to its beck and call. Isn't this the jungle law of survival par excellence? Isn't this helping the imperialists in their nuclear blackmail? Isn't this openly forbidding people to make revolution? . . .

The Khrushchev revisionists maintain that a single spark in any part of the globe may touch off a world nuclear conflagration and bring destruction to mankind. If this were true, our planet would have been destroyed time and time again. There have been wars of national liberation throughout the twenty years since World War II. But has any single one of them developed into a world war? . . .

The Khrushchev revisionists claim that if their general line of 'peaceful coexistence, peaceful transition and peaceful competition' is followed, the oppressed will be liberated and 'a world without weapons, without armed forces and without wars' will come into being. But the inexorable fact is that imperialism and reaction headed by the United States are zealously priming their war machine and are daily engaged in sanguinary suppression of the revolutionary peoples and in the threat and use of armed force against independent countries. The kind of rubbish peddled by the Khrushchev revisionists has already taken a great toll of lives in a number of countries. Are these painful lessons, paid for in blood, still insufficient? . . .

We know that war brings destruction, sacrifice and suffering on the people. But the destruction, sacrifice and suffering will be much greater if no resistance is offered to imperialist armed aggression and the people become willing slaves. The sacrifice of a small number of people in revolutionary wars is repaid by security for whole nations, whole countries and even the whole of mankind; temporary suffering is repaid by lasting or even perpetual peace and happiness. War can temper the people and push history forward. In this sense, war is a great school. . . .

. . . Of course, every revolution in a country stems from the demands of its own people. Only when the people in a country are awakened, mobilised, organised and armed can they overthrow the reactionary rule of imperialism and its lackeys through struggle; their role cannot be replaced or taken over by any people from outside. In this sense, revolution cannot be imported. But this does not exclude mutual sympathy and support on the part of revolutionary peoples in their struggles against the imperialists and their lackeys. Our support and aid to other revolutionary peoples serves precisely to help their self-reliant struggle. . . .

The u.s. imperialists are now clamouring for another trial of strength with the Chinese people, for another large-scale ground war on the Asian mainland. If they insist on following in the footsteps of the Japanese fascists, well then, they may do so, if they please. The Chinese people definitely have ways of their own for coping with a u.s. imperialist war of aggression. Our methods are no secret. The most important one is still mobilisation of the people, reliance on the people, making every one a soldier and waging a people's war.

We want to tell the u.s. imperialists once again that the vast ocean of several hundred million Chinese people in arms will be more than enough to submerge your few million aggressor troops. If you dare to impose war on us, we shall gain freedom of action. It will then not be up to you to decide how the war will be fought. We shall fight in the ways most advantageous to us to destroy the enemy and wherever the enemy can be most easily destroyed. . . .

4. Kwangtung CCP Committee Meeting on Mao's Instruction (August 1966)*

The Kwangtung Provincial ccp Committee recently held an enlarged meeting of the Standing Committee which seriously studied

* Text of report broadcast on Canton regional service, No. 2, at 04.40 GMT, August 13, 1966. Translation, with minor abridgement, from BBC *Summary of World Broadcasts*, FE/2247/B/3.

Chairman Mao's great instruction and decided to adopt ten measures to implement it resolutely. . . .

The great, far-reaching significance of Chairman Mao's instruction. The meeting held: Chairman Mao's instruction constitutes an extremely important and brilliant document of historical significance, a further development and a new outline of the theory [he] put forward concerning the general line, the great leap forward and the people's commune, a new epoch making development of Marxism-Leninism. This document will have an extremely far-reaching influence on promoting the three great revolutionary campaigns: the socialist revolution, and socialist construction, and on consolidating national defence. This document exhibits to us a magnificent blueprint of communism, points out the concrete road to the elimination of the three great differences and the transition to communism. This is a programme for the thorough completion of the socialist revolution and the transition to communism in China. It is also a programme for the future realisation of communism in the whole world. The implementation of this instruction of Chairman Mao will accelerate the revolutionisation of the workers, peasants, soldiers, students and commercial circles. All factories, enterprises, offices, schools, army units, people's communes will all become big communist schools for studying Mao Tse-tung's thinking, big schools for learning politics, military affairs and culture. This will accelerate the revolutionisation of the masses of people on the broadest breadth and to the greatest depth, making all the 700 million people, armed with Mao Tse-tung's thinking, critics of the old world and builders and defenders of the new world. The implementation of this instruction of Chairman Mao will link all our current work with diminishing the three great differences step by step and the transition to the great ideal of communism, raise spontaneity and overcome blindness, and steadfastly advance towards communism along the socialist road. Previously, we always thought that the scientific prediction of Marx and Engels on the elimination of the three great differences was a matter of the distant future. Having studied this instruction of Chairman Mao, we feel that it is already on our agenda, and something quite tangible. The implementation of [his] instruction . . . will greatly speed up the socialist revolution and socialist construction of our country. China, with a population amounting to one-fourth of the whole world's, is raising high the great Red flag of Mao Tse-tung's thinking, promoting what is proletarian and eliminating what is bourgeois, preventing and opposing revisionism, rooting out thoroughly feudalism, capitalism and revisionism and steadily promoting ideological revolutionisation. This will produce great spiritual as well as material forces, bringing about a great liberation of the productive forces. It will be possible to make comprehensive use of all manpower and resources, fully tapping the potentials of socialist production, spurring on the development of production and creating large quantities of material wealth for the State, thus making our country the greatest and strongest socialist power.

The implementation of this instruction of Chairman Mao will greatly strengthen combat preparedness, giving full play to the great might of people's war. Once war breaks out all people will be soldiers, guaranteeing victory over the enemy under any circumstances and making our country forever invincible.

The implementation of his instruction . . . will also bring closer the relationship between cadres and the masses, between the army and the people, and between the leadership and the led. It will greatly promote the revolutionisation of the offices, so that the socialist superstructure will offer still better service for the socialist economic basis, promoting the consolidation and development of the socialist system. The great instruction of Chairman Mao is the guiding orientation of all our work. We loyally support this instruction, and will resolutely implement it in all actual work. . . .

The ten great measures for the implementation of Chairman Mao's instruction.

A. The most fundamental measure is to turn the whole province into a big school for the study of Mao Tse-tung's thinking. It is necessary to raise still higher the great Red flag of Mao Tse-tung's thinking, and do still better in the creative study and application of Chairman Mao's works, to promote the revolutionisation of people's thinking. Chairman Mao's instruction demands that we promote what is proletarian and eliminate what is bourgeois, create conditions step by step to finally abolish all exploiting classes and exploitation systems and effect the transition to communism. People who are not revolutionised cannot shoulder this great historical task. Hence, workers, peasants, soldiers, students and commercial circles, and all sectors of the economy, must all implement completely Chairman Mao's instruction. They must, in their own work posts, take an active part in class struggle, in the socialist education campaign, and in the great proletarian cultural revolution, and criticise the bourgeoisie. Meanwhile they should also learn politics, military affairs and culture, becoming truly worker-peasant wielding both pen and sword. This is the general key link. Apart from this, the various fields should, in the light of their own characteristics, carry out their respective concrete tasks.

B. *Factories, mines and enterprises:* (1) All enterprises with suitable conditions should introduce in a big way the worker-peasant labour system, particularly factories, mines and enterprises with close relation with agriculture in the rural areas, county seats and townships. Existing enterprises and those built or extended in future should, in the light of the characteristics of their trade, respectively adopt the system of rotation workers, temporary workers, seasonal workers, or contracted workers with the communes and brigades, and gradually turn a number of permanent workers into worker-peasant workers. In building and construction departments and in highway maintenance work, a voluntary work system should be introduced step by step. All factories, mines and enterprises must make great efforts to improve their backward state and strive to reach progressive levels rapidly, to facilitate the introduction of the worker-peasant, pen-sword system. (2) In a methodical manner, remove some factories to the rural areas, particularly the existing processing industry which depends on farm and sideline products as raw materials, such as canning, preserved fruit, preserved food and vegetables, etc. These should either set up processing centres in the countryside where the raw materials are produced, or actively develop the processing industry within the collective economy. (3) All factories, mines, and enterprises with suitable conditions should engage in farm and sideline production. They should actively integrate the factory with the communes, having the factory lead the commune, etc., on a trial basis, thus integrating industry with agriculture. It is necessary to promote mutual support and co-operation between state and collective economy. State enterprises must energetically support collective economy. Under the united leadership of the Party committees the factories should lead the rural areas in four aspects, i.e., in politics, culture, production and technique. The population of cities, townships, and factories must be controlled.

C. *Finance and trade departments:* (1) Commercial points and networks in rural areas should hand over some of their work, such as being agents for purchasing, selling, storing . . . and most processing of subsidiary foodstuffs, to the rural communes, brigades and productions teams. (2) The basic-level finance and trade units should put into effect the system of rotation workers who will be recommended by the collective. These will include workers for commerce, food, supply and marketing, finance and tax-collection, banking and the granting of loans. The production teams will select youths of good origin, good politics and thinking and with a certain cultural level to become workers by rotation. For temporary labour force, use widely seasonal workers, temporary workers and assistant workers, who will help on market days. Put into effect also the worker-peasant system in being agents for purchasing and selling. (3) All small business and peddling in the basic-level commerce in the countryside of the province must be thoroughly reformed.

D. *State-run agricultural, forestry and reclamation farms:* (1) In future the development of state-run farming, forestry and reclamation must follow the line of joint management by the State and the commune, doing more with less funds. All experimental or model farms and fine-strain seed cultivation farms may also adopt this method. Existing state-run farms, forestry and reclamation farms must also at the same time be people's communes. (2) Existing state-run agricultural, forestry and reclamation farms must energetically introduce the system of rotation workers and temporary workers, having the farms lead the brigades, integrating the farms with the communes, going step by step towards ownership by the whole people. (3) All agricultural, forestry and reclamation farms must diversify their economy with agriculture as the main pursuit, so that, under their respective conditions they will step by step succeed in becoming self-supporting in management expenses, and in staple and non-staple foodstuffs such as grain, edible oil, meat etc. (4) All enterprises of the agricultural system such as management structures of dykes and reservoirs must all do production work as a sideline, so that they will become step by step more than self-supporting.

E. *Rural people's communes:* (1) In accordance with the characteristics of the communes which are big and public, a combination of government administration and commune, and comprising worker, peasant, soldier, student and commercial circles, the communes should step by step develop into basic level organisations with agriculture as the main pursuit and at the same time running industry and wielding pen and sword. At the same time, in accordance with the principle of comprehensive management and overall development of agriculture, forestry, animal husbandry, sideline production and fishery, they should, with agriculture as the main pursuit, run one or two major industrial and sideline productions in the light of local conditions; with food grains as the main crop, they should grow one or two major industrial crops. In the light of local conditions, step by step set up small farms, small forestry farms, agricultural science centres and agricultural machinery stations. Fishery and agriculture should pursue comprehensive management. The present state of fishery and agriculture being divided among families along the coast should be changed.

(2) Actively and methodically develop commune industry, handicraft industry and joint management of industry and handicrafts by commune and brigade, by several brigades jointly, or by individual brigades. The provincial industrial departments are determined to help communes to develop industry through running small sugar refineries, small paper mills, small pottery factories, small electric power stations, small processing factories and short-distance transport teams. This is a correct orientation. (3) Every year the communes must spontaneously and methodically send peasants to factories to be rotation workers, seasonal workers or temporary workers, to join the army, to attend various schools or training courses, to be 'political apprentices', to take part in various political campaigns, etc. so that the people's communes will foster more and more all-round master hands, accelerating the realisation of mechanisation and raising the standard in science and technology, making the commune a basic level unit of workers, peasants, soldiers, students and commercial circles.

F. *Education:* (1) Schools must first solve the problem of the leadership. Through the socialist education campaign and the great proletarian culture revolution the leadership of the schools must be truly in the hands of the proletariat. Schools in the countryside should, under the leadership of the commune Party committees and the brigade Party branches, take an active part in the three great revolutions. (2) Reform the education system of schools, resolutely implementing the principles of education serving proletarian politics and education integrating with productive labour, so that schools truly become sites for carrying out the three great revolutionary struggles. The school years are to be shortened. Students must learn industry, agriculture, and military affairs, becoming labourers with culture. Existing work-farmwork-study schools must be run well. All-day schools must be methodically and gradually transformed into work-farmwork-study schools. Schools built in future must all be located in the countryside without exception. Universities, colleges and middle schools in the cities must go to factories and the rural areas to do labour at fixed periods. (3) Factories and enterprises must run spare-time universities: counties must set up labour universities, communes must set up agricultural middle schools. Students should come from the communes and go back to them, and be fostered into new-type labourers that combine mental and manual labour. In the rural areas, farmwork-study primary schools are to be developed actively on the basis of the village, and state-run and folk-run primary schools are to be unified gradually.

G. *Cultural and art activities:* (1) Launch widely worker-peasant-soldier cultural and art activities, the launching and support of which should be regarded as the major task by cultural and art offices and bodies. Outstanding cultural and art activists among the workers, peasants, soldiers, should be the main source of future professional cultural and art workers. (2) Culture and art must serve the worker, peasant and soldier masses. Professional cultural and art workers must, for long periods, unconditionally go among the worker, peasant and soldier masses, regarding the rural areas as their basic points, taking root in the countryside and pursuing part-time farmwork and part-time cultural and art work, so that a truly proletarian cultural and art contingent can be fostered. Cultural and art bodies must adopt more often the form of light cavalry teams to serve the workers, peasants and soldiers directly and constantly in factories, the rural areas and the army units. Cultural and art workers should go deep into life in factories, the rural areas and the army units and create works that reflect the revolutionary struggle and production struggle of the workers, peasants and soldiers. (3) Rectify and reform old opera troupes. Old county opera troupes, in principle must be all turned into light cavalry cultural and art propaganda teams, presenting revolutionary modern-theme operas and serving the worker, peasant and soldier masses and proletarian politics.

H. *Tap labour potentials:* Organise the idle labour forces that are divorced from production, and send them to the front line of production to reclaim wasteland, till the land and do farmwork, forestry, animal husbandry and sideline production. In cities and towns, set up street industry and handicraft production.

I. *Militia work:* Further give prominence to politics, study Chairman Mao's works in a big way, study Chairman Mao's strategic and tactical thinking on people's war, strengthen militia building in all sectors of economy and the necessary military training, make a success of putting militia work on a solid basis politically, organisationally and militarily, so that the militia will truly become a production force in peacetime and a fighting force in wartime.

J. *Accelerate the revolutionisation of offices and cadres:* The superstructure must serve better the economic basis. Structures should be resolutely stream-lined and organisation systems reformed in accordance with the spirit of Chairman Mao's instruction, putting into effect the revolutionisation of offices. Lids are to be removed in a big way, sweeping away all ideas, viewpoints, regulations and systems that are unfavourable to the diminishing of the three differences, the realisation of the worker-peasant, pen-sword system and the development of the all-people and collective economy and establishing in a big way new ideas, viewpoints, regulations and systems. Party and government leadership offices of the provincial, special districts, municipalities and counties must streamline the management and simplify administration. Office cadres must still better go deep into the basic levels to stay at points, strengthen the mass viewpoint, and make a success of investigations and study. Cadres must particularly be made to take part in productive labour. The system of cadres taking part in physical labour ruled in the past by the Centre and Provincial CCP Committee, must be persisted in.

5. *Make Experiments on Agricultural Science in the Midst of Production*

By Liu Keng-ling and Chian Chao-yü*

Beginning in the spring of 1960, together with other units concerned, we set up a rural base point in Ch'iyang *hsien*, Hunan province, and studied there the problem of controlling the 'autumn sedentariness' of rice plants in slime fields. After several years of efforts, the problem has eventually been solved. How was it solved? What enlightening lessons have we agricultural scientific and technical personnel learned?

I. Agricultural Science Research must Serve Agricultural Production. In the past, when a number of agricultural scientific and technical personnel conducted scientific research, they mostly copied foreign practices. They spent by far the greater part of their energy reading documents, observing and analysing samples, drawing charts, and writing theses and reports. They studied what other countries were studying. When results were obtained, these research workers would compare them with foreign documents. They would consider the results established if they agreed with the research results obtained by foreigners. If the results did not agree, they themselves would not dare believe in them. Accustomed to such a practice, some agricultural science workers even thought that this was the only way to catch up with the international standards of science. We youths once came under their influence.

Not long after the liberation, for instance, some people wanted very much to apply a foreign farming system to China. They did

* Published in *Hung-ch'i*, No. 13, December 6, 1965: translation, with minor modifications, from SCMM, No. 505.

so without any regard for conditions and possible results, and thought that this was the direction for research on agricultural science and techniques. We remember that, when we had just graduated from university, we tried to adopt this farming system in a district, but we were criticised and opposed by the farm workers and the masses around. Full of enthusiasm, we had wanted to do some work for the people, but we met with this setback the moment we left school. We felt very unhappy. We asked a teacher about this, and he said: 'Those who conduct scientific research have to bear criticism. Many great scientists in history were criticised. There is nothing strange about this. Just stand your ground.'

These words sounded very soothing at the time. But the more we thought about them afterward, the more they appeared to be improper. Agricultural science and techniques personnel were to serve the people. How could they 'stand their ground' and take no heed of the criticism of the people? . . . Reading our minds, the leadership promptly pointed out to us that, to make our agricultural science research work welcomed and supported by the masses, we must first establish clearly the policy of letting agricultural science serve production and the masses. In order to develop, agricultural science must be combined with the practice of agricultural production. . . . At this time, we also repeatedly studied Chairman Mao's teachings concerning the need for educated youths to combine themselves with the workers and the peasants, and discussed the policy of letting science serve production. Only then did we give up many personal plans and make up our minds to defy hardship and difficulty. We would go to the rural areas and into the midst of practice. We would go to the front line of agricultural production to conduct research.

In the spring of 1960, the Scientific and Technical Commission of Hunan Province, the Provincial Department of Agriculture and the Academy of Agricultural Science organised a force jointly with the comrades of our Soil and Fertiliser Research Institute of the Chinese Academy of Sciences. This force went to Kuanshanp'ing production brigade, Wenfushih people's commune, Ch'iyang *hsien*, and set up a base point of agricultural science research there. It was to study improvement of low-output rice fields in the south.

At the time, a cold wave had just set in, and the masses were taking emergency measures in protecting seedlings from the cold. We actively plunged ourselves into this struggle of the masses. In the middle of the night, together with the masses, we applied fertiliser and covered the seedlings with grass, lighted fires and made smoke, dug ditches to drain off water, and observed changes in the temperature of the slime and that of water. After more than ten days of struggle to protect the seedlings, we made a good impression on the masses. We ate, lived, laboured, and held discussions together with the masses. We laboured actively and with initiative. We chose the hardest jobs to do. We were not afraid of filth or hard work. Some commune members said to us: 'You wear glasses and leather shoes. But you are really modest and work really hard.' We felt very glad to hear these words. We knew that we had done right. We were all in high spirits, and our relations with the masses became closer. Many poor peasants and lower middle peasants confided their secrets to us, and told us about the problems in local production. They entertained high hopes of experiment and research on the improvement of low-output fields. This greatly encouraged us and filled us with strength.

Actively supported by the masses, we proceeded to learn the characteristics of local production. We discovered that, in a large number of slime fields after winter drying, 'autumn sedentariness' of rice plants was a problem which needed urgently to be solved. By 'autumn sedentariness' is meant that, after transplanting, rice seedlings did not resume a green colour for a long time, during which their blades turned yellow, their tips withered, their roots turned black and they ceased to grow. The result of this would be a sharp decrease in output. This phenomenon . . . was more prevalent in the south. In Ch'iyang *hsien*, for instance, over half of all the rice fields were threatened by it. Serious harm could result. Once the phenomenon occurred, the damage could not be undone by means of ordinary technical measures. A serious decrease in rice output would result. Only 100 to 200 catties could be gathered per *mow*. What is more, no successful crop could be gathered for two to three years in a row. The local peasants said: 'One dry winter, three fruitless years.' . . . [but] After several years of efforts, . . . [it] was eventually solved. This greatly raised the local grain output. In Kuanshanp'ing production brigade, the grain output, which was 350 catties per *mow* on an average in 1960, rose to 680 catties per *mow* in 1964.

II. Summing Up Masses' Production Experiences, Learning Nature's Laws. Is it possible to accomplish something worthwhile by conducting scientific research in the rural areas? At first, we were sceptical. We had a metaphysical viewpoint. We set production and science against each other and experience and theory against each other. We thought that 'the rural areas could only carry out production; they could not produce science', and that 'the experiences of the masses will always be experiences only; they cannot rise to the status of scientific theories'. Though we had studied Chairman Mao's *On Practice* and though we agreed with the words that practice was the foundation of theory and the criterion of truth, yet in our minds we never felt assured but were half sceptical as to whether or not production practice could give rise to science, and whether or not the experiences of the peasants had scientific value.

As a result of several years of practice, we have come to realise gradually that the vast rural areas are the principal grounds for agricultural science activities, and that the summed up production experiences of the masses of peasants, are the foundation on which the development of agricultural science is advanced. Our original doubts were dispelled one by one.

How did we proceed with the research work after we had chosen the control of 'autumn sedentariness' of rice plants as our research topic? At first, we merely studied books, searched for documents and looked up reference materials. The books, though offering an abundance of explanations and hypotheses of various kinds, did not afford many practical methods. Some books stated that 'autumn sedentariness' was due to lack of sulphur in the soil. Other books stated that it was due to lack of silicon. Still others stated that it was due to the fact that 'the soil is lacking in humus so that good granular structures cannot be formed'. Yet others stated that it was due to 'ferrous poisons resulting from prolonged soaking'. We tested all the methods mentioned by the books, but the results were disappointing. What should we do? As taught by Chairman Mao, we consulted the masses. We began by summing up the experiences of the masses of peasants. We conducted investigation extensively and discussed and studied the matter together with the peasants. We first conducted a survey in Kuanshanp'ing. Next, we gradually extended the survey to the whole of Ch'iyang *hsien* and then to other *hsien*, including Ch'itung, Hengyang and Shaotung.

From these surveys and from our direct experience of participation in labour, we acquired an abundance of perceptual knowledge. For instance, concerning the laws of occurrence of 'autumn sedentariness' of rice plants, the masses told us that, where the topographical situation was the same, 'autumn sedentariness' occurred in slime but did not occur in yellow mud; that, among slime fields, only those which were dry in winter gave rise to 'autumn sedentariness', while those which were soaked in winter did not give rise to it; that, in slime fields which were dry in winter, the rice seedlings which were transplanted earlier developed 'autumn sedentariness' to a greater extent, while those which were transplanted later developed it to a lesser extent; that, among seedlings which were transplanted late, those which were transplanted at a time when the atmospheric temperature and the earth temperature were low developed 'autumn sedentariness' to a greater extent, while those transplanted at a time when the atmospheric temperature had risen developed it to a lesser extent; and that 'autumn sedentariness' occurred to a greater extent in fields with accumulations of cold water and to a smaller extent in fields without accumulations of cold water. In view of these phenomena, we realised that the 'autumn sedentariness' of rice plants was closely connected with environmental conditions and agricultural technical measures.

But what technical measures were to be adopted to prevent 'autumn sedentariness'? Chou P'ei-hsiang, an old poor peasant in Kuanshanp'ing, told us that he had obtained good results from application of small quantities of chicken or duck excreta to seedling bases. Hsü Hsien-hsiu, an old peasant in the mountainous district of Ch'iyang *hsien*, told us that good results could be obtained from application of pulverised old bricks to fields. . . . The old peasants in Ch'itung *hsien* told us that good results could be obtained from application of pulverised cow bones to the roots of seedlings. Other experiences showed that 'autumn sedentariness' of rice plants could be reduced by application of bits of burned clay, soot or rice husk ash to bases. We made scientific experiments on the basis of these experiences of the masses, and proved that all these methods were effective for reducing the 'autumn sedentariness' of rice plants. The effect of pulverised cow bones . . . was particularly pronounced. By analysis, we found that this was due to the effect of phosphorus.

In 1961, we made an experiment with calcium phosphate. The experiment worked the very first time, resulting in a marked increase in output. Application of 40 to 50 catties of calcium phosphate per *mow* could increase rice output by 100 to 150 catties. After that, 157 experiments were made in 14 production brigades, and similar results in terms of output increases were yielded. From the experience of application of phosphorous fertiliser . . . we realised that the 'autumn sedentariness' of rice plants was caused by the lack of phosphorus in the soil. But for the light shed by the experiences of the masses, we could not have learned that it was caused by this; while, if we had simply repeated the masses' methods of applying bits of chicken or duck excreta, applying pulverised old bricks, and applying pulverised cow bones, not only would the shortage of these materials have made application over a vast surface impossible, but our ignorance of the real cause would have hindered adoption of measures suited to the local conditions, flexible adoption of the methods, and further improvement. . . .

Appendix B. 5. Make Experiments on Agricultural Science . . .

Chemical analysis showed that the phosphorus content of the soil in the fields affected by 'autumn sedentariness' was not small. The reason why the supply of phosphorus was inadequate was that, in the process in which slime dried up, effective phosphorus became solidified and could not be absorbed and assimilated by the plants. Hence, activation of solidified phosphorus became another important research task. Analysis and experiment showed that the peasants could increase the content of effective phosphorus of the soil by 30–50 per cent by storing water to soak the fields in winter. By means of frequent plowing, frequent raking and breaking up of soil lumps, the peasants could shorten the period of soaking and speed up the activation of phosphorus. The peasants had the experience of making compost with mountain plants and applying pig manure. It had the effect of breaking up soil lumps, activating phosphorus, and preventing solidification of phosphorus. . . .

Through summing up the experiences of the masses, we acquired a great deal of knowledge about the laws governing the internal changes of the soil in slime fields. As a result, we could take a great deal more initiative when studying technical measures for the control of 'autumn sedentariness' of rice plants. For activating the phosphorus in the soil and increasing organic matter in the soil, we thought of planting green manure crops in addition to increasing the application of pig manure and gathering mountain plants. But planting green manure crops called for digging ditches to drain off water. This meant conversion of winter water fields into winter dry fields and was contradictory to the local experience of storing water to soak the fields in winter. As these fields dried up in winter, the phosphorus in the soil was solidified. Lack of phosphorus in the soil would not only prevent the growth of green manure crops but also cause 'autumn sedentariness' of rice plants grown in the following year. This would mean a decrease in output.

Bearing this special fact in mind, we solved the problem by means of letting big fertility feed on small fertility. When green manure crops were grown, a small quantity of phosphorous fertiliser was applied first. This caused the green manure crops to grow. Secretions from their root systems and organic acids produced by the process of decomposition then activated the solidified phosphorus in the soil. The facts proved that this was a correct method. Green manure crops developed very rapidly. In 1964, green manure acreage accounted for over 60 per cent of the total rice acreage in Kuanshanp'ing. A new farming system was thus put into practice, and the soil was enriched. In fields where green manure crops were grown in three or four years successively, effective phosphorus was abundant, and rice output was comparatively high even where no phosphorous fertiliser was applied. Thus, planting green manure crops was a basic measure for improving slime fields liable to 'autumn sedentariness' of rice plants.

How should we apply the law that the phosphorus in the soil is activated by raising of soil temperature, so as to insure the healthy growth of the seedlings? The experiences of the peasants were that an attempt should be made to grow a late crop of rice in slime fields which dried up in winter. Transplanting of the rice seedlings was to wait until the soil temperature had risen. Where there were accumulations of cold water in the fields, these should be drained off. These measures were effective for safeguarding the growth of the seedlings. However, in July and August, the soil temperature rose, and a large quantity of phosphorus in the soil was activated. At such a time, if only one rice crop a year was grown, the rice plants would not need phosphorous fertiliser, and that which was applied would be wasted. Following this clue, we studied development of double cropping of rice. During the growth of the early rice crop, the soil temperature was very low, and not much of the phosphorous in the soil was activated. During its growth, the early rice crop needed phosphorous nutrients set free by green manure. As for the late rice crop, it needed only the phosphorous nutrients released by the soil.

The facts showed that this double rice cropping and green manure system was an economic and rational system in this district. It turned to full account the latent fertility of the soil. After experiments and demonstrations, the double rice cropping acreage of Kuanshanp'ing production brigade increased continuously. By 1965, it had developed to account for over 80 per cent of the total rice acreage. In many hitherto low-output slime fields, the two rice crops yielded a total of over 1,000 catties per *mow*.

III. Popularising Fruits of Research, Developing Agricultural Science. When research had borne fruit, what was the next step to be taken? According to past practices, our task would have been completed the moment we completed the thesis or report and submitted it to the higher levels. In the past, we completely depended on the agricultural administration departments and techniques popularisation departments to apply the fruits of research. We erroneously thought that it would do more harm than good for research personnel to do the work of demonstration and popularisation. The leadership repeatedly pointed out to us that the purpose of scientific research was to develop production, and the purpose of cultivating demonstration plots was to guide the surface from a point. We must popularise the fruits of research among the masses before we could comprehensively examine the degree of accuracy of these fruits and enrich them with the experiences and suggestions of the masses which were to be absorbed. In our practical work, we gradually realised ourselves that popularisation of the fruits of research was actually a continuation of the work of scientific research and evaluation in the midst of the masses and in a bigger scope. We could not further perfect the fruits of research except by examining them, revising them, making them more complete and improving them in the midst of the production practice of the masses. . . .

During the past few years, under the leadership of the Party committee of Ch'iyang *hsien* and because we attached importance to returning the fruits of research into the midst of production practice in big fields, we carried out a great deal of work for popularising the fruits of scientific research. In 1963, the whole *hsien* organised 50 thousand *mow* of phosphorus fertiliser experimental fields. In 1964, it organised 70 thousand *mow* of phosphorous fertiliser demonstration fields. . . . The results of the demonstration and popularisation also showed that application of phosphorus fertiliser not only produced marked effects in slime fields but also produced good effects in over ten types of soils including heavy clay and poor soils with accumulations of cold water. This enriched our experiences concerning suiting application of phosphorus fertiliser to each particular type of soil. . . .

From 1960 to the present, under the leadership of Party committees at various levels in Hunan province, and on the basis of summing up the experiences of the masses, we discovered effective ways for controlling 'autumn sedentariness' of rice plants in slime fields; Ch'iyang *hsien* improved 180 thousand *mow* of low-output fields and raised output by 30 per cent. Hunan province energetically popularised the experiences of Ch'iyang *hsien* in parts of Hengyang, Lingling, Shaoyang and Hsiangt'an administrative districts where the conditions were similar. The production increasing effect was also very conspicuous. Five years' practice of research on control of 'autumn sedentariness' of rice plants in slime fields has made us realise deeply that we agricultural scientific and technical personnel must regard the thought of Mao Tse-tung as our weapon, go deep into the front line of agricultural production, sum up the experiences of the masses of peasants, grasp the key production problems which need urgently to be solved, and conduct research on them. Only thus can we develop agricultural science and advance agricultural production.

6. *Basic Experience in Revolutionising the Tach'ing Oil Field*

By Hsü Chin-ch'iang*

Under Party leadership and thanks to the concern and support of various related quarters, workers of the Tach'ing Oil Field in the 1960–63 period overcame innumerable difficulties and succeeded in completing this huge oil field [development] at a very high speed. . . . A first-class, modern and huge petroleum base has been built, a force of revolutionised workers, armed with the thought of Mao Tse-tung, has been trained and tempered, and, at the same time, there has been established a socialist mineral exploitation area of a new type, combining town and countryside, industry and agriculture, and government and enterprise. The victory of the battle for creating Tach'ing Oil Field is a victory for the thought of Mao Tse-tung, a victory for the Party's general line.

The road along which [the creators of] Tach'ing Oil Field [have] travelled is a road for the operation of socialist enterprises according to the thought of Mao Tse-tung. For the past several years, Tach'ing has always used the thought of Mao Tse-tung as its guide, persevered in the Party's general line for socialist reconstruction, and taken class struggle and the struggle between the two roads as the level. It has learned from the PLA in a big way, brought politics to the fore and opened up a road for China's industrialisation. . . .

In order to persist in this correct direction and way, it is imperative to draw a line of demarcation with capitalism and revisionism. This is the struggle between two ideas and two roads for running a socialist enterprise. . . . After six years of hard work, we have gained, in the main, the following nine points of understanding with respect to the realisation and continual deepening of the revolutionisation of the enterprise:

I. Class Struggle Must Be Used as the Key Link. . . . Our enterprise is a socialist enterprise. It is one where the proletariat make revolution and undertake construction. It is a ground for the three great revolutionary movements: class struggle, production struggle and scientific experiment. This ground must be occupied by us employing the proletarian stand, viewpoint and method and proletarian

* Published (under the general slogan heading, 'Hold High the Great Red Banner of the Thought of Mao Tse-tung: Further Deepen the Revolutionising of Enterprises') in *Chin-chi Yen-chiu* (Economic Research), No. 4, April 20, 1966; translation, with minor modifications, from SCMM, No. 538.

ideas and style of work. . . . Extremely fallacious are the viewpoint and practice which hold that an enterprise is engaged in nothing but production and which separate revolution from construction and class struggle from the production struggle and scientific experiment. Without carrying out class struggle, there will not be revolution; instead, there will be capitalism and revisionism. . . .

To carry out class struggle, we must rely on the masses, ferret out the landlords, rich peasants, counter-revolutionaries and wicked elements hidden among the workers, and isolate them politically. We must strengthen the supervision of them by the masses and reform them through labour. . . . To carry out class struggle, we must give attention to preventing the emergence among certain cadres of the ideas of bureaucracy, graft, and abuse of authority, ideas which cause one to degenerate. To carry out class struggle, we must wage a resolute struggle against the exploiting classes' idea among a number of intellectuals that 'those who work with their brains should rule those who work with their hands'. To carry out class struggle, we must criticise the bourgeois individualist ideology of various shades and colourings and promote the socialist spirit which takes the principle of integration of collective interests with personal interests as the criterion for all words and deeds. . . .

II. Learn from PLA and Bring Politics to the Fore. In the operation of an enterprise, whether or not we should bring proletarian politics to the fore is a basic question of whether we should take the socialist road or the capitalist road. An enterprise run by the bourgeoisie exploits the workers by depending on the discipline of hunger and the policy of buying off [union leaders], while an enterprise run by the revisionists relies on material incentives and actually takes the road of capitalist restoration. . . . In order to put politics to the fore, we must wholeheartedly, honestly and unreservedly learn from the experience of the Liberation Army. . . . [Accordingly], we have concentrated on doing the following things well:

1. Primarily we grasped the creative study and application of Chairman Mao's works. To bring politics to the fore is to bring the thought of Mao Tse-tung to the front, that is, to arm the people with the thought of Mao Tse-tung. . . . We must persistently and untiringly turn the creative study and application of Chairman Mao's works into a regular mass movement, continuously raise the people's consciousness, and gradually turn the study of Chairman Mao's works into a conscious action. In this connection, the most fundamental thing is to study Chairman Mao's theory on class struggle and his philosophical thought, to transform the objective world while transforming the subjective world, and solidly establish

the revolutionary outlook on life and on the world. In studying Chairman Mao's works, we must make a special effort to apply them, and achieve five combinations: the combination of the study of Chairman Mao's works with the study of the Party's policies and guidelines; . . . with the study of the PLA's experience; . . . with the analysis of the situation and the task of one's unit; with criticism and self-criticism as well as thought reform; . . . and with the summing up of work experience.

2. It is necessary consciously to place politico-ideological leadership above all work. Politics is the commander and the soul; it must be used to command work and techniques. . . . Whether you are in charge of administrative work or technical work, you must first of all grasp politico-ideological leadership and through it give leadership to administrative or technical work. . . . Only in this way can work and techniques pass the test. . . .

3. It is necessary to make the political work organ really a command headquarters for politico-ideological work under the leadership of the Party committee. In putting politics first and strengthening politico-ideological work, we must establish an effective political work organ and institute a set of political work systems. . . .

4. Everybody must grasp living ideas. . . . An enterprise is faced with a host of problems which fall into two categories: ideological and production problems. But production problems often are caused by ideological problems. It would not be enough to depend for the prompt solution of these problems on the political work organ and political cadres alone. It is imperative to trust and rely on the masses; to mobilise everyone to do politico-ideological work and grasp living ideas; and to grasp the living ideas of everyone. . . . For instance, when one wins a battle, one is liable to slacken; so it is necessary to educate the workers to advance from victory to victory. When one finds the going smooth, one is liable to benumb oneself; so it is important to teach the workers to raise their vigilance. When the going is rough, one is likely to show fear of difficulties and hope for luck; so it is necessary to educate the workers in the need for hard work and plain living and to establish their confidence in their ability to win. When one is commended, one is likely to feel complacent; that is why we must energetically seek out the gaps and continuously raise the standards and requirements. When one suffers setbacks, one is liable to succumb to despair; that is why we must do everything to encourage exertion of big efforts. When a contest is on, one is likely to chase after big and quick results without paying attention to quality; and this is the reason why we stress top priority to quality. When there are many new hands, accidents are

likely to occur; so it is necessary to unfold technical training and pay heed to safety. And so on and so forth.

5. Grasp the five-good movement and intensify basic-level construction. The five-good movement (for five-good workshops and five-good workers) has as its principal content the following basic-level work in an enterprise: to bring politics to the fore and strengthen regular politico-ideological work in coordination with the enterprise's tasks at various periods; to better develop the role of the Party branch as the fighting fortress and reinforce Party building; to provide a greater scope for the enthusiasm and creativeness of the workers in the enterprise and set in motion the mass activities of comparing with, learning from, catching up with and surpassing the advanced and helping the backward; and to strengthen the single leadership of the enterprise's Party committee, to pay attention to the basic level, improve the style of leadership, and train cadres. Hence, the Party committee must provide stronger leadership over the five-good movement. In developing the five-good movement, we must set up standard-bearers, provide examples, create images of the proletariat, establish proletarian ideas, fill the political atmosphere with vigour, and let more good people and good things emerge. Living examples are most convincing and are something that the masses can see or touch. Standard-bearers and examples must be set up clearly and the thought of Mao Tse-tung given expression in conjunction with the three great revolutionary movements in the enterprise. We must make clear what must be promoted and what must be opposed. We must set an example in a honest way for only when examples are well set and experience well introduced can they command people's attention. . . .

6. Select young and outstanding cadres and foster Red and expert successors to the revolution. How to select young and outstanding cadres? The most important thing is to test, understand, and select cadres in the course of the three great revolutionary movements. A cadre must be judged on the basis of his basic qualities and the principal aspect of his character. We must boldly promote truly outstanding cadres to positions of responsibility in strict accordance with the five conditions laid down by Chairman Mao for fostering successors to the proletarian revolution. This is a major strategic measure for insuring that our ranks will forever be loyal to the thought of Mao Tse-tung. Five-good standard bearers and five-good cadres who have been tested many times provide the main and inexhaustible source for the selection of cadres. Those who are good politically and ideologically must be selected first. Newly promoted cadres must be fully trusted and boldly assigned to work.

Strict demands must be made on and warm assistance given to them. They must be allowed to take up heavy burdens in the three great revolutionary movements; they must be given a free hand to work and positively supported in their ventures and work. But strict political and ideological demands must be made on them. . . . It is necessary to place the cadres under the supervision of the masses before we can guarantee that they will not degenerate. We should enable them to live and work alongside the masses.

III. It Is Essential To Follow the Mass Line and Conduct a Large-Scale Mass Movement. A socialist enterprise is an enterprise of the labouring people. An enterprise of the labouring people must be run by the masses of the people, by the working class. The revisionists turn an enterprise practically into the private property of the bourgeois privileged stratum; they manage an enterprise by dictatorial means and control the masses by commandism, the imposition of penalties and the enforcement of rigid systems. These are two kinds of ideas and two kinds of roads for operating an enterprise. In operating an enterprise we respect, trust and rely on the masses, we take the mass line and conduct the mass movement on a grand scale. . . .

The battle at the Tach'ing Oil Field has been a large-scale mass movement. For the past several years, we have consistently abided by Chairman Mao's teachings, persevered in the mass movement, and consequently maintained a favourable revolutionary situation throughout. How to carry out a large-scale mass movement?

1. Mobilise and rely on the masses. In order to conduct the mass movement with success, we must really let the masses run their own house. To this end, we must:

(a) Opportunely reform those rules and systems which bind the hands and feet of the masses and impede the development of productivity. Appropriate rules and systems are needed, for they can unify our actions and help us to work according to the objective laws. It is for this reason that rules and systems must come from reality and the masses, and must be revised and perfected in keeping with the changes in production. Such rules and systems are flexible as they are capable of giving full play to the enthusiasm and creativeness of the masses and promoting the development of productivity. . . .

(b) Prevent the bureaucratic style of organs. An organ must serve production, the basic level and the masses, making the cadres and workers at the basic level devote themselves wholly to winning the battle in production. Hence, we should pay heed to overcoming the bureaucratic practice among certain organ cadres of sitting high above, issuing orders and demanding service from the basic level.

Appendix B. 6. Revolutionising the Tach'ing Oil Field

(c) Get rid of the bourgeois authoritative complex of a part of intellectuals. The practice of the three great revolutionary movements among the masses of people is the source of all knowledge. However, in an enterprise there are often some people who, influenced by the ideology of the exploiting class, think they are superior to others because they have a little knowledge, use this little knowledge to frighten the masses, and look down upon labour. Such ideas must be criticised and their influence eliminated.

2. Unreservedly promote democracy in politics, production and economy. Promoting political democracy is aimed principally at insuring that the whole body of workers, led by the Party, will continue to enhance their proletarian political consciousness and fully exercise 'five major rights':

(a) the right to struggle against all acts which run counter to the policies and guidelines of the Party and the State and against foul wind and evil atmosphere; (b) the right to examine the revolutionisation of leading organs and the observance of rules and regulations by the leading cadres; (c) the right to criticise the cadres at any conference; (d) the right to hear and discuss reports by leading cadres on work; and (e) the right to elect basic-level cadres through the democratic process. . . .

In order to safeguard the right of the workers to run their own house, Tach'ing has provided for workers at production posts 'five big functional rights':

(a) the right to refuse to take orders having nothing to do with their production posts; (b) the right to refuse to operate a machine which is due for overhaul; (c) the right to refuse to let unqualified personnel operate a machine; (d) the right to report immediately to the higher level on hidden dangers in production and, should the higher level fail to give any instruction or take any action, to suspend production when suspension is the only way to avoid accidents; and (e) the right to refuse to commence production where there are no working regulations, quality standards and safety measures

As for capital contruction workers, they are also empowered not to carry out construction under five conditions; namely: (a) they may not start operation if their task is not clearly defined and the construction blueprints are not clear; (b) they may not start operation if the quality, specifications and technical measures are not clear; (c) they may not start operation when the materials necessary for construction are not well prepared; (d) they may not start operation if the construction equipment is not in good condition; and (e) they may not start the next operation sequence if the quality of the previous operation sequence is not up to standard.

Promotion of economic democracy is designed to insure that the masses will take part in the economic and food management of the enterprise and exercise four rights: (a) the right to fight against all phenomena of extravagance and waste; (b) the right to participate in the economic accounting of the enterprise; (c) the right to participate in the mess hall management and to examine the accounts of the mess hall; and (d) the right to participate in the distribution of farm and subsidiary production.

3. Carry out a mass movement on a large scale in combination with the strengthening of centralised leadership. . . .

4. Foundation work must be realistically done. . . . As we see it, in the course of the vigorous mass movement, it is necessary to take a firm grip on foundation work in the following five respects: (a) Secure first-hand data and master the laws of production; (b) improve the quality of work and work to insure success in the revolution; (c) streamline the management of equipment and see to it that every machine is in perfect working order; (d) intensify technical training in order to acquire real, tough skills; and (e) adhere strictly to the system of responsibility at individual posts. . . .

IV. It Is Necessary To Develop the Party's Revolutionary Traditions of Hard Work and Plain Living. Chairman Mao has taught us, saying: 'It will take several decades of hard work to make our country rich and strong. Among other things, we must adopt the policy of practising austerity and opposing waste a policy of building the nation along industrious and economical lines.' . . . In order to promote the Party's revolutionary traditions of hard work and plain living, we must oppose those who put industry in a privileged position because they think they have more workers, more funds and more things to work with; those who one-sidedly seek modern, tall, large and novel projects and indulge in extravagance; those who spend money carelessly, give no attention to the upkeep of equipment and materials, and carry out production and construction regardless of cost; and those who cling to the bourgeois ideas of extravagance and waste, pursuit of material comforts, and fear of hardships and fatigue. . . .

How to promote the Party's revolutionary traditions of hard work and plain living? . . . Whether it is plant construction or living facilities, we must give attention to practicality and must not chase after formalism and grandeur. We should not build tall buildings including office buildings, auditoriums, hostels, and reception houses. Size should be determined by local conditions and local materials must be used. We must save construction funds for the State and establish the idea of taking pride in plain living among the workers. . . . We must develop the spirit of sewing, washing and mending old clothes, repairing the old and utilising the waste. . . . We must not waste one drop of oil, one unit of electricity, one tael of coal, one inch of steel or timber. Everybody must practise austerity. Austerity must be practiced everywhere, in everything, and at all times. . . .

V. It Is Essential To Integrate Revolutionary Zeal With a Scientific Attitude. How to integrate a high degree of revolutionary zeal with a strict scientific attitude? The most fundamental thing is for all of us to study and apply Chairman Mao's philosophy creatively. Chairman Mao's philosophy is the philosophy of the worker and peasant masses, the philosophy of the proletariat, and the broad masses of workers must be organised to study and master it. Throughout the battle at Tach'ing, *On Practice, On Contradiction* and the *Law of One Dividing into Two* were studied and applied in a big way to oppose metaphysics and scholastic philosophy. . . . From the battle itself we have gained the following points of understanding:

We must grasp the principal contradictions and concentrate forces for fighting a battle of annihilation. . . . In the early days of the battle, since the foundation of the petroleum industry was weak, manpower, material and financial resources from various petroleum plants, mines, institutions, and schools in the whole country were concentrated on this main battlefield of Tach'ing so that this battle of annihilation could be fought to a successful conclusion. Thus, by turning the relative inferiority of the whole situation into an absolute superiority in a partial situation, we enabled the workers to bring their skyrocketing zeal into full play so as to eliminate the backwardness of the petroleum industry. . . . The whole situation was turned into an active situation, and a favourable prospect was opened up for the petroleum industry for the whole country. . . .

It is necessary to sum up our experiences continuously so that we may be brave and resourceful. All new-born things must be tested. We must gradually know the objective laws by engaging in repeated practice and continuously summing up experiences. Only by doing so can we find out the conditions, have a great determination and the right methods of work; can we be brave and resourceful, make inventions and discoveries and go on creating and advancing.

We must divide one into two and continue to advance. In dealing with anything we must divide one into two. Particularly in dealing with victories and difficulties, we must all the more divide one into two. In this way we shall stand high and see far, neither feeling conceited when we win nor feeling despondent when we lose.

We must carry on the revolution and go on advancing forever.

VI. It Is Necessary to Launch the Technical Innovation and Technical Revolution Movement on a Large Scale and Catch Up with and Surpass the Advanced World Levels. . . . How to carry out a technical innovation and technical revolution movement?

1. We must be brave in practice and daring in creation. . . . To create things, we must wrestle with difficult technical problems and with the most advanced levels in foreign countries. We must dare to touch the hind quarters of a tiger and never concede defeat. . . . To create things, we must fight for time and strive to raise our standards. . . . To create things, we must break down conventions and eliminate those out-moded rules which retard man's creativity. We must discard all conservative policies. We must provide full scope for man's subjective conscious activity. . . . To create things, we must not have selfish ideas and must not be afraid of taking risks. . . . To create things, we must acquire a strict scientific attitude. We must seek truth from facts, start from reality in doing everything, and subject everything to test. In face of scientific problems, we must be honest men who do honest things; we must carry out arduous research and do things according to the laws of objective things. We cannot accomplish anything if we are careless, impetuous and subjective. To create things, we must have tough basic skills. We must master the fundamental theories and have a specialised knowledge. We must commit to memory basic data, formulae in common use and technical rules, and aply them with flexibility so as to pass the test when called upon to do so. . . . To create things, we must seriously study the strong points of others. . . .

2. In catching up with and surpassing the world levels, we must have a strategic objective. . . .

3. We must direct our attention toward production and serve production. Our purpose in carrying out technical innovations and technical revolution is to promote and develop production. Therefore, all subjects relating to technical innovations and technical revolution must originate from production. When results have been gained, they must be tested, summed up, modified and improved in the course of production. It is best for scientific and research personnel to come from production fields. Because they have participated in production practice, carried heavy burdens in production, been more or less familiar with production and shared common feelings and a common language with the workers, they are likely to think in terms of production and work in the best interests of production.

4. 'Triple combination' is the most effective way for technical

innovations and technical revolution. In effecting this 'triple combination', it is essential to bring into full play the roles of the leading cadres, workers and technicians. 'Triple combination' must be effected from investigation and study, formulation of plans, drafting of designs, organisation of supply of equipment and materials, manufacture of equipment, experiments on the spot and application of results of experiments in production all the way to the summarisation and popularisation of results of experiments. The workers call this 'a dragon's triple combination'.

VII. It Is Necessary To Establish a Revolutionary Style of Work. . . . In forming the . . . revolutionary style, the most crucial question is for us to be strict, careful, correct and energetic.

By being strict, we mean first of all being strict politically and ideologically, doing things according to the Party's principles and not making any concession on questions of principle. . . . By having a strict style of work, people will become the motive power to push work forward. When the leadership is strict, everyone will also be strict, work energetically, have a sense of responsibility and display fighting power. Being strict is a prerequisite for making specifications, producing techniques, imposing high standards and producing good products. Being strict is the requirement of the revolution, of class interests and of socialist construction. Being strict does not mean that we should open our eyes wide and look stern and resort to the imposition of penalties and to commandism, but that we should conduct ideological education regularly, continuously and patiently.

Being careful means that we must, in accordance with Chairman Mao's teachings, do economic work with increasing care. We must do all work in a very careful and highly meticulous manner. In producing petroleum, we carry out a great many underground operations in high temperature and at a high atmospheric pressure. Many projects are undertaken below the ground surface. The production processes are highly complicated, and the solution of many problems has to depend on the analysis of large amounts of data and on our judgments of them. All this calls for great care. When we work carefully, we will get a complete and true picture of the conditions, our work will conform more to the objective realities, and we will succeed in achieving high quality and a high level. Should we approach our work in a rough and crude attitude, we will be unable to stand an inspection and will do harm to the State.

Being correct means that we must look at problems correctly and do our work correctly. This is the foundation for correctly

231

solving problems and correctly directing production. To be correct, we must make a serious study of the thought of Mao Tse-tung and the policies and guidelines of the Party centre, conduct arduous research, do penetrating thinking, and strive to solve problems thoroughly. We must go to the basic level, penetrate into reality, and go deep among the masses to conduct investigations and studies seriously so as to find out the conditions below as they are. If we fail to see and grasp a problem correctly, we will commit subjectivism and issue commands with closed eyes.

Being energetic means that we must work with great vigour to the end and will not stop until results are produced. In dealing with a problem or a piece of work, if we find out the conditions clearly, we will then have to make up our minds to tackle it boldly and persistently. If we are afraid of the dragon in front and the tiger behind, if we hesitate and let opportunities slip by, then we will accomplish nothing in our lives. We must also be energetic in rectifying shortcomings and mistakes. We must adhere to the correct things to the end. When we make a mistake, we must correct it quickly. We must bravely acknowledge and promptly correct our shortcomings and mistakes.

These four points constitute the principal content of the style of work mentioned above. They reflect the objective demands for modernised production and construction at Tach'ing Oil Field, giving expression to the integration of the revolutionary spirit with the scientific attitude and to the aspirations of the broad masses of the workers. If we do our work correctly, carefully, strictly and energetically, then, with the passage of time, the style of our ranks will be further improved, their outlook will undergo a new change, their organisation and discipline will be further strengthened, and their fighting power will be still greater. They will improve their work further as an industrial army should.

VIII. It Is Necessary to Revolutionise the Leadership and Organs. . . . Leading cadres must persist in staying at selected spots and regard this as a system. Through staying at selected spots, they must continuously seek to understand the work the masses are doing, what they think and what they want. They must grasp thinking, note the signs and trends, set examples, cite typical cases and sum up experiences. We must combine centralised leadership with mobilisation of the broad masses and general calls with specific guidance, so that the opinions of the masses may be gathered together and any decision reached on the basis of these opinions may be implemented among the masses. In this way, correct leadership can be realised. . . .

Appendix B. 6. Revolutionising the Tach'ing Oil Field

Tach'ing has upheld the principle laid down by Chairman Mao to the effect that 'big power must be centralised while small power must be decentralised. Decisions reached at the Party committee must be implemented by various quarters, and they must be implemented resolutely and on the basis of principles. The Party committee should be responsible for inspection of work.' . . . The principal leading cadres of the Party committee of the oilfield . . . do not command production directly and do not concern themselves with complicated routine affairs. Instead, they attach special importance to bringing politics to the fore. In the main they are faced with five tasks: they must acquaint themselves with the thought of Mao Tse-tung, the policies and guidelines of the Party centre and the directives of the higher authorities concerned; they must go to the basic level to stay at selected spots and carry out investigations and research; they must size up the general situation, see the main stream, point out the direction and grasp the central issues; they must examine and assist in the work of the 'first line', seek out the shortcomings and mistakes, and sum up experiences. . . .

For introduction of face-to-face leadership, there are the following forms: (a) To handle office work on the spot, 'five things are done on the spot'—political work is carried out on the spot, production command is exercised on the spot, designing work is done on the spot, supplies are arranged on the spot, and livelihood service is rendered on the spot; (b) to organise a command structure at the front so as to direct operations on the spot; (c) to assign personnel to the spot to solve problems there; (d) to simplify organs, reduce intermediary levels, and command the basic level directly.

Insist that leading cadres abide by 'three agreements'. These . . . are as follows:

(a) To persevere in the fine traditions of hard work and plain living without claiming any special privileges. They will not build office buildings, auditoriums, hostels and reception houses; they will live in 'make-shift dwellings' or single-story houses. They will hold no parties and present no gifts; they will neither dance nor put a sofa in their office. They will eat in collective dining rooms. And they will teach their children not to seek privileges for themselves.

(b) They must persist in participating in physical labour and must never be bureaucrats sitting high above the people. Cadres should participate in labour at fixed hours. They must submit to the leadership of team and group leaders. They must create material wealth. Moreover, they must effect 'five combinations': combination of participation in labour with leadership work, with work on experimental plots, with the carrying out of investigations and studies and the solution of problems, with the learning of operating techniques, and with their own administrative work.

(c) Persist in being 'honest' and 'strict'; never feel conceited or tell lies. They must persist in staying at selected spots and step up investigations and studies, consult with the masses when common problems arise; insist on using the 'law of one dividing into two' as a weapon for summing up work continuously; and regularly call meetings of Party groups, examine the conditions of execution of 'three agreements', make criticism and self-criticism, and oppose liberalism. . . .

The basic question of revolutionisation is a question of the service viewpoint. After several years of practice in revolutionisation of organs, we have gradually made clear five relationships concerning the work of organs. (a) . . . Administrative work and production. All administrative work in an enterprise must proceed from production; all the work is for winning the battle at the production front. Therefore, the administrative work of organs must be subordinated to production requirements. (b) . . . Organs and the basic level. An organ must establish the idea of serving the basic level and through this service make a success of management. (c) . . . Strictness and flexibility. In the enforcement of systems, the principle must be strict while the concrete methods must be flexible.

(d) . . . Restraint and promotion. Rules and systems must have a restraining force, aimed at mobilising the initiative and creativeness of the workers and promoting production. (e) . . . Targets and work. A target is a fighting goal, showing the result to be achieved from doing a large amount of practical work. The realisation of targets must depend on the implementation of work. Therefore, an organ must direct all its efforts to grasping work; it must not spend the whole day making target calculations. After these [five] relationships are clearly defined, the service viewpoint of an organ will be strengthened. It will enable the organ to rely on the masses, break the old framework of 'management', and establish an integral set of work systems with service to the basic level and the masses as the core. . . .

When it comes to the arrangement, examination and summing up of work, we put special emphasis on attaching first importance to summing up. . . . The work of summing up at Tach'ing has produced a set of systems: a monthly big examination and summing up is carried out for the system of responsibility at individual posts and for the five-good movement. When a drilling team completes a well or a construction team completes an engineering project, it invariably makes a summing up. A big examination and a big summing up of work and a five-good preliminary assessment are carried out once every half year. At the end of each year, a general summing up and five-good general assessments are made. . . .

IX. Combine Industry with Agriculture and Town with Countryside, and Progressively Reduce the Three Differences. When an enterprise is built by us, it means a new ground for socialism is added. We must give full play to the leading role of the working class, pursue the general policy of developing the national economy with industry as the leading factor and agriculture as the foundation, strengthen the ties between industry and agriculture, use industry to support agriculture and hasten its development, and speed up socialist construction in an overall manner. Therefore, a socialist industrial enterprise does not merely produce products for the State; it must also develop its role as socialist position fully—politically, ideologically and economically.

If we build an industrial or mining enterprise of a foreign pattern, we shall have to build or expand a city; we shall have to build a welfare district with tall buildings and use walls to keep the peasants away. This is bound to lead to separation from the masses to a serious extent and to expansion of the differences between industry and agriculture and between town and countryside; it will jeopardise the worker-peasant alliance and be harmful to socialist construction and the transition to a communist society. From the very beginning, Tach'ing Oil Field has firmly refused to do things of such a foreign pattern.

In the course of an inspection tour of Wuhan Steel Works in 1958, Chairman Mao had directed: Such a large enterprise as Wuhan Steel Works could be gradually expanded into a comprehensive complex. Apart from producing a greater variety of iron and steel products, it should also produce some machines, chemicals and building materials. Such a large enterprise, in addition to industrial production, should also engage on a modest scale, in agriculture, trading, education and military training. When other leading comrades of the Party centre visited Tach'ing Oil Field for an inspection, they also indicated that the construction of the mining district must be based on the principle of integrating industry with agriculture and town with countryside for the benefit of production and the people's livelihood. Workers' living quarters should be scattered and not concentrated in one area. A large city should not be built. The dependents of the workers must be properly organised to take part in labour and develop production. It is by following these directives of Chairman Mao and other leading comrades of the Party centre that we have proceeded with the construction of the

235

mining district. At present, Tach'ing has preliminarily built a new socialist mining district where town and countryside, industry and agriculture, and government and interprise are integrated.

Tach'ing does not build a concentrated urban area; instead it has built residential points in scattered places. At the moment, it has completed three workers' towns and several dozen central residential points (each consisting of 300–400 households) and residential points (each with 100–200 households). Every central residential point with four or five residential points surrounding it becomes a livelihood base. Within this base are set up a mechanised farming station, an agricultural technical research station, a primary school, a part-work (farming) and part-study middle school, a bookstore, a health clinic, a nursery, a mess hall, a food shop, a flour mill, a commercial store, a barber shop, a bath house, a shoe repair shop, a sewing and mending unit, a post and tele-communication agency, and a savings office. These are establishments for production, livelihood, culture, education and health. Their presence contributes to production and to the improvement of living standards. Within residential points all houses built are single-storey houses of earth.

Tach'ing Oil Field does not mean to move the dependants of workers into a city from the countryside or turn them from producers into consumers. Instead, it organises them to take the path of revolutionisation and participate in productive labour. At present, the dependants whom the Oil Field has organised to take part in various kinds of collective productive labour represent 95 per cent of the total number of dependents with labour capacity. They are engaged in farm and subsidiary production in the entire mining district. In addition, they are also charged with the task of maintaining several hundred kilometres of highways; they work in industry as auxiliary labourers and are engaged in service trades. Today, the residential points and production teams are managed by the dependants themselves—and are managed well. The dependants constitute an important force for the construction of the mining district. Their spiritual outlook has undergone a marked change. The overwhelming majority . . ., who formerly were concerned only with their small families, are now concerned with the important affairs of the State and the world. They are concerned with the cause of the revolution. Because they have revolutionised their thinking, large groups of five-good dependants and five-good production teams have emerged. In 1965, among the dependants 192 joined the Party and 162 joined the League. Revolutionised, the dependants become an important force for politico-ideological work.

In organising the dependants to engage in productive labour,

Appendix B. 6. Revolutionising the Tach'ing Oil Field

Tach'ing has put into force the principle of 'taking the team as the foundation, practising unified accounting, assessing work performance and recording work points, and paying according to work'. All products are without exception delivered to the proper authorities. Whether they are engaged in industry or agriculture or engage in service work or work as teachers, the dependants do not receive salaries; their work is assessed and work points are recorded for them, and those who work more are paid more. Cadres engaged in work looking after the dependants also participate in labour and their work is assessed and work points are recorded for them in the same way. There will be year-end summing up, assessment, comparison and distribution.

Tach'ing Oil Field is actively enforcing two systems of labour and two systems of education. Today, it has introduced universal primary education and junior middle education and established an education network ranging from primary school to university, including primary schools, part-farming and part-study junior middle schools, part-work and part-study schools and a part-work and part-study petroleum college. Whatever school is needed has been established, and personnel have been trained to meet the requirements of production. Since the Oil Field is in need of well-drilling and extraction personnel, it has established a school for training such kind of personnel. Since medical and health personnel are short in the oil field, a medical school has been set up, where not only Chinese traditional medicine but also western medicine are studied. In this school, the students, besides studying medicine, also study nursing. In order to meet the needs of mechanisation of farm production, it has established a tractor drivers' training school for the dependants, who study during slack seasons and farm during busy seasons.

In order to strengthen centralised and unified leadership in the mining district, Tach'ing has established a government in the mining district so as to effect integration of government with enterprise. The Party committee of the Oil Field is the Party committee of the mining district. The work of the government and that of the enterprise are carried out under the unified leadership of the Party committee. . . .

Although Tach'ing has obtained definite results in its work these years, it still has many shortcomings. Now, the whole country is learning from Tach-ing, but what should Tach'ing do? We feel the enormity of the pressure. We are determined to continue to hold high the great red banner of the thought of Mao Tse-tung and the red banner of the general line, bring politics to the fore, and take class struggle as the key link. We must learn from the PLA, Tachai and

237

other advanced units. Using the law of one dividing into two as a weapon, we must promote the achievements and overcome the shortcomings. Prudent and humble, we must continue to deepen our revolutionisation and march forward bravely to win greater victories.

7. Comment on Sun Yeh-fang's Reactionary Political Stand and Economic Progress*

By Meng K'uei and Hsiao Lin

As in other domains, serious and sharp class struggle exists in the nation's economic circles. A black line which is against the Party, against socialism and against the thought of Mao Tse-tung has for a long time predominated in economic circles. . . . Sun Yeh-fang, Director of the Economic Research Institute, Chinese Academy of Sciences, is a figure assuming command of this black line in economic circles. . . .

Sun Yeh-fang is a representative of the bourgeoisie who has wormed his way into the Party. He has an immense hatred for the socialist system. Shortly after the 20th Congress of the CPSU, he visited the Soviet Union in 1956, sought for experiences and accepted the black ware of Khrushchev revisionism lock, stock and barrel. After his return, echoing the adverse current of international revisionism and collaborating with the bourgeoisie at home, he openly fluanted a black flag against the Party, socialism and the thought of Mao Tse-tung in economic circles. In his "Beginning with 'the Total Value of Production'" and "Place the Plans and Statistics on the Basis of the Law of Value", published in that year, he wantonly attacked the socialist system and put forward such ideas of capitalist restoration as placing profit in command and doing away with the planned economy. Sun Yeh-fang is a big rightist that slipped out of the net.

In 1958 and 1959, under the wise leadership of the Party Centre headed by Chairman Mao the whole nation held aloft the great red banner of the general line, took a big leap forward on each front and established people's communes on a big scale. It was at that time that Sun Yeh-fang released two big poisonous weeds—"If One Wants to Understand Economics One Must Acquire Some Knowledge of Philosophy", and "On Value"—viciously attacking

* Article published in *Hung-ch'i*, no. 10, October 1966. Translation, abridged, from *Survey of China Mainland Magazines* (SCMM), no. 539.

Chairman Mao's great teaching on contradictions, classes and class struggle in the socialist society, frantically opposing the command of proletarian politics, the Party's general line, the big leap forward and the people's commune. Sun Yeh-fang is a right opportunist pure and simple.

At the time when our country experienced temporary economic difficulties, the class enemies at home and abroad launched frantic attacks on our Party and the socialist system. Believing that the time for restoring capitalism had come, Sun Yeh-fang carried out activities and spread poison everywhere and, together with all ogres at home, blew the 'wind of individual farming' and the 'wind of reopening cases' and fomented 'three freedoms and one guarantee'. During the period in question Sun Yeh-fang visited the Soviet Union on two occasions and had extensive contacts and secret talks with the revisionists of the Soviet Union. After his return from abroad he released a mass of 'internal research reports', put forward a whole set of revisionist economic programmes, clamoured for open 'discussion' of his proposal and frantically demanded extensive 'experiments' in his vain attempt to restore capitalism in our country. Sun Yeh-fang is an out-and-out counter-revolutionary revisionist. . . .

Sun Yeh-fang's Black Line against the Thought of Mao Tse-tung. Comrade Mao Tse-tung is the greatest Marxist-Leninist of the contemporary age. The thought of Mao Tse-tung is Marxism-Leninism of the era in which imperialism is heading for collapse and socialism is heading for world victory, is our guide to the socialist revolution and socialist construction, and is a powerful ideological weapon for defeating imperialism and modern revisionism. . . . The class enemies at home and abroad have the greatest fear and immense hatred for the thought of Mao Tse-tung. Sun Yeh-fang has consistently and violently opposed [it] so as to make his dream of capitalist restoration come true.

Glossing over the Class Contradiction and Denying the Class Struggle. . . . On the first anniversary of the publication of Chairman Mao's great work, "On the Correct Handling of Contradictions among the People", Sun Yeh-fang wrote . . . an article entitled "If One Wants to Understand Economics One Must Acquire Some Knowledge of Philosophy". . . . Adopting the favourite tactics of the bourgeoisie and the revisionists, Sun Yeh-fang obliterated the class contradiction with the 'contradiction between man and thing' and denied class struggle. He did his best to preach that the 'contradiction between man and thing' was 'the deepest contradiction inherent in the socialist economy' and was the 'deepest and most far-reaching common root-cause' of various economic contradictions. . . . Lest people did not know what his spearhead was directed against, Sun Yeh-fang deliberately added a sub-title: "Several Points of Under-standing after Re-reading Comrade Mao Tse-tung's 'On the Correct Handling of Contradictions among the People'". . . .

. . . He generalised the 'contradiction between man and thing' into this formula: $\dfrac{\text{Products}}{\text{Labour Hours}}$. He praised this formula as a wonderful 'new discovery'. He said: 'Not only are all the secrets of economic problems contained in this formula' but the question of who wins in the struggle of socialism against capitalism was 'in the final analysis' 'how to reduce the denominator and enlarge the numerator'. . . .

Sun Yeh-fang's fantastic and strange theory is nothing new. To cover up their brutal class struggle against the Soviet People, the Khrushchev revisionist clique talked such rubbish as 'the socialist society is one without class struggle' and 'in the socialist society the unity of various classes takes the place of class struggle that has existed since the ancient time'. They accused our Party of 'stubbornly looking for class struggle in the socialist society'. Sun Yeh-fang sang the same tune as the Khrushchev revisionist clique, and his object, too, was to cover up the frantic attacks of the ogres on the Party and socialism in his vain attempt to make the revolutionary people throw off their guard against such attacks, to give up the class struggle and to let capitalism stage a comeback.

He Is Against Placing Politics in Command. Chairman Mao teaches us that politics is the commander and the soul. Political work is the lifeline of all economic work. Sun Yeh-fang regards political command as a thorn in his flesh. He viciously attacked political command for 'dealing with politics without regard to economics and substituting political explanation for economic explanation—which is not only an idealist view but, it may be said, is also the thought of lazy-bones in economics'. He picked up the worn-out weapon which Bukharin used for attacking Lenin and which was thoroughly refuted by Lenin, and made the charge that political command 'has only explained problems in the political sense but not in the economic sense'. And he advocated the need for both 'explanation in the political sense' and 'explanation in the economic sense'.

All such are fallacies. Chairman Mao said: 'Economics is the base while politics is the concentrated expression of economics.' Such is our fundamental view of the relationship between politics and economics,

Chairman Mao pointed out. In the socialist society there still exist class struggle, the struggle of two roads and the danger of capitalist restoration. All class struggles are political struggles. If the proletariat wants to defeat the bourgeoisie in this struggle of two roads, it must bring politics to the fore and persist in placing the thought of Mao Tse-tung in command. Otherwise, it will lose its bearings in the grave class struggle, a nation-wide counter-revolutionary restoration will emerge, and there will be a danger that the Party and the State will go into extinction and the heads of millions will fall on the ground. . . .

Sun Yeh-fang's reactionary class sense of smell is very strong. Fearing that placing the proletarian politics in command will destroy everything on which they depend for life, he came forward and opposed placing politics in command. He never wearied of talking about 'economics' and 'law' as if some 'economics' was divorced from politics and as if only he himself comprehended the mystery of economic laws. As a matter of fact, all these were excuses for opposing political command. He made this nonsensical statement: 'The relationship between cost and function is one in which the maximum effect is achieved with the minimum expenditure of labour (living labour and materialised labour). This means placing politics in command, does it not?' He even said downright that placing politics in command 'should be included in the concept of economic effect'. . . . Placing proletarian politics in command means placing the thought of Mao Tse-tung in command. In attacking the proletarian politics assuming command, Sun Yeh-fang attacked the thought of Mao Tse-tung assuming command. He slandered political command as 'idealism' and 'lazy thinking'. Is not this a blatant charge that placing the thought of Mao Tse-tung in command is 'idealism'? . . .

Sun Yeh-fang's fallacies against placing politics in command are obtained wholesale from the poisonous company of Khrushchev (whom Sun Yeh-fang called his 'master') revisionism. Khrushchev revisionists charged that placing politics in command is a 'theory that will-power is everything' and 'overlooks objective economic laws'. Sun Yeh-fang also made the charge that placing politics in command is 'idealism' and is 'denial or belittlement of objective economic laws'. Khrushchev revisionists made the charge that acting according to Chairman Mao's directives means 'one does not have to think' and 'mechanical carrying out of the will of others'. Sun Yeh-fang, too, made the charge that listening to Chairman Mao's words and explaining things with the thought of Mao Tse-tung is 'lazy thinking'. Khrushchev revisionists talked such rubbish as 'comparison between cost and effect is the soul of economics'. Sun Yeh-fang, too, talked rubbish, declaring that the relationship between cost and function means 'placing politics in command'. All this shows that Sun Yeh-fang is in every sense a 'yes' man to Khrushchev revisionism.

Attacking the General Line, the Big Leap Forward and the People's Commune. . . . Sun Yeh-fang launched vicious attacks on the general line. He brought up this charge: 'The Party's general line and walk-on-two-legs policy, etc., are limited to the super-structure and political science' and are not reflections of 'economic relations' and are 'subjectivist'. Resorting to subterfuge Sun Yeh-fang openly stated that 'the law of value is actually another way of presenting the general line' and 'the general line for building socialism means uniting cost and function and achieving the maximum effect at the minimum cost'. A clear-sighted person can readily see through the vain attempt of Sun Yeh-fang to substitute capitalist way of business for our Party's general line for socialist construction, his objective being to openly restore capitalism.

Sun Yeh-fang launched violent attacks on the big leap forward. Imperialism, Khrushchev revisionism and the right opportunists, and 'Three-Family Village' counter-revolutionary gang at home denounced the big leap forward for 'placing exclusive reliance on will', 'regarding economic laws with indifference', 'causing disproportions', 'undermining the economy', 'blowing hot air' and 'talking big'. Sun Yeh-fang threw mud at the big leap forward, saying that it caused 'serious disproportions', 'turned the already created national wealth into waste' and 'ate all the capital'. He slandered the big leap forward as 'a hot head getting dizzy'. He was so conscienceless as to speak Russian, in the presence of foreign revisionists and without the help of an interpreter, to describe the big leap forward as a product of 'a head getting dizzy'. . . .

Sun Yeh-fang also launched frenzied attacks on the people's commune. The people's commune is a new social organisation of great significance, created by our people under the leadership of Chairman Mao to meet the need of development of productive forces and is an inevitable product of the political and economic development of our country. Immediately it emerged from the broad horizon of China like the morning sun in 1958, Sun Yeh-fang viciously attacked the people's commune movement, saying that 'it deals with the relations of production without regard to the productive forces and tries to be the largest in size so as to leap to the skies at one step', and 'it is an error of reckless advance and subjective idealism'. He slandered: 'In agriculture, at best we still use draught animals to plough the field and are still at the same backward level of productive forces as found in the Ch'in dynasty. This level must be taken into account in the collectivisation movement but at that time we seemed to take the view that the bigger the better.' He also blatantly made the charge that Chairman Mao's scientific conclusion that the people's commune is 'large and just' was 'questionable'. Sun Yeh-fang's attack on the people's commune was cast from the same mould as the absurdities uttered by the right opportunists and the revisionists that our people's communes 'were set up too soon and were a failure', 'they went beyond the level of social development and level of mass consciousness', 'they came from subjective imagination and skipped over phases'.

Barking could not sully the light of the sun. Now the whole world can see that it is precisely because we held aloft the great red banner of the thought of Mao Tse-tung and stuck to the general line, the big leap forward and the people's commune that we have fulfilled the Second Five-Year Plan ahead of schedule, that we have triumphed over serious natural calamities for three years in succession, that we have smashed the disruptive activities of the Khrushchev revisionist clique against our economic construction, that we have created the Tach'ing Oil Field and removed the label of 'oil poverty', that we have turned out 12,000-ton hydraulic presses, that we have successfully carried out nuclear explosions on three occasions. The great achievements of the general line, the big leap forward and the people's commune can by no means be obliterated by the outcries of a few reactionaries. . . .

Crazily Clamouring for 'Declaration of War' on Mao Tse-tung's Thought. Sun Yeh-fang hates the thought of Mao Tse-tung to the bone. He viciously slandered Chairman Mao's writings as 'dealing with only "abstraction"', and 'endlessly indulging in idle talks on "abstraction", thus turning abstraction into emptiness or nothingness'. Like all the revisionists he flaunted the banner of opposing 'traditional dogmatism' and opposed Marxism-Leninism and the thought of Mao Tse-tung. For many years he has consistently styled himself a valiant opponent to 'traditional dogmatism'. He said that in economics 'traditional dogmatism' means the 'theory of natural economy'. . . . He also said that the system of economic management for more than ten years in China had been drawn up under the 'guidance' of the 'theory of natural economy'. . . .

Against what was the spearhead of Sun Yeh-fang's attack on the 'theory of natural economy' directed? . . . Obviously, what Sun Yeh-fang attacked as the 'traditional dogmatism' was the thought of Mao Tse-tung. The so-called 'theory of natural economy' which occupied a 'monopolistic position', as he charged, was the Marxist-Leninist economic doctrine, Chairman Mao's economic theory. . . .

The thought of Mao Tse-tung is our guide to revolution and construction while the thought of the bourgeoisie and the revisionist thought are instruments which the ogres of all kinds use to restore capitalism. . . . Simultaneously with cursing the commanding position of Mao Tse-tung's thought, Sun Yeh-fang openly wanted people to learn from the 'wise' capitalists, saying that Khrushchev revisionism had given him 'the greatest revelation'. He shouted: 'It cannot be said that all the revisionist wants we may not want.' This precisely shows that Sun Yeh-fang wanted the bourgeois and revisionist thoughts to monopolise the ideological position and shaped public opinion in favour of capitalist restoration.

Chairman Mao is the red sun in our hearts and is our life-line. Every word of Chairman Mao's is truth. We most ardently love and adore the thought of Mao Tse-tung and have boundless faith in it. We will forever study, publicise, carry out and safeguard the great thought of Mao Tse-tung. Whoever dares to oppose Chairman Mao and oppose the thought of Mao Tse-tung we will resolutely fight to the end! We will hold aloft the great red banner of the thought of Mao Tse-tung and completely knock down the counter-revolutionary revisionists like Sun Yeh-fang and his ilk.

Sun Yeh-fang's Economic Programme for Capitalist Restoration. Sun Yeh-fang viciously attacked the thought of Mao Tse-tung and the leadership of the Party with the object of restoring capitalism in our country. This criminal attempt finds its concentrated expressions in a whole set of revisionist economic programmes he has put forward. . . . Proceeding from this point, Sun Yeh-fang has brought forward a set of economic programmes for restoring capitalism. His programmes have the following basic contents: profit as the commander, autonomy of enterprises, free market, guarantee of production by households, the law of value as the primary.

This stuff of Sun Yeh-fang's is nothing new. It is complete parrotry and is copied from Khrushchev revisionism. He shamelessly said that his 'basic views' were copied 'from the Soviet comrades'. Sun Yeh-fang is China's Liberman. He declared without sense of shame that he 'is the same' as Liberman, the notorious revisionist economist of the Soviet Union, and 'is more thoroughgoing than Liberman'. What Sun Yeh-fang loudly advocates is precisely what is now carried out by Khrushchev revisionism in the Soviet Union.

The question of profit is one talked about with the biggest noise by Sun Yeh-fang since 1956. He makes the charge that we are so enchanted by 'magic' that we take 'capital and profit' as 'capitalist concepts' and 'get frightened whenever profit is mentioned' and that this causes the 'evil consequences' of 'disregarding cost and universally belittling the economic results'. Shouting himself hoarse, he clamours for 'restoration of the reputation of the socialist profit indicator' and 'raising the position of the profit indicator in the system of the planned economic management'. . . .

Sun Yeh-fang stands for taking the amount of profit as the sole criterion for measuring whether an enterprise is advanced or backward. He says: 'Profit is the most concentrated expression of the way an enterprise is managed' and 'the most ingenious indicator' and that 'the rate of socially averaged profit on funds is the level to be reached by every enterprise, and those exceeding this level of average profit on funds are advanced and those which fail to reach this level are backward'.

Sun Yeh-fang also advocates that the direction in which social investments are made should be determined according to the amount of profit. He considers that in determining 'the amount of investments' in various departments of the entire national economy, 'economic comparison should be made. That is to say, the average rate of profit on funds should be taken into consideration.' This means that investments should be made in the department whose profit rate is high and little or no investments should be made in the department whose profit rate is low.

This stuff of Sun Yeh-fang's is completely the capitalist and revisionist one of placing profit in command. In the eyes of the capitalists in the capitalist society, profit is indeed 'the most concentrated expression of the way an enterprise is managed' and 'the most ingenious indicator'. The only aim of the capitalists is to make money. Where the capitalists invest their capital is determined entirely according to the level of profit rate. If the capitalist economy is compared to an 'ox', then profit is indeed the 'ox nose' for all the economic activities of capitalism depend on profit.

The socialist economy is absolutely not allowed to follow the capitalist pattern. We run enterprises and undertake construction not for making money but in the interests of the Chinese revolution and world revolution. All our economic work can only follow the general guiding principle for economic and financial work as formulated by Chairman Mao, that is, 'develop economy to insure supply' and can by no means follow the example of the capitalists who seek only profit, do more business if profit is high, less business if profit is low and no business if there is no profit.

The distribution of construction funds can only be determined according to the political task of our Party and State and according to the development of the national economy and the needs of people's livelihood. We can by no means distribute construction funds and determine the direction of investments according to the profit rate and sacrifice the fundamental interests of the proletariat and the labouring people as advocated by Sun Yeh-fang.

The central link that sets all things in motion in the socialist economy can only consist in placing proletarian politics in command. Only by bringing politics to the fore, placing the thought of Mao Tse-tung in command and promoting revolutionisation of man's mind can the socialist direction of the enterprises be insured and can the revolutionary enthusiasm and creative power of the worker masses be summoned and the quality and quantity of products raised to the greatest extent. The task of an enterprise is not only to turn out products but also to train personnel and create experiences. Simultaneously with developing production, an enterprise must prepare not only material conditions but also spiritual conditions for communism to come. For this reason, the most fundamental criterion for measuring whether an enterprise is advanced and how it is managed is whether it brings politics to the fore and brings the proletarian politics to the fore. Enterprises of Tach'ing type are good and advanced because they have brought the thought of Mao Tse-tung and the proletarian politics to the fore. . . .

Advocating Autonomy of Enterprise. Autonomy of enterprise and profit assuming command are twins delivered by Sun Yeh-fang from the poisonous womb of capitalism. To place profit in command and restore capitalism is bound to undermine the centralised and unified leadership of the Party and the State over the socialist economy, disintegrate the ownership by the whole people and make every enterprise an independent kingdom. For this reason, like the renegades Tito and Khrushchev, Sun Yeh-fang ferociously attacks the centralised and unified leadership of the Party and the State over the socialist economy. He slanders the socialist economy under the unified and centralised leadership as 'natural economy' like the 'primitive commune' and says the 'unified and centralised planning organ takes the place of the leaders in the economy of primitive clans and leads the economic activities of the whole society'. He accuses the Party and State leadership over enterprises of 'binding the hands and feet of enterprises and restricting their initiative'. He launches vicious attacks on our Party management of economy, saying: 'As soon as the Party lays hold on the economy, the economy dies, the Party worries; when it worries, it relaxes the hold; when it relaxes the hold, the economy is in disorder; when the economy is in disorder, the Party lays a firm hold on it—now one thing now another.' In the eyes of Sun Yeh-fang, the socialist economy has entered a blind ally and the only way out is to ask this gang of counter-revolutionary revisionists to restore capitalism.

Under the signboard of dividing authority into 'big authority' and 'small authority', Sun Yeh-fang stands against the centralised and unified leadership of the Party and the State over the national economy and advocates giving enterprises 'function and power to handle all their economic affairs independently'. He says that 'small authority' belongs to enterprises and 'big authority' belongs to the State. The 'small authority' he has in mind includes specifically: First, enterprises have the authority to draw up their production plans and the State should not set enterprises planned indicators of variety, quantity and quality. Second, enterprises have the authority to dispose of all their depreciation funds and decide on maintenance and renewal of their fixed assets and even the authority to 'buy and sell fixed assets freely'. Third, cancel the system of unified State allocation of supplies; enterprises have authority to arrange supply and marketing relations and to buy and sell products freely. In this way, Sun Yeh-fang gives the State 'big authority' and to manage only two things: investing funds and collecting profits.

According to what Sun Yeh-fang advocates, the relationship between the State and the enterprises will virtually change into one between the lending capitalists and industrial capitalists. Investing funds and collecting profits is the business of the State. After obtaining funds the enterprises will decide how to produce and how to do business, and the State need not and has no right to interfere. If things are done like this, then what socialist ownership by the whole can there be? What socialist planned economy can there be?

Fomenting Free Market and Guarantee of Production by Households. Sun Yeh-fang and his ilk could not reconcile themselves to the fact that more than 500 million peasants have embarked on the royal road to socialism. With a view to disintegrating the socialist economy owned by the collective, Sun Yeh-fang, exploiting the Economic Research Institute under his thumb, organised personnel to carry out 'investigations', write 'reports', hold 'discussion meetings' and foment 'opening free markets extensively'. Sun Yeh-fang and his ilk did not conceal what was on their minds when they said: 'Suppose there are speculative activities, what is the harm? At worst the speculators are allowed to make some money.' They even openly wanted our Party to 'govern without interference' with regard to the free market. . . . .

During the period of temporary economic difficulties in our country, the class enemy blew up the 'guarantee of production by households' black wind in the countryside. Sun Yeh-fang, who consistently hated the people's commune to the bone, hurriedly leapt forward and, co-ordinating with the attack by the ogres of all kinds, advocated 'guarantee of production by households' in his vain attempt to overthrow the system of people's communes. Sun Yeh-fang said: 'One step too much was taken and it is now necessary to go back by two steps—to a smaller size.' Where should the communes fall back? Back to 'guarantee of production by households', i.e., to individual farming, to capitalism. . . . [He] said that the 'masses have lost confidence in the collective'. This was rubbish and a gross slander to the broad masses of our country. The broad masses of peasants, particularly the poor and lower-middle peasants deeply realised from their own experience that the collective economy was their life-line and the people's commune was the royal road to communism. They knew that 'guarantee of production by households' or individual farming would mean going back to capitalism and sinking into the abyss of suffering. The 'masses' referred to by Sun Yeh-fang were actually a handful of landlords, rich peasants, counter-revolutionaries, bad elements and rightists, a handful of persons who stubbornly followed the capitalist road. . . .

Sun Yeh-fang once again made a wrong assessment of the situation and laughed too early. Not long afterwards, under the wise leadership of the Party Centre headed by Chairman Mao the people of our country beat off the frenzied attacks by the capitalist force and the remnant force of feudalism, consolidated the collective economy, developed agricultural production and made the socialist world ever more stable. And those like Sun Yeh-fang and his ilk, who preached retrogression, advocated 'three freedoms and one guarantee' and desperately recalled the soul of the capitalist system, came to grief.

The Law of Value Is Primary. Sun Yeh-fang racked his brains to clothe in 'theory' his economic programme for restoring capitalism. This garment is the 'theory of the law of value' he has repeatedly preached. He said: 'Of all laws, the law of value is primary.' The law of value 'signifies a combination of politics, economics and techniques'. That is to say, the law of value means everything, and the socialist system, Party leadership, political command and planned and proportional development of the national economy may be cast to the winds.

Sun Yeh-fang denies the fundamental principle of Marxist-Leninist political economy that the law of value is the economic law for commodity production. He lies prostrate before the law of value, worships it and cries 'Long live the law of value!' In his view, the law of value plays the role of 'promoting technical progress and developing the productive forces' and the 'role as a regulator of production', both in the capitalist and in the socialist society and even in the communist society. He cries against denial of the 'common character' of capitalism and socialism, saying that 'to deny value is to deny the common character . . . and deny the most fundamental thing in the socialist society'. Sun Yeh-fang deliberately confuses the different roles played by the law of value under two social systems. The socialist economy is based on public ownership of the means of production and the economy is developed in planned and proportional ways. Although the law of value functions to a certain degree, yet its role is subjected to strict restriction, so much so that it cannot play the role as a regulator of production, still less is it 'the most fundamental thing'. . . .

Sun Yeh-fang ardently demands that the socialist planned economy be 'placed on the basis of the law of value' and 'enterprises be allowed to produce cheap-priced and fine-quality goods automatically . . . under the predominant role of the law of value'. He is fully aware that as long as the law of value is elevated to a predominant position and is allowed to play the 'role as the regulator' blindly and spontaneously, the whole society will sink into a state of competition and anarchy and into the quagmire of capitalist 'liberalisation'. . . .

NOTES AND REFERENCES

Full publication details of Western works referred to will be found in Works Cited, pages 265 et seq.

Abbreviations

CB: *Current Background*, United States Consulate General, Hong Kong.

CL: *Chinese Literature*, English-language monthly published in Peking.

CQ: *China Quarterly*, London.

FLP: Foreign Language Press, Peking.

JMJP: *Jen-min Jih-pao* (People's Daily), Peking.

PR: Peking Review, English-language weekly, published in Peking.

SCMM: *Survey of China Mainland Magazines*, United States Consulate General, Hong Kong.

SCMP: *Survey of China Mainland Press*, United States Consulate General, Hong Kong.

Chapter II. Problems and Policies

1. Cf. Alec Nove, *The Soviet Economy*, London and New York 1961, pp. 146, 290.

2. Cf. Robert Tung, in *Far Eastern Economic Review*, Vol. LIII, no. 10, September 8, 1966.

3. See Roderick MacFarquhar, *The Hundred Flowers*, London and New York 1960.

4. Mao Tse-tung, *On the Correct Handling of Contradictions Among the People*, FLP, Peking 1957.

5. Cf. Li Ch'eng-jui, *Draft History of the Agricultural Taxes of the Chinese People's Republic* (in Chinese), Peking 1959.

6. Cf. Roy Hofheinz, "Rural Administration in Communist China", *CQ*, no. 11, July–September 1962, pp. 150–55.

7. Cf. T'ao Chu, "The People's Communes are making progress", *Hung-ch'i* (*Red Flag*), February 26, 1964; see abridged text in Appendix B. 2, pp. 179 et seq.

8. Cf. Joan Robinson, "Organisation of Agriculture" in Ruth Adams (ed.), *Contemporary China*, New York 1966, p. 321.

9. *Hung-ch'i*, December 16, 1961 [*SCMM*, no. 295].

10. *Shih-shih Shou-ts'e* (*Current Affairs*), November 21, 1961 [*SCMM*, no. 296].

11. *Chung-kuo ch'ing-nien* (*China Youth*), March 1, 1962 [*SCMM*, no. 307].

12. *Hung-ch'i*, November 16, 1962. It is notable that this article, after analysing Lenin's statements on class-struggle in the post-revolutionary situation, becomes an attack on Yugoslavia and therefore, by implication, on the Soviet Union. This suggests the close connection, which persisted throughout the Cultural Revolution, between domestic issues and the anti-Soviet polemic. It is a curious and characteristic fact that the Chinese party, in conducting this polemic, took the trouble to republish in translation, for the guidance of its members, works by Kautsky, Bernstein and Kardelj, as well as by John Dewey.

13. *Shih-shih Shou-ts'e*, October 21, 1962 [*SCMM*, no. 346].

14. *Chung-kuo ch'ing-nien*, December 1, 1962 [*SCMM*, no. 347].

15. Ibid., February 10, 1963 [*SCMM*, no. 355].

16. *Shih-shih Shou-ts'e*, December 1, 1963 [*SCMM*, no. 403].

17. J. Chester Cheng (ed.), *The Politics of the Chinese Red Army*, Stanford, Calif. 1966.

18. *Quotations from Chairman Mao*, FLP, Peking 1966.

Chapter III. *The Thought of Mao Tse-tung*

1. Franz Schurmann, in his *Ideology and Organisation in Communist China*, Berkeley, Calif. 1966, discusses with great insight Mao's use of the idea of the 'unity of opposites'. One such unity which he might have discussed is that which represents Mao's attempt to transcend, in his own theory of knowledge, the two theories which, coming to China almost simultaneously, gave rise to the greatest of the controversies which raged in his youth: Marxism, and the pragmatism of John Dewey. At the intellectual level, Mao's theory of knowledge may be seen as a characteristic attempt to get the best

of both worlds—of the unifying ideology of Marxism and of the powerful practical force of pragmatic habits of thought.

2. Schurmann, op. cit., and John Wilson Lewis, *Leadership in Communist China*, Ithaca, N.Y. 1963.

3. Stuart R. Schram, *Mao Tse-tung*, Harmondsworth and Baltimore 1966, p. 76.

4. Jack Gray, "Political Aspects of the Land Reform Campaign in China", *Soviet Studies*, October 1964.

5. Schurmann, op. cit.

6. Richard Harris, in *The Times*, February 17, 1967.

7. *The High Tide of Socialism in the Chinese Countryside* (in Chinese), Peking 1956.

8. A. Donnithorne, *China's Economic System*, London and New York 1967, p. 337.

9. "In Praise of Norman Bethune" and "Serve the People", in Mao Tse-tung, *Selected Works*, Vol. III, New York 1953.

Chapter IV. The Revolution in Culture

1. Chu Kuang-ch'ien, "My Understanding", *CL*, 1957, no. 4, p. 173.

2. See especially Stuart R. Schram, *Mao Tse-tung*, op. cit., (ch. 3, note 3); and *The Political Thought of Mao Tse-tung*, New York and London 1963.

3. For the therapeutic use of drama see, for example: Ai Ssu-ch'i et al., *Yang-ko lun-wen hsuan-chi*, Dalien 1947, pp. 55–7; J. Prusek, *Die Literatur des befreiten Chinas und ihre Volkstradition*, Prague 1955, p. 361 et seq.; Chou Yang, "The People's New Literature" (report of 1949), in *The People's New Literature*, FLP, Peking 1950, pp. 109–10.

For the epochal role of literature, see: Mao Tse-tung, *Talks at the Yenan Forum on Art and Literature* (hereafter referred to as *Yenan Talks*), originally delivered in May 1942, and published in *Mao Tse-tung on Art and Literature*, FLP, Peking 1960, p. 97; Chou Yang, *Wo kuo she-hui chu-i wen-hsueh i-shu ti tao-lu* (report of July 22, 1960), Peking 1965, pp. 11–12.

4. The negative functions of literature are referred to in Mao's *Yenan Talks*, op. cit., p. 110; and, in more general terms, in "Never Forget the Class Struggle", editorial in *Chieh-fang-chün Pao*, May 4, 1966, translated in *The Great Socialist Cultural Revolution in China*, FLP, Peking 1966, 1, p. 25.

5. The main sources for literary and cultural policy today are the following works by Mao: *Yenan Talks*, op. cit., and relevant passages from *On New Democracy* (1940), *On the Current Handling of*

Contradictions among the People (1957), and *Speech at the Propaganda Conference of the Communist Party of China* (1957). The first three of these may be consulted in the compendium *Mao Tse-tung on Art and Literature*, op. cit. (Note 3). The fourth has been published in English as a separate pamphlet.

For a useful summary of the main positions in the period of anti-revisionism, see Chou Yang, op. cit. (Note 3).

6. For the 'change of heart', see Mao's *Yenan Talks*, op. cit., pp. 81–2. The policy of popularisation in 1958 is discussed in *JMJP* editorials of April 26 and May 8, 1958, reprinted in *Hsin-hua Pan-yueh k'an*, 1958, no. 132, pp. 126–7, 141. Similar points are made editorially in *Wen-i Pao* (Literary Gazette), October 1962, no. 10, pp. 2–4. Educational policy can be studied in documents in C. T. Hu (ed.), *Chinese Education under Communism*, New York 1962.

7. For Mao on 'national form', see his: "The Role of the Chinese Communist Party in the National War" (October 1938), "On New Democracy" (January 1940), and "Oppose the Party Eight-Legged Essay" (February 1942), in *Mao Tse-tung on Art and Literature*, op. cit., pp. 8–9, 32–3, 66–8, respectively. See also Chou Yang's speech at the Eighth Congress of the CCP (September 25, 1956),"The Important roles of Art and Literature in the Building of Socialism", *CL*, 1957, no. 1, esp. 184–6.

8. For 'revolutionary romanticism', see: Chou Yang, "The new Folk Song has opened up a new road for poetry and song", *Hung-ch'i*, 1958, no. 1; Mao Tun's report of July 24, 1960 to the National Congress of Literary and Art Workers [*CB*, no. 632, p. 17]; Lin Mo-han, "Hold even higher the Banner of Mao's Tse-tung's Thinking on Literature and Art", *JMJP*, January 21, 1960; and Kuo Mo-jo, "Lang-man chu'i ho hsien-shih chu'i", *Hung-ch'i*, 1958, no. 3, reprinted in *Hsin-hua Pan-yueh-k'an*, 1958, no. 14, pp. 139–43. Fokkema discusses this in *Literary Doctrine . . .*, pp. 196–202 (see Note 10 below). Note that Chou Yang was already advocating revolutionary romanticism in his speech of September 25, 1956, op. cit. (Note 7), p. 183.

9. Realism is discussed in Mao's *Yenan Talks*, op. cit., 112–13. The point about assent and dissent is summed up by Chang T'ien-yi, "Writing about Contradictions", *CL*, 1957, no. 3, 211–12.

10. See especially D. W. Fokkema, "Chinese criticism of humanism: campaigns against the intellectuals, 1964–65", *CQ*, 1966, no. 26; and his *Literary Doctrine in China and Soviet Influence, 1956–60*, The Hague 1965.

11. For education in contemporary China, see: C. T. Hu (ed.), op. cit., and his "Politics and Economics in Chinese Education", in

Werner Klatt (ed.), *The Chinese Model*, Hong Kong 1965, pp. 31–47; also T. H. Chen, "Education in Communist China: Aims, Trends and Problems", and C. H. G. Oldham, "Science and Education in China", both in Ruth Adams (ed.), *Contemporary China*, op. cit. (ch. 2, Note 8).

For Chinese statements, see Lu Ting-yi, "Education must be combined with productive labor" (1958), and "Our schooling system must be reformed" (1960), translated in C. T. Hu (ed.), *Chinese Education . . .*, op. cit. Note also Yuan Hsi-liang, "Physical labor and mental labor in socialist society", *Ching-chi Yen-chiu*, 1965, no. 11 [*SCMM*, no. 507]; and his "Transforming intellectuals into laborers", *JMJP* editorial, October 15, 1960 [*CB*, no. 642].

12. The class character of the student body is reported in: *JMJP* editorial, July 3, 1958; ibid., August 29, 1962, p. 1; and Kuo Mo-jo, "In refutation of an anti-socialist scientific program", ibid., July 6, 1957, translated in C. T. Hu (ed.), *Chinese Education . . .*, op. cit.

13. Cf. Chou Yang, report of 1960, op. cit. (Note 3), p. 19.

14. Idem, "The fighting task confronting workers in philosophy and the social sciences", speech of October 26, 1963 [*CB*, no. 726, esp. pp. 4–13]. Here Chou Yang defined and discussed 'modern revisionism'. Lu Ting-yi referred to the special danger to youth in his introductory speech (July 22, 1960) to the Third National Congress of Literature and Art Workers [*CB*, no. 632, p. 2].

15. See, in particular: Franz Schurmann, op. cit. (ch. 3, Note 1), pp. 297, 398–9, 492; Stuart R. Schram, "The Man and his Doctrines", in *Problems of Communism*, September–October 1966, p. 5; Dennis Doolin, "The Revival of the 100 Campaign: 1961", *CQ*, 1961, no. 8; John Wilson Lewis, "Revolutionary Struggle and the Second Generation in Communist China", *CQ* 1965, no. 21.

16. For rehabilitation of rightists, see *JMJP*, December 17, 1961, recording a Central Committee decision of September 16, 1959. See also Chou Yang's 1960 report, op. cit., p. 17.

17. The best known statement giving weight to 'expertise' was that of Vice-premier Ch'en Yi in September 1961. See also articles on 'redness' and 'expertise' by Ai Huang and Cheng Chih in *Chung-kuo ch'ing-nien*, September 17 and 18, 1961 [*SCMM*, no. 285]. On 'elevation', see: Mao Tun, "Hsueh jan-hou chih pu tsu", *Jen-min Wen-hsueh*, 1962, no. 2, p. 15; and Li Huan-chih, "Elevation and Promotion", *Kung-jen Jih-pao*, May 19, 1962, [*CB*, no. 685].

18. Chiao Yü-lu, publicised as the ideal type of *hsien* (district) party secretary, was featured in *JMJP*, January 1, 1966 [*SCMP*, no. 3616].

19. For the 'Learn from the Army' campaign and the army's political work, see J. Gitting's, *The Role of the Chinese Army*, London and New York 1967; and his "The 'Learn from the Army' Campaign", *CQ*, 1966, no. 18, pp. 153–9.

20. Material on the rural edition of the Kwangtung newspaper *Nan-fang Jih-pao* (a project begun in January 1963), is given in that paper's issue of April 14, 1963 [*SCMP*, no. 2980]. Regarding the dimensions of press campaigns: an estimated 2,131 items were published during the anti-Hu Feng campaign of 1955; and over 230 press articles on the film *Early Spring in February* appeared about October 1964 according to a comment in *JMJP*, November 8, 1964.

21. Chiang Ch'ing's speech was published in the army journal *Chieh-fang-chün Pao*, May 10, 1967, and in *Hung-ch'i*, 1967, no. 6 [*PR*, 1967, no. 20]. It does not appear in the official collection of material on the revolution in opera, *A Great Revolution on the Cultural Front*, FLP, 1965.

22. Mao's statements (*Instructions*) were allegedly made on December 12, 1963 and June 27, 1964; see *PR*, 1967, no. 23. ✓

23. For discussion of the Yang Hsien-chen affair, see D. J. Munro, *CQ*, 1965, no. 22, pp. 75–82. Six Chinese articles of 1964 on the 'Two into One' question were translated in *CB*, no. 745.

24. Chou Ku-ch'eng's original article, "The historical position of art creation", was published in *Hsin Chien-she*, 1962, no. 12.

25. For material on Feng Ting and Chou Ku-ch'eng, see *CB*, nos. 750 and 747 respectively. The Chou controversy was summarised in *JMJP*, July 18, 1964 [*CB*, no. 747].

26. Wu Han's original article, "Lun Hai Jui" (On Hai Jui), was published in *JMJP*, September 19, 1959. For subsequent discussion, see: Wu Han, "Shuo tao-te" and "Tsai shuo tao-te", *Ch'ien Hsien*, Peking 1962, nos. 10 and 16 (not seen). Hsu Ch'i-hsien took these up in *Kuang-ming Jih-pao*, August 15, 1963, p. 5; to which Wu replied ("San shuo tao-te") in the same paper, August 19, 1963, p. 2. Wang Ssu-chih reopened the discussion in the paper, June 3, 1964, p. 4. Wu replied on June 17 to Wang and to Hsing Yü's article in the paper (May 29), repeating his point on July 9. For the discussion early in 1966, and for a survey of the whole campaign against *The Dismissal of Hai Jui* and *Hsieh Yao-huan*, see *JMJP*, February 28 and March 11, 1966. For a review of the controversy by Yueh Hua, see *Pei-ching Jih-pao*, December 18, 1965 [*SCMP*, no. 3668]. Note also criticism of the great magistrate-investigators of popular fiction by Liu Shih-te and Teng Shao-chi in *Chung-kuo Ch'ing-nien pao*, June 13, 1964 [*SCMP*, no. 3252].

27. Reported in article "'Ch'ing Kuan' wen-t'i t'ao-lun chung ti pa chung i-chien", *JMJP*, February 28, 1966.

28. See Jan Shao-te, "Kuan-yü 'Shi Chih: You-hsia lieh chuan' jen-wu ti p'ing-lun wen-t'i", *Kuang-ming Jih-pao*, June 3, 1964, p. 4.

29. J. A. Harrison, "Communist Interpretations of the Chinese Peasant Wars", *CQ*, 1965, no. 24, pp. 92–118.

30. Figure given in *China Reconstructs*, Peking, September 1965, Vol. xiv, no. 9, p. 37. Provision of films in rural areas was first promoted on a large scale in 1958. The size of the film audience as a whole was put at 4,100 million seats occupied during the year 1959; see Chou Yang's report of 1960, op. cit. (Note 3), p. 10.

31. Hsieh T'ieh-li's filmscript (*Erh-yueh*, February) was published in *Tien-ying Ch'uang-tso*, 1962, no. 3, pp. 20–40, and was dated Peking, April 19, 1962. Several critical articles were published in the reconstructed film journal *Tien-ying I-shu*, 1964, no. 4. Five critical articles were translated in *CB, 196 , no. 749*, the most important being Ho Ch'i-fang, "An appraisal of the novel *February* and the film *Early Spring in February*", *JMJP*, November 8, 1964 [*CB*, no. 749, pp. 9–24].

32. Hsia Yen commented on the adaptation of the novel in "Tui kai-pien wen-t'i ta k'o wen", *Tien-ying Chü-tso*, 1963, no. 6, p. 3. For a discussion of Jou Shih and his work, see T. A. Hsia, *The Enigma of the Five Martyrs*, Berkeley, Calif. 1962, esp. pp. 38–47.

33. The text of the filmscript was published in *Chung-kuo Tien-ying chü-pen hsuan-chi*, Peking 1961, Vol. v, pp. 3–46. A translation of the original story is included in Mao Tun, *Spring Silkworms and Other Stories*, FLP, Peking 1956, pp. 113–63. For critical material in translation, and for details of the film's re-exhibition, see *CB*, no. 766.

34. See Hsia Yen, op. cit., p. 5; also CB, no. 766, p. 11.

35. This revival of interest was noted, for example, in Li Ni's review of *Draft History of the Development of the Chinese Cinema*, 2 vols., in *Tien-ying I-shu*, 1963, no. 2, p. 70n. Ch'ü Pai-yin's article "Soliloquy on the problems of creation in the film" (ibid., 1962, no. 3, pp. 50–7), severely attacked in 1966, expressed general interest in higher standards, and Ch'ü referred to disagreement in the Chinese film world on whether there was, in fact, a 'revolutionary tradition' in the cinema, and whether it was worth 'inheriting' (p. 56). It is noteworthy that a revival of films of the 1930s and 1940s took place in 1956, another period of relative relaxation; cf. *CL*, 1957, no. 3, pp. 218–19.

36. *Laying Siege to the City* (*Ping lin ch'eng hsia*) has been frequently revised, one such revision being published in Peking in 1963; see its "Final Note" (*Hou chi*), pp. 126–7.

37. For a discussion of Wu Ch'iang's novel *Red Sun*, see T. A. Hsia, "Heroes and Hero-worship in Chinese Communist Fiction", *CQ*, 1963, no. 13, pp. 125–38. An excerpt, translated as "Prelude to Victory", was published in *CL*, 1960, no. 7, pp. 3–67. Ch'ü Pai-yin's filmscript was published by Wen-i Ch'u-pan She, Shanghai, 1961. For criticism of the film *Red Sun*, see: Kao Chü, in *JMJP*, April 24, 1966; and Ming Ching (of the People's Liberation Army), ibid., May 29, 1966 [both articles translated in *CB*, no. 798].

38. Contemporary material on Shao Ch'üan-lin's views has not been found. Mu Yung's views (expressed in his article, "Ts'ung Shao Shun-pao, Liang San Lao-han suo hsiang-tao ti", *Wen-i Pao*, September 1962) were attacked by Lin Chih, "Ch'uang-tsao wo-men shih-tai ti ying-hsiung hsing-hsiang", ibid., December 1962. Lin Chih here also referred to two other articles on this theme in *Huo-hua*, October 1962. Liu Pai-yü, an important figure, wrote in support of heroic literature in *Wen-i Pao*, 1964, no. 5, and in *Hung-ch'i*, 1964, no. 19. Refutation of 'middle-character' writing was the main content of *Wen-i Pao*, 1964, no. 8–9, pp. 3–20, and 1966, no. 4.

39. Mao Tun discussed the correct weight to be given to positive, negative and minor characters, and the avoidance of a 'style' of literature dealing with 'minor characters', in his speech to the 1960 National Congress of Literary and Art Workers [*CB*, no. 632, p. 17]. Lin Chih, op. cit. (Note 38), p. 23, referred to the 'simplistic theory': one class, one type.

40. Yang Han-sheng's filmscript *A Chiangnan in the North* (*Pei-kuo Chiang-nan*) was published in *Tien-ying Chü-tso*, 1963, no. 6, pp. 10–42. A general report on the discussion of the film was carried in *Wen-i Pao*, 1964, no. 8–9, pp. 31–5 [*SCMM*, no. 449].

41. According to *JMJP*, August 5, 1966 [*CB*, no. 806, p. 25], 'Lin Mo-ch'en' is a pseudonym of Lin Shan and collaborators. *Two Families* was filmed in the Ch'ang-ch'un studios in 1963.

42. Mao Tun, "A general review of the short stories published in 1960", *Wen-i Pao*, 1961, nos. 4, 5 and 6 [*CB*, no. 663, pp. 32–3]. The question of humour and comedy was discussed by Cheng Hung and Yen Chi-chou, *Tien-ying I-shu*, 1962, nos. 4 and 5.

43. The text of *Big Li, Young Li and Old Li* (*Ta Li, Hsiao Li ho Lao Li*) was published in *Tien-ying Ch'uang-tso*, 1962, no. 2, pp. 2–22. For criticism, see Chü Hung in *Kung-jen Jih-pao*, June 15, 1966 [*CB*, no. 798].

44. No text of *Football Fans* (*Ch'iu Mi*) has been traced. For critical material (notably an article by Ch'i Hsing-kuang, *T'i-yü Pao*, Peking, August 17, 1966), see *CB*, no. 806.

45. Quotation from *JMJP*, August 17, 1966 [*CB*, no. 806, p. 14].

46. Among other films criticised were: *Nightless City* (*Pu yeh ch'eng*), criticised in June 1965 [*CB*, no. 767]; *Sisters of the Stage* (*Wu-t'ai chieh-mei*), cf. *Kuang-ming Jih-pao*, May 12 and June 1966 [*CB*, no. 798]; *Pressganging* (*Chua Chuang-ting*), cf. *Kuang-ming Jih-pao*, May 21, 1966 [*CB*, no. 798, and *SCMM*, no. 535]; *A Thousand Miles against the Wind* (*Ni feng ch'ien li*), cf. *JMJP*, June 15 and 25, 1966 [*CB*, no. 798]; *Peach Blossom Fan* (*T'ao hua shan*), cf. *JMJP*, July 12, 1966 [*CB*, no. 798]; *Prairie Fire* (*Liao Yuan*) cf. *JMJP*, April 28, 1967 [*SCMP*, no. 3934].

Material on the criticism of films is given in *Wu-ch'an chieh-chi wen-hua ta ko-ming tzu-liao hsuan*, San-lien Shu-tien, Hong Kong 1966, Vol. 1.

47. Wu Han's *Dismissal of Hai Jui* (*Hai Jui Pa-kuan*), written in 1959–60, was published in 1961. (The author's preface is dated August 8, 1961.) It was performed, apparently only a few times, in February 1961 by the Pei-ching Ching-chü Chü-t'uan (Opera Company of Peking). Wu Han's interesting account of the process of revision is printed with the text.

48. T'ien Han's *Hsieh Yao-huan* (author's preface dated August 2, 1961) was reprinted in *Kuang-ming Jih-pao*, February 2, 1966 as material for criticism.

49. Yao Wen-yuan's key article "On the new historical opera, *The Dismissal of Hai Jui*" first published in *Wen Hui Pao*, Shanghai, November 10, 1965, was reprinted in *JMJP*, November 30 [*CB*, no. 783, pp. 2–18]. This issue also published four other articles from the campaign. For an account of the earlier stages of the campaign against Wu Han, see Stephen Uhalley, Jr, "The Wu Han Discussion: Act One in a new Rectification Campaign", *China Mainland Review*, Hong Kong, Vol. 1, no. 4, pp. 24–38.

50. The key attack on T'ien Han was by Yun Sung, "Tien Han's *Hsieh Yao-huan* is a Big Poisonous Weed", *JMJP*, February 1, 1966 [*CB* no. 784, pp. 1–15]. This issue also contained three other articles from the campaign.

51. For renewed criticism of Hsia Yen, see *CB*, no. 786.

52. Yao Wen-yuan attacked the 'Three-family clique' of Teng T'o, Wu Han and Liao Mo-sha in "On *The Three-Family Village*", *JMJP*, May 11, 1966 [*CB*, no. 792, pp. 22–44]. For translations of five items on this subject, and an index to twenty others in *SCMP* and *SCMM*, see *CB*, no. 792.

53. The most detailed indictment of Teng T'o and his articles of 1961–62 was by Lin Chieh and others, "Teng T'o's *Evening Chats at Yenshan* is anti-party and anti-socialist Double-talk", *Chieh-fang-chün Pao* and *Kuang-ming Jih-pao*, May 8, 1966, translated in *The*

Great Socialist Cultural Revolution in China, op. cit., 2, pp. 12–49.

54. For the attack on *Ch'ien Hsien* and *Peiching Jih-pao* and on the insufficient criticism of April 1966, see Ch'i Pen-yü, "On the bourgeois stand of *Front Line* and *Peking Daily*", *Hung-ch'i*, 1966, no. 7, translated in *The Great Socialist Cultural Revolution in China*, op. cit., 2, pp. 50–65.

55. For translations of attacks on Chou Yang, and for references to other items in *SCMP* and *SCMM*, see CB, no. 802.

56. For a review of these events, see three articles in *CQ*, 1966, no. 27; Ellis Joffe, "China in mid-1966: 'Cultural Revolution' or Struggle for Power?"; Merle Goldman, "The Fall of Chou Yang"; Stephan Uhalley, Jr, "The Cultural Revolution and the Attack on *The Three-Family Village*". See also W. A. C. Adie, "China: Government by Permanent Rebellion", *Government and Opposition*, 1967, Vol. II, no. 2, pp. 219–39.

57. According to *PR*, 1967, no. 25, p. 8, more than 29 million sets of Mao's works were printed in China in the first five months of 1967, and about 23 million during 1966. See also *CL*, 1967, no. 5–6, pp. 170–1.

58. Criticism of Stalin made at the Forum on Work in Literature and Art in the Armed Forces, convened by Chiang Ch'ing in Shanghai, February 1966; for a summary of the proceedings, see PR, 1967, no. 23 p. 13.

59. Some of the forty-two operas and plays put on at the North China Festival of Modern Drama and Opera, held in Spring 1965, are sketched in Li Lun, "Socialist Times, Socialist Heroes, Socialist Drama", *China Reconstructs*, August 1965.

The 'eight revolutionary exemplary works' are: (1) *Taking the Bandits' Stronghold* (*Chih ch'ü wei hu shan*), a new revolutionary Peking opera adapted in Shanghai from the novel *Lin Hai Hsueh Yuan*. It deals with the eradication of a Kuomintang bandit gang in Manchuria c. 1946–49. First staged in 1957, it was revised in 1964, and a further revision was published in Shanghai in January 1965. A later text was published in *Kuang-ming Jih-pao*, May 25, 1967. T'ao Hsing described the revision process in *JMJP*, June 5, 1964; see also "A new Blossoming of revolutionary Peking Opera", *China Reconstructs*, March 1967, pp. 8–11.

(2) *On the Docks:* text not traced. A revolutionary Peking opera, it deals with Shanghai dockers and is set in 1963.

(3) *The Red Lantern* (*Hung Teng Chi*), text translated in *CL*, 1965, no. 5, pp. 3–48; a revolutionary Peking opera. Set in Manchuria sometime between 1931 and 1945 it tells how a Red railwayman and his family fulfil a mission for the party despite Japanese railway

authorities. For material on its revision and interpretation, see *Ching-chü "Hung Teng Chi" p'ing-lun chi*, Peking 1965.

(4) *Shachiapang*, a revolutionary Peking Opera adapted from Wen Mu's Shanghai Opera (Hu-chü) *Lu-tang Huo-chung*. It deals with the fight between Red and puppet troops in south Kiangsu during the Anti-Japanese War. For comment and interpretation, see *Ching-chü "Shachiapang" p'ing-lun chi*, Peking 1965. Text given in *JMJP*, March 18, 19, and 20, 1965. Trans. *CL*, 1967, no. 11.

(5) *The Raid on the White Tiger Regiment*, a revolutionary Peking Opera dealing with the Korean War. Trans. *CL*, 1967, no. 10.

(6) *The Red Detachment of Women (Hung-se Niang-tzu Chün)*. A revolutionary ballet, presumably adapted from the film of the same title, it is set in Hainan Island during the civil war of 1927–37.

(7) *The White-Haired Girl (Pai mao nü)*, a revolutionary ballet based on the famous opera of that name; see *JMJP*, April 28, 1966, p. 5.

(8) *Shachiapang*, a revolutionary oratorio based on the same material as the opera (see 4 above); described in *PR*, 1967, no. 28, pp. 33–4.

Performances of these works were attended by leaders of the Cultural Revolution, including Mao Tse-tung, in the spring of 1967. For illustrations of scenes from them, see *PR*, 1967, no. 23, pp. 42–4. For a translation of anti-imperialist work, see *War Drums on the Equator* by Li Huang and others of the Naval Political Department, *CL*, 1965, no. 7, pp. 3–72.

60. Reportage (*pao-kao wen-hsueh*) was urged in *Wen-i Pao*, 1962, no. 10, pp. 3–4. For the link between reportage and mass creativity, see Mo Kan, "Reportage in Contemporary Chinese Writing", *CL*, 1965, no. 2, pp. 79–85. Its importance in literary policy is made clear in the attack on Yang Han-sheng, *JMJP*, December 27, 1966 [*SCMP*, no. 3857, p. 9]. For mass creative writing, a field in which successes have been claimed since 1958, see: Hung Yu's article on the Shanghai periodical *Meng-ya* (Buds) in *CL*, 1965, no. 10, pp. 108–11; articles from *Wen-i Pao*, 1965, nos. 1 and 10 [*SCMM*, no. 485, pp. 13–15, and no. 511, pp. 21–8]; and from *Min-chien Wen-hsueh*, 1966, no. 1 [*SCMM*, no. 527, pp. 23–7].

61. Speeches and articles on the 1964 festival are translated in *A Great Revolution on the Cultural Front*, op. cit. (Note 21). The 1967 festival is discussed in *PR*, 1967. no. 23. The descriptions of the festival's role quoted here are from "Hold high the Great Red Banner of Mao Tse-tung's Thought, and actively participate in the Great Socialist Cultural Revolution", *Chieh-fang-chün Pao*, April 18, 1966, cited in *The Great Socialist Cultural Revolution in China*, op. cit.,

1, p. 6, and *Ching-chü "Hung Teng Chi" p'ing lun chi"*, op. cit., p. 5.

62. See Note 59, under (8), and Note 65 below.

63. The *Rent Collection Court* and its revision are described in *JMJP*, November 27, 1965 and December 3, 1966, and in *Hung-ch'i*, 1966, no. 3. The *Tashu* tableau is described and illustrated in *CL*, 1967, no. 5–6, pp. 154–8; see also *JMJP*, October 11, 1966.

64. *The Red Detachment of Women* is described in *JMJP*, October 7, 1964, p. 6; and both it and *The White-Haired Girl* in *JMJP*, April 28, 1966 and April 27, 1967. See also Note 59 under (6) and (7).

65. For a description of the 'struggle' for this work, see *PR*, 1967, no. 28, pp. 33–4.

66. Chin Ching-mai's interview with Ch'en Yi and T'ao Chu was reported in *JMJP*, February 27, 1966.

67. The novel's Chinese title is *Ouyang Hai chih ko*, author's post-face dated October 1965. By April 1966, one million copies had been published; and *Kuang-ming Jih-pao*, May 29, 1966, also refers to a 'rural edition'. Excerpts from the novel were published in *CL*, 1966, nos. 8–11. For evaluations by Kuo Mo-jo and Liu Pai-yü, see *Wen-i Pao*, 1966, no. 4. For the original figure of Ouyang, see *JMJP*, February 7, 1964, p. 2. For a comment on the lack of full-length works for young readers, see Chiang Kuei-ying, *Shou-huo*, no. 1 [*SCMM*, no. 520, pp. 33–5].

68. These heroes have been the subject of a very extensive literature, especially in the press. Selected sources: for Lei Feng, see Chen Kuang in *CL*, 1967, nos. 1 and 2; for Ts'ai Yung-hsiang, see *China Pictorial*, 1967, no. 3, and *JMJP*, November 26, 1966, p. 6; for Liu Ying-chün, see *Kuang-ming Jih-pao*, July 14, 1966; for Lu Hsiang-pi, see *PR*, 1967, no. 28; for Chiao Yü-lu, see "Hsien Party Secretary Chiao Yü-lü, *PR*, 1966, no. 9.

69. For the 'five' or 'four' histories, see Meng Teng-chin and Miu Hsin-fang, "The epistemological significance of Five-History Education", *Che-hsueh Yen-chiu*, 1964, no. 4 [*SCMM*, no. 432]. For an interesting account of a 'historical worker's' stay of nine months in 1964–65 in a Shansi village, see Hsia Hsiang, "Write mass history, and write history for the masses", *Li-shih Yen-chiu*, 1965, no. 5 [*SCMM*, no. 511]. The historical work of Canton army units is described in articles in *Yang-ch'eng Wan-pao*, Canton, December 29, 1965 [*SCMP*, no. 3616].

70. The leading attack on the historical establishment came in *JMJP* June 3, 1966, translated in *The Great Socialist Cultural Revolution in China*, op. cit., 4, pp. 20–5. For details, see Chin Ch'un-hain-"*Historical Studies* is a reactionary bulwark of bourgeois historical circles", *JMJP*, October 23, 1966 [*SCMP*, no. 3813].

71. See Mao Tse-tung, *Four Essays on Philosophy*, FLP, 1966.

72. For the educational reform of 1966, see *PR*, 1966, no. 26.

73. "The Chinese Communist Party Central Committee's (draft) Provisions concerning the current Great Proletarian Cultural Revolution in Institutes of Higher Learning (for discussion and trial use)", *Hsin Pei-ta* (organ of the Peking University Cultural Revolution Committee), March 14, 1967 [*SCMP*, no. 3939].

Chapter V. The Crisis, 1966–67

1. The *Summary of World Broadcasts, issued by the* BBC, is the broadest single source for events in China, for it covers not only the national but the provincial Chinese stations. In addition, during the height of the crisis, when our knowledge of events depended primarily on Japanese and East European correspondents in Peking the BBC in a specialised subsection of the *Summary* reported broadcasts on China from Tokyo, Moscow, Belgrade, Sofia and Prague. Information provided by the Kyodo (Japan) and Tanjug (Yugoslavia) agencies was especially good. As far as possible, references in this chapter have been related to material in the *Summary*, since this is more readily available in libraries. (FE—Far East). The references are not intended to do more than guide the interested reader through this rich and fundamental source of information.

2. Tanjug, January 4, 1967: FE/2358/C/1.

3. BBC, *Summary of World Broadcasts*, passim, nos. 2185–234.

4. Foochow broadcast, July 19, 1966, reporting on Fukien Provincial Committee meeting on the Cultural Revolution: FE/222/B/1.

5. Kyodo, February 1, 1967: FE/2382/C/1; BTA, February 16, 1967: FE/2395/C/2.

6. Tokyo broadcast, January 7, 1967: FE/2361/C/4.

7. "The Principal Document of the Great Proletarian Cultural Revolution", *Hung-ch'i*, 1966, no. 10.

8. New China News Agency (NCNA), in Chinese, August 18, 1966: FE/2244/B/3.

9. Ibid.: FE/2244/B/5.

10. Stuart R. Schram, articles in *Far Eastern Economic Review*, Hong Kong, Vol. LIII, no. 5.

11. NCNA, in Chinese, September 1, 1966, reporting Chou's speech at the Teacher's Loyalty to Mao rally of August 31: FE/2254/B/5.

12. Kyodo, January 27, 1967: FE/2379/C/2.

13. NCNA, in Chinese, August 25, 1966: FE/2253/B/3.

14. CTK, January 6, 1967: FE/2361/C/2.

15. Tanjug, in English, January 10, 1967: FE/2363/C/1
16. Tokyo broadcast, January 23, 1967: FE/2374/C/4.
17. Tanjug, in English, January 9, 1967: FE/2362/C/1.
18. *Observer*, London, January 22, 1967.
19. BTA, February 27, 1967: FE/2405/C/1.
20. Czech broadcast, January 2, 1967: FE/2357/C/1.
21. Kyodo, February 6, 1967, based on Red Guard posters in Shanghai: FE/2386/C/1.
22. Ibid., January 26, 1967: FE/2379/C/1.
23. Ibid., January 27, 1957: FE/2379/C/1.
24. BTA, March 3, 1967: FE/2410/C/1.
25. Ibid., March 14,1967: FE/2418/C/1.

WORKS CITED

For guide to periodical-abbreviations used, see Notes and References page 251. For Chinese material, the most convenient English translation is given where possible. In such cases, the original Chinese source is given in the Notes and References.

Adie, W. A. C., "China: Government by Permanent Rebellion", *Government and Opposition*, London 1967, Vol. II, no. 2.

Adams, Ruth (ed.), *Contemporary China*, Vintage Books, New York 1966.

Ai Huang, article on 'redness' and 'expertise' (1961), *SCMM*, no. 285.

Ai Ssu-ch'i et al., *Yang-ko lun-wen hsuan-chi*, Dalien 1947.

Chang T'ien-yi, "Writing about Contradictions", *CL* 1957, no. 3.

Chen Kuan, article on Lei Feng, *CL* 1967, nos. 1 and 2.

Chen, T. H., "Education in Communist China: Aims, Trends and Problems", in Adams, Ruth (ed.), q.v.

Cheng Chih, article on 'redness' and expertise' (1961), *SCMM*, no. 285.

Cheng Hung, article on humour and comedy, *Tien-ying I-shu* 1962, no. 4.

Cheng, J. Chester (ed.), *The Politics of the Chinese Red Army*, Stanford University Press, Stanford, Calif. 1966.

Ch'i Hsing-kuang, article (1966) criticising film *Ch'iu Mi* (Football Fans), *CB*, no. 806.

Ch'i Pen-yü, "On the bourgeois stand of *Front Line* and *Peking Daily*", in *The Great Socialist Cultural Revolution in China*, 2, q.v.

Chiang Ch'ing, speech on revolutionary drama (1964), *PR* 1967, no. 20.

Chiang Kuei-ying, article on youth and heroic literature (1966), *SCMM*, no. 520.

Chin Ching-mai, *Ouyang Hai chih ko* (The Song of Ouyang Hai, novel), Peking 1965–66.

Chin Ch'un-hsin, "*Historical Studies* is a reactionary bulwark of bourgeois historical circles" (1966), *SCMP*, no. 3813.

"Chinese Communist Party Central Committee's (draft) Provisions concerning the current Great Proletarian Revolution in Institutes of Higher Learning . . ." (1967), *SCMP*, no. 3939.

Ching-chü "Hung Teng Chi" p'ing-lun chi, Peking 1965 (on the Peking opera *Hung Teng Chi* [The Red Lantern].

Ching-chü "Shachiapang" p'ing-lun chi, Peking 1965 (on the Peking opera *Shachiapang*).

Chou Ku-ch'eng, "The historical position of art creation", *Hsin Chien-she* 1962, no. 12.

Chou Yang, "The People's New Literature" (1949 report), in *The People's New Literature*, FLP 1950. "The Important Roles of Art and Literature in the Building of Socialism" (1956 speech), *CL* 1957, no. 1. "The New Folk Song has opened up a new road for poetry and song", *Hung-ch'i* 1958, no. 1. "The fighting task confronting workers in philosophy and the social sciences", *CB* 1963, no. 726. *Wo kuo she-hui chui-i wen-hsueh i-shu ti tao-lu* (1960 report), Peking 1965.

Chu Kuang-chi'en, "My Understanding", *CL* 1957, no. 4.

Chü Hung, article (1966) criticising the film *Big Li, Young Li and Old Li*, *CB*, no. 798.

Ch'ü Pai-yin, script of film *Red Sun*, Wen-i Ch'u-pan She, Shanghai 1961. "Soliloquy on the problems of realism in the film", *Tien-ying I-shu* 1962, no. 3.

Donnithorne, A., *China's Economic System*, Allen and Unwin, London 1967; Praeger, New York 1967.

Doolin, Dennis, "The Revival of the 100 Flowers Campaign: 1961", *CQ* 1961, no. 8.

Fokkema, D. W., "Chinese Criticisms of Humanism: Campaign against the Intellectuals, 1964–65", *CQ* 1966, no. 26. *Literary Doctrine in China and Soviet Influence, 1956–60*, Mouton, The Hague 1965.

Gittings, J., *The Role of the Chinese Army*, Oxford University Press, London and New York 1967. "The 'Learn from the Army' Campaign", *CQ* 1966, no. 18.

Goldman, Merle, "The Fall of Chou Yang", *CQ* 1966, no. 27.

Gray, Jack, "Political Aspects of the Land Reform Campaign in China", *Soviet Studies*, Glasgow 1964, no. 2.

Great Revolution on the Cultural Front, A, FLP 1965.

Great Socialist Cultural Revolution in China, The, FLP 1966.

Harris, Richard, article in *The Times*, February 17, 1967.

Harrison, J. A., "Communist Interpretations of the Chinese Peasant Wars", *CQ* 1965, no. 24.

Ho Ch'i-fang, "An Appraisal of the novel *February* and the film *Early Spring in February*", *CB*, no. 749.

Hofheinz, Roy, "Rural Administration in Communist China", *CQ* 1962, no. 11.

"Hold High the Great Red Banner of Mao Tse-tung's Thought . . .", *The Great Socialist Cultural Revolution in China*, 1, q.v.

Hsia Hsiang, "Write mass history, and write history for the masses" (1965), *SCMM*, no. 511.

Hsia Yen, "The Shop of the Lin Family" (filmscript), *Chung-kuo Tien-ying chü-pen hsuan-chi*, Peking 1961, Vol. v. "Tui kai-pien wen-t'i ta k'o wen", *Tien-ying Chü-tso* 1963, no. 6.

Hsia, T. A., *The Enigma of the Five Martyrs*, University of California Press, Berkeley, Calif. 1962. "Heroes and Hero-worship in Chinese Communist Fiction", *CQ* 1963, no. 13.

Hsieh T'ieh-li, "Erh-yueh" (filmscript), *Tien-ying Ch'uang-tso* 1962, no. 3.

"Hsien Party Secretary Chiao Yü-lu", *PR* 1966, no. 9.

Hsing Yü, article criticising Wu Han, *Kuang-ming Jih-pao*, May 29, 1964.

Hsu Ch'i-hsien, article criticising Wu Han, *Kuang-ming Jih-pao*, August 15, 1963.

Hu, C. T. (ed.), *Chinese Education under Communism*, Teachers' College, Columbia University Press, New York 1962. "Politics and Economics in Chinese Education", in Klatt, Werner (ed.), q.v.

"Hung Teng Chi" (The Red Lantern, Peking opera text), *CL* 1965, no. 5.

Hung Yu, article on mass creative writing, *CL* 1965, no. 10.

Jan Shao-te, "Kuan-yu 'Shi Chih' . . .", *Kuang-ming Jih-pao*, June 3, 1964.

Joffe, Ellis, "China in mid-1966: 'Cultural Revolution' or Struggle for Power?", *CQ* 1966, no. 27.

Kao Chü, article (1966) criticising the film *Red Sun*, *CB*, no. 798.

Klatt, Werner (ed.), *The Chinese Model*, Hong Kong University Press, Hong Kong 1965.

Kuo Mo-jo, "In refutation of an anti-socialist scientific program" (1957), in Hu, C. T. (ed.), q.v. "Lang-man chu-i ho hsien-shih chu-i", *Hung-ch'i* 1958, no. 3. Article appraising *Ouyang Hai chih ko*, in *Wen-i Pao* 1966, no. 4.

Lewis, John Wilson, *Leadership in Communist China*, Cornell University Press, Ithaca, N.Y. 1963. "Revolutionary Struggle and the Second Generation in Communist China", *CQ* 1965, no. 21.

Li Ch'eng-jui, *Draft History of the Agricultural Taxes of the Chinese People's Republic* (in Chinese), Peking 1959.

Li Huan-chih, "Elevation and Promotion" (1962), *CB*, no. 685.

Li Huang et al., *War Drums on the Equator*, *CL* 1965, no. 7.

Li Lun, "Socialist Times, Socialist Heroes, Socialist Drama", *China Reconstructs*, Peking, August 1965.

Li Ni, review of *Draft History of the Development of the Chinese Cinema*, in *Tien-ying I-shu*, 1963, no. 2.

Lin Chieh et al., "*Teng T'o's Evening Chats at Yenshan* is anti-party and anti-socialist Double-talk" (1966), in *The Great Socialist Cultural Revolution in China*, q.v.

Lin Chih, 'Ch'uang-tsao wo-men shih-tai ti ying-hsiung hsing-hsiang", *Wen-i Pao*, October 1962.

'Lin Mo-chen': *see* Lin Shan.

Lin Mo-han, "Hold even higher the Banner of Mao Tse-tung's Thinking on Literature and Art", *JMJP*, January 21, 1960.

Lin Shan et al., filmscript of *Two Families*, 1963.

Liu Pai-yü, articles on heroic literature, *Wen-i Pao* 1964, no. 5; *Hung-ch'i* 1964, no. 19. Article appraising *Ouyang Hai chih ko*, *Wen-i pao* 1966, no. 4.

Liu Shih-te, article on 'good official' (1964), *SCMP*, no. 3252.

Lu Ting-yi, "Education must be combined with productive labor" (1958), and "Our schooling system must be reformed" (1966), in Hu, C. T. (ed.), q.v.

MacFarquhar, Roderick, *The Hundred Flowers*, Stevens, London 1960; published in USA as *The Hundred Flowers Campaign and the Chinese Intellectuals*, Praeger, New York 1960.

Mao Tse-tung, *The High Tide of Socialism in the Chinese Countryside* (in Chinese), Peking 1956. "In Praise of Norman Bethune", in *Selected Works*, Vol. III, International Publishers, New York 1953. "On Contradictions", in *Four Essays on Philosophy*, FLP 1966. *On New Democracy*, FLP 1954. "On Practice", in *Four Essays. . . . On the Correct Handling of Contradictions Among the People*, FLP 1957 (also in *Four Essays . . .*). "Oppose the Party Eight-Legged Essay", in *Mao Tse-tung on Art and Literature*, FLP 1960. *Quotations from Chairman Mao*, FLP 1966 "Role of the Communist Party in the National War", in . . . *Art and Literature*. "Serve the People", in *Selected Works*, Vol. III. *Speech at the*

Propaganda Conference of the Communist Party of China, FLP 1957. "Talks at the Yenan Forum on Art and Literature", in . . . *Art and Literature*. "Where do Correct Ideas come from?", in *Four Essays*. . . .

Mao Tun, *Spring Silkworms and Other Stories* (including the story *The Shop of the Lin Family*), FLP 1956. "Report to the National Congress of Literary and Art Workers" (1960), *CB*, no. 632. "A general review of the short stories published in 1960" (1961), *CB*, no. 663. "Hsueh jan-hou chih pu tsu", *Jen-min Wen-hsueh* 1962, no. 2.

Meng Teng-chin, and Niu Hsin-fang, "The epistemological significance of Five-History Education" (1964), *SCMM*, no. 432.

Ming Ching, article (1966) criticising the film *Red Sun*, *CB*, no. 798.

Mo kan, "Reportage in Contemporary Chinese Writing", *CL* 1965, no. 2.

Mu Yung, "Ts'ung Shao Shun-pao, Liang San Lao-han suo hsiang-tao ti", *Wen-i Pao*, September 1962.

Munro, D. J. "The Yang Hsien-chen Affair", *CQ* 1965, no. 2.

"New Blossoming of revolutionary Peking Opera, A", *China Reconstructs*, Peking, March 1967.

Nove, Alec, *The Soviet Economy*, 1961; rev. edn., Allen and Unwin, London 1966; Praeger, New York 1966.

Oldham, C. H. G., "Science and Education in China", in Adams, Ruth (ed.), q.v.

Pai Jen et al., *Ping lin ch'eng hsia* (Laying Siege to the City, 1959), revised version, Peking 1963.

"Principal Documents of the Great Proletarian Cultural Revolution, The", *Hung-ch'i* 1966, no. 10.

Prusek, J., *Die Literatur des befreiten Chinas und ihre Volkstradition* (translated from Czech by P. Eisner and W. Gampert), Artia Press, Prague 1955.

Robinson, Joan, "Organisation of Agriculture", in Adams, Ruth (ed.), q.v.

Schram, Stuart R., *The Political Thought of Mao Tse-tung*, Frederick A. Praeger, New York 1963; Pall Mall Press, London 1963. *Mao Tse-tung*, Penguin, Harmondsworth and Baltimore 1966. "The Man and his Doctrine", *Problems of Communism*, Washington D.C., September–October 1966. Article in *Far Eastern Economic Review*, Hong Kong (1966), Vol. LIII, no. 5.

Schurmann, Franz, *Ideology and Organisation of Communist China*, University of California Press, Berkeley, Calif. 1966.

T'ao Chu, "The People's Communes are making progress", *Hung-ch'i*, February 26, 1964.

269

T'ao Hsing, article on revision of *Chih ch'ü wei hu shan* (Taking the Bandit's Stronghold), *JMJP*, June 5, 1964.

Teng Shao-chi, article on 'good official' (1964), *SCMP*, no. 3252.

Teng T'o, *Yen-shan Yeh-hua* (Evening Chats at Yenshan), 5 vols., Peking 1961–63, published under the pseudonym Ma Nan-t'sun.

T'ien Han, *Hsieh Yao-huan* (1961), reprinted in *Kuang-ming Jih-pao*, February 2, 1966.

Tung, Robert, article in *Far Eastern Economic Review*, Hong Kong, September 8, 1966, Vol. LIII, no. 10.

Uhalley, Stephen (Jr), "The Wu Han Discussion: Act One in a New Rectification Campaign", *China Mainland Review*, Hong Kong 196 , Vol. I, no. 4. "The Cultural Revolution and the Attack on *The Three-Family Village*", *CQ* 1966, no. 27.

Wang Ssu-chih, article criticising Wu Han, *Kuang-ming Jih-pao*, June 3, 1964.

Wu Ch'iang, "Prelude to Victory", excerpt from *Red Sun*, *CL* 1960, no. 7.

Wu Han, "Lu Hai Jui", *JMJP*, September 19, 1959. *Hai Jui Pa-kuan* (Dismissal of Hai Jui), Peking 1961. "Shuo tao-te", *Ch'ien Hsien* 1962, no. 10. "Tsai shuo tao-te", ibid. 1962, no. 16. "San shuo tao-te", *Kuang-ming Jih-pao*, August 15, 1963: and articles on same theme, ibid., June 17 and July 9, 1964.

Wu-ch'an chieh-chi wen-hua ta ko-ming tzu-liao hsuan, San-lien Shu-tien, Hong Kong 1966, Vol. I.

Yang Han-sheng, filmscript of *Pei-kuo Chiang-nan* (A Chiangnan in the North), *Tien-ying Chü-tso* 1963, no. 6.

Yao Wen-yüan, "On the new historical opera *The Dismissal of Hai Jui*" (1965), *CB*, no. 783. "On *The Three-Family Village*" (1966), *CB*, no. 792.

Yen Chi-chou, article on humour and comedy, *Tien-ying I-shu* 1962, no. 5.

Yü Ling et al., filmscript of *Ta Li, Hsiao Li ho Lao Li* (Big Li, Young Li and Old Li), *Tien-ying Ch'uang-tso* 1962, no. 2.

Yuan Hsi-liang, "Transforming intellectuals into laborers" (1960), *CB*, no. 642. "Physical labor and mental labor in socialist society" (1965), *CB*, no. 507.

Yueh Hua, summary of *Hai Jui* controversy (1965), *SCMP*, no. 3668.

Yun Sung, "Tien Han's *Hsieh Yao-huan* is a Big Poisonous Weed", (1966), *CB*, no. 784.

INDEX

The abbreviation c.r. stands for Cultural Revolution

Index

Cadres, 19, 47, 55, 67, 84, 121; army, 47, 117; rural, 28, 40, 42, 59, 117, 139; production, 36, 63; revolutionary, 115, 139

Canton, 5, 6, 7; in c.r., 112, 141, 142, 143, 144

Capitalism, Chinese, 13, 40

Castro, Fidel, 55

Census (1953), 28

Central Committee, CCP, 34, 53; Tenth Plenum (1962), 39–40, 52, 58, 83–4, Appendix B. 1; in c.r., 113, 118, 119, 121, 137, 139, 140, 142; attacked by Red Guards, 129; General Propaganda Dept., 130, 131; Military Affairs Committee, 122; South-West Region Bureau, 118; struggle in, 114, 115, 116, 121; see also Sixteen Point Directive

Central control, problem of, 3, 19, 21–3

Central Institute of Arts, 128

Centralism, democratic, 38, 40; Mao's theory of, 60–2

Chang Chün-chao, 140

Chang Kuo-hua, 134, 140

Chang P'ing-huan, 131

Ch'en Chiung-ming, 3

Ch'en Yi, 111, 131, 139, 140

Ch'en Po-ta, 128, 129, 130, 132, 140

Ch'en Tsai-tao, 131, 134

Ch'en Tu-hsiu, 4

Ch'i Pen-yü, 112

Chiang Ch'ing: see Mme Mao

Chiang Kai-shek, 6–8, 9, 10, 11, 19

Chiangnan, 101

Chiao Yü-lu (hero figure), 112

Chieh-fang-chun Pao: see *Liberation Army Daily*

Ch'ien Hsien: see *Front Line*

Ch'ien Po-ts'an, 112

Ch'ien San-t'ai (character), 97, 98

Chin Ching-mai, 111

China, Republic of (1911), 3; People's Republic of (1949), 11

China Youth, 38, 40

Chinese Workers' Party, 134

Ch'inghai, 144

Chingkangshan Soviet, 53, 63

Chou En-lai, 121, 123, 126, 127, 132, 142, 145; and new govt. (1967), 140–1; and Red Guard, 124, 130, 137–40; conversations with Mao, 138–9, 140

Chou Ku-ch'eng, 87

Chou Yang, 82, 85, 103–4, 106–7, 137

Ch'u Pai-yin, 93

Chu Teh, 129

Ch'ü Yüan (play), 105

Chungking, 9, 10; university, 118

Chung-kuo ch'ing-nien: see *China Youth*

Cinema, films, 83, 86, 90ff., 108, 148; audiences, 90; rural themes in, 95–9

Civil strife, in c.r., 132ff.

Civil Wars: c. 1911, 3; 1929–31, 8; 1946–49, 11, 17, 18, 44, 53, 77; in arts, 93, 94

Class line, in arts, 94

Class struggle, 39–40, 42, 84, 87, 89; and c.r., 119, 121; and nationalism, 53–4; in arts, 97, 98; in historical studies, 112; Mao's theory of, 51–6

Collectives, collectivisation, 17, 18, 23ff., 31, 33, 34, 40–2, 52, 63, 64, 82, 83; and c.r., 119, 136, 145, 147; in arts, 96–9

'Combine two into one', 87

Comedy, humour, 97–8, 99–100

Comintern, 5, 9

Commerce, socialisation of, 26

Communes, 31, 32–7, 42, 44, 61–2, 64–5, 68, Appendix B. 2; and c.r., 115, 117, 119, 120, 136, 137, 138, 140, 143, 145; in arts, 102, 104; in historical studies, 112

Communications, 35; political, social, 56–7, 81, 141

Communist Party, Chinese (CCP): pre–1949, 4, 5ff., 17–18; post–1949, 18–20, 145; concept of

272

Index

Index

Index